W9-BGL-494

WITHDRAWN

ARGUMENTS WITH ETHNOGRAPHY

ARGUMENTS WITH ETHNOGRAPHY

COMPARATIVE APPROACHES
TO HISTORY, POLITICS & RELIGION

IOAN M. LEWIS

LONDON SCHOOL OF ECONOMICS MONOGRAPHS ON SOCIAL ANTHROPOLOGY

Volume 70

THE ATHLONE PRESS
London & New Brunswick NJ

First published in 1999 by
THE ATHLONE PRESS
1 Park Drive, London NW11 7SG
and New Brunswick, New Jersey

© I. M. Lewis 1999

British Library Cataloguing in Publication Data
*A catalogue record for this book is available
from the British Library*

ISBN 0 485 19570 4

Library of Congress Cataloging in Publication Data

Lewis, I. M.
   Arguments with ethnography ; comparative approaches to history,
politics, and religion / Ioan M. Lewis.
      p.   cm. -- (Monographs on social anthropology : no. 68)
   Includes bibliographical references.
   ISBN 0-485-19570-4 (cloth : alk. paper)
   1. Ethnology--Philosophy.   2. Ethnology--History.   3. Ethnology-
-Religious aspects.   4. Political anthropology.   I. Title.
II. Series.
GN345.L48   1999
305.8'001--dc21   98-54619
                                                                          CIP

Distributed in the United States, Canada and South America by
Transaction Publishers
390 Campus Drive
Somerset, New Jersey 08873

Typeset by Bibloset, Chester
Printed and bound in Great Britain by
Cambridge University Press

'Those impressive and all-explanatory theories which act upon weak minds like revelations.'

Karl Popper, *Conjectures and Refutations*

CONTENTS

PREFACE

At a public lecture he gave in London in the early 1970s, I asked Lévi-Strauss how he explained the popularity of structuralism in France (at that time). 'Oh,' he replied modestly, 'you know, in France every few years we need some new enthusiasm.' Vogues in anthropology, of course, are hardly a French monopoly, and their sequential patterns over time are not without interest, particularly if they can be shown to relate to wider factors in the environment in which anthropologists fashion theory.

In British social anthropology, although evolutionism has, in the main, long since fallen out of fashion, it nevertheless still accurately enough describes the succession of theoretical vogues in our subject. So, just as functionalism replaced, and was claimed to render otiose, diffusion and evolutionism, functionalism in its turn was superseded, according to their enthusiasts, by structuralism, Marxism, and 'structural Marxism' (cf. Ortner, 1984). These movements in their turn gave ground to reflexive anthropology, new ethnography and, more generally, post-modernism.

In this evolutionary process, functionalism acquired a particularly negative aura – being identified in popular anthropological mythology (especially in North America) with colonialism – and thus became (like 'tribalism' in nationalist circles) a convenient term of abuse (see Chapter 1). However, despite the profusion of rival banners, advertising 'new theory', functionalism (again like 'tribalism' and other forms of particularist loyalty) lingers on and frequently materialises unbidden as the (unrecognised) basis of arguments claiming that one set of social circumstances has specific (often allegedly intended) social consequences (cf. Chapters 1 and 9).[1]

This is not surprising since, as I argue here, any viable comparative social anthropology which seeks to explore the correlates of different social formations is bound to employ functionalist assumptions about praxis, and the more explicit these are the better. Such analysis can proceed within a historical time-frame legitimately, and often more fruitfully, than within a particular temporal period in the 'ethnographic present'. By 'functionalism' here, I should emphasise, I mean simply how social institutions work through the engagement and interests of individuals in different roles and positions. I do not mean a deterministic functionalism which confuses effects and causes, and treats social institutions as existing solely to maintain the identity and character of particular structures. The same institutions can have different functions, in my sense, at different times and places (cf. I.M. Lewis, 1968a, xxiv).

As fashion succeeds fashion in the gamut of rival anthropological theories, there is, naturally, a general presumption that each new, and more advanced, stage automatically decommissions its predecessors. As in other disciplines, this, of course, is encouraged by academic 'priestcraft', whereby enthusiastic teachers seek to promote their favourite theoretical 'discourse' which is, by definition, always novel. This evolutionary process (as pedagogy presents it) naturally encourages the neglect of earlier work however intrinsically relevant that may in fact be. As I recall from my own training with Evans-Pritchard, unless they are taken with a pinch of salt, such didactic attitudes tend to foster a rather uncritical and unscholarly presentism which neglects to teach young researchers how to control and assess sources, past and present – except in what are virtually ahistorical, ideological terms. This can have serious consequences. Hence, an informed knowledge of the existing literature, and the means to critically assess its relevance to the task in hand, are essential if progress in our subject is to be maintained. Without these essential elements of intellectual equipment, as a cumulative discipline, based on well-informed theories systematically tested against empirical data, social anthropology is at risk of losing its substantive anchorage and disciplinary rigour. To be taken seriously in the social sciences, social anthropology has to be more than merely a succession of transient vogues.

In the 1960s anthropological publications had a strongly comparative character and were studded with ethnographic references to other peoples and cultures. In the 1970s and 80s, however, this emphasis on comparative analysis declined markedly. References to peoples were replaced by copious citations of persons, often themselves not anthropologists, whose usually obscure (and sometimes quite unintelligible) writings (seldom read in the original language) had acquired totemic status on the philosophical fringe of anthropology. Many anthropologists (particularly those who were relatively junior) evidently sought to establish their intellectual credentials by impressive citation of such intellectocratic figures, rather than by demonstrating a convincing grasp of the relevant comparative ethnographic literature.

These introductory comments (elaborated in the concluding chapter) are in my view especially relevant to the 'post-modernist' ethnography of the 1980s and 1990s. This, I believe, has infected a wider range of anthropological practice than that produced by self-declared adherants of the tendency, fostering a general debasing of the currency of social anthropology. Reflecting partly a shortage of research funds, field work tends to be conducted over shorter periods than in past British practice, by researchers with less linguistic competence and scholarly preparation. Seeking to make a virtue out of financial constraints and the insecure post-colonial circumstances in many exotic field sites, this 'post-modernist' approach risks abandoning serious scholarly standards in the representation of other cultures. Fortified, as it usually is, with a dash of politically correct neo-Marxism, it advocates what amounts to a 'zombification', a process in which local communities are ethnocentrically drained of their distinctive vitality and 'agency' (see further below, p.140). Our objective, on the contrary, should be to seek to understand other worlds, and not, in the name of high-sounding theory and inadequate ethnographic reporting, to shroud these in meretricious mystery, nor to project on to them interpretations which are manifestly ethnocentric (and even worse, egocentric). Obviously, I do not agree with those who claim that all cross-cultural interpretations are inevitably ethno/egocentric and consequently equally valid, or invalid.

This new collection of essays on history, politics and religion argues that such subjective anthropology can itself be viewed as an extreme development of exaggeratedly patronising (and misleading) assessments of the anthropologist's creative role in the construction of theory. But theory-building, as I maintain here (chapters 1 and 9), is actually more dependent than is usually recognised on the inspiration of the peoples anthropologists study. This is a further justification for the kind of empirically based comparative social anthropology which, like its predecessor on religion (I.M. Lewis, 1986), this collection of essays advocates. We thus concentrate our examination of the construction of theory in this book on what I like to call the 'fieldwork mode of production (and reproduction)'.

Chapter 1 argues that theoretical directions in social anthropology, which is ultimately an empirically based discipline, result from the interaction of actors and agencies in at least three overlapping arenas. These are principally: the subjective ethnographer and his application of current theoretical assumptions; the ethnographic 'facts' elicited in fieldwork; and the geographical and historical context in which field-work is conducted. Within this tripartite schema, the chapter proceeds to examine the increasingly conspicuous presence of a historical dimension in the work of British anthropologists. It explores how this emphasis on diachronic processes has developed unequally over time in different ethnographic regions, where the presence or absence of a vernacular literate tradition is a further variable.

I have myself carried out a considerable amount of oral and documentary historical research in Somalia where I have worked since the 1950s, and have also, *faute de mieu*, written an extended political history of Somali society and culture from pre-colonial times to the present (I.M. Lewis, 1965b; 1988; 1994). This experience of tracing continuities and discontinuities in Somali political history makes me very aware of the contribution which history can make to the comparative study of social institutions (cf. I.M. Lewis, 1968a).

Contrary to commonly held assumptions, this attention to the light the past sheds on the present, and the opportunities this perspective affords of exploring how social institutions register and respond to changing circumstances over time, is by no means a new development in our subject. The long-standing presence of this historical tendency in British social anthropology, and the inclusion where appropriate of the local impact of Western imperialism, throws into serious doubt the claims for novelty made in the late 1980s and 1990s by some 'political economy' and 'subaltern studies' anthropologists working in Africa (e.g. Comaroff and Comaroff, 1991) and elsewhere. Naturally, however, as Chapter 2 emphasises, by comparing Evans-Pritchard's treatment of exotic mystical beliefs with those of two eminent European contemporaries working in different intellectual traditions, such historically conscious British functionalists were not consistently even-handed in their utilisation of the two disciplines.

As I hope will be plain, throughout this book I maintain that a continuous dialogue between theory and empirically observed data is the essential basis of a vigorous, substantive social anthropology. In this spirit, the third chapter explores the 'meaning' of descent, in terms of its operational significance (or 'functions') in different social systems where it is a prominent principle of political identification. It argues that this analysis can only be made effectively by rigorous comparison of a set of clearly defined variables which, in this kinship context, should include gender as a factor governing patrilineal loyalty and status. As the contemporary German kinship specialist Muller (1981, pp. 73–81) has pointed out, this is an aspect of patrilinearity which had not been considered in earlier male-focused discussions.

In similar style, again discounting cultural particularities and concentrating on structure rather than form, Chapter 4 examines what I take to be the fundamental political structure of post-colonial African states. It argues that the principal effect of colonisation and decolonisation has been to establish the type of culturally plural polity – for which Ethiopia provides an indigenous model – as the dominant strain on the continent and where, in the absence of mono-ethnic nationalism, territorial sovereignty plays a crucial role. With its complex scriptural heritage, Ethiopia is also, as we shall see, an ideal testing ground for theories of nationalism whose ambiguous relationship with literacy is explored in Chapter 5. (This unintended effect of colonisation, in promoting cultural pluralism, of course, is all the more remarkable in that the European powers which established this pattern of pluralistic state in Africa were themselves dedicated in Europe to the principle of mono-cultural nationalism.)

Mono-cultural political formations are not, however, less African (less 'authentic') – only less common now, with possible implications for social cohesion and governance. Chapter 4 naturally reflects a point of view influenced by my studies of Somali nationalism, in which case as Chapter 5 demonstrates, contrary to the situation in Ethiopia, literacy was far from being a simple determinant. Unfortunately, as events in Somalia have shown all too dramatically, the political benefits of a shared national culture may be offset by other political factors such as powerful centrifugal forces (e.g. the Somali segmentary lineage system which played a major role in the collapse of the Somali state in 1990 – cf. I.M. Lewis, 1994; 1997c; 1998). In this case, state formation (Somali independence in 1960) and state dissolution (in 1990), in their different ways, threw revealing light on the extraordinary resilience and historical continuity of lineage organisation in a traditionally acephalous society.

The contribution which evidence of historical processes can make to the comparative analysis of social institutions and ideologies is further illustrated in Chapters 6 and 7 which deal, respectively, with the changing significance of possession cults in north-east Africa (including the Sudan), and with predisposing factors involved in the conversion of Africans to Islam. The first of these essays combines a historical and regional approach to explore the genesis and changing meaning of spirit-possession among the various peoples of north-east Africa, arguing that the well-documented pattern of possession in Ethiopia invites some re-evaluation of the classic anthropological accounts of Nilotic religion by Evans-Pritchard and Lienhardt.

This chapter also raises practical issues concerning the psychiatric significance of possession, its incidence and its treatment. It poses – but does not resolve – the question of the possible relationship between radical social change and possession afflictions. Although recorded long before the 1990s epidemic of Multiple Personality Disorder in North America, these African data provide an illuminating comparative dimension in evaluating this 'new' western syndrome (cf. Littlewood, 1996).

Inspired by similar ideas of the social dynamics of religious change, Chapter 7 seeks to highlight the limitations of the 'intellectualist' model of religious conversion, advanced by Robin Horton and others, which treats religion as essentially an explanatory (i.e. cognitive) system of beliefs, and underestimates religion's role as a spiritual force and badge of identity. Chapter 8, in turn, adopts a broader cross-cultural approach to examine gender roles in the context of shamanism and spirit-possession. It concludes, tentatively, that the role of human husband *vis-a-vis* spirit wife, rather than spirit husband *vis-a-vis* human wife is not a decisive index of the difference between shamanism and possession.

Our concluding Chapter 9 returns to the general discussion of the generation of theory in social anthropology in the light of our simple tripartite model. Drawing on my own personal acquaintance with those generally regarded today as the founding fathers of our subject, as well as upon written sources which are in the public domain, I explore here the distinctive characteristics of British Social and American cultural anthropology. I argue that, to a significant degree, their contrasting features reflect the fieldwork situations and wider political circumstances in which they originated. Although I examine it in a more schematic fashion, I suggest also that similar processes linked to the nature of French colonialism ('direct rule' in contrast to British 'indirect rule') are reflected in dominant trends in French anthropology. In both the French and American schools of anthropology, the notion of 'culture', associated with cultural assimilation, reflected a wider general experience of cultural pluralism and the assumption that peoples' salient differences arise from cultural, rather than social, determinants. As cultural and ethnic pluralism has become as prominent in Britain as in America and France, and with other shared factors affecting fieldwork in the

Third World, there has been a globalisation of the culture principle in anthropology.

However, it is a profound paradox that, as I contend, the formation of theory in social anthropology has never actually been culture-free. Rather, theory bears the traces of the cultures in which it has been forged. In addition, most theories seem to have their anonymous, amateur 'backroom boys' who are often the ultimate authors of these cultural constructs launched into international anthropological discourse by serendipitous professionals. With a more explicit awareness of this underlying dependence on culture, and the congruence of the wider socio-political forces influencing anthropologists of both schools, both at home and in exotic field situations, the merging of the social and cultural approaches in the 1980s no longer seems surprising.

The arguments in these chapters, which span history, politics and religion, have developed over a number of years, and I have naturally been greatly stimulated by many colleagues at home and overseas. Especially in relation to chapters 1 and 9 and without seeking to apportion blame, I would like particularly to thank: John Argyle, David Brokensha, Richard Brown, Raymond Firth, Chris Fuller, Bernhard Helander, Johnny Parry, Julian Pitt-Rivers, Isaac Schapera, Warren Shapiro, and George Stocking. I am especially grateful to my old friend William Shack for the invitation to deliver the Hitchcock Lecture from which Chapter 9 has developed. I am similarly indebted to my friends at the Catholic University in Lisbon in relation to chapter 4. In editing and preparing this material for publication in this form, I have found the comments of Charles Stafford and his anonymous reader most helpful. It is, finally, also a pleasure to acknowledge the editorial help I have received from Peggie Froere and the London School of Economics (LSE) research fund, and the meticulous copy-editing of Anstice Hughes.

NOTES

1 Thus a recent critique of media reporting on the collapse of the Somali state in the post-modernist journal, *Cultural Anthropology*, by Besteman ('Representing violence and "Othering" Somalia', *Cultural Anthropology*, 11 (1996): 120–35) baldly claimed that journalistic accounts of Somali violence were designed to discredit Somalis in racist fashion and to bolster US notions of national superiority. How this alleged effect was achieved was neither explored nor explained in this unconsciously functionalist and palpably unconvincing account (see Lewis, 1998).

ACKNOWLEDGEMENTS

Chapter 1 is a revised version of an article, 'Die zukunft der Vergangenheit in der Britischen Sozialanthropologie', published in *Wiener Beitrage zur Ethnologie und Anthropologie*, Band 2, 1985, originally delivered to the Vienna Conference on History and Anthropology. As may be apparent, the present title reflects the influence of George Stocking.

Chapter 2 is based on my contribution 'Comprendere il Mistero delle Credenze Degli "Altri"' to the International Conference on Ernesto De Martino in European Culture, held in Rome and Naples in November–December 1995. I am grateful to Clara Gallini for the invitation to participate and the permission to publish an English version here.

Chapter 3 was originally published as 'Problems in the comparative study of unilineal descent', in M. Gluckman and F. Eggan (eds), *The Relevance of Models in Social Anthropology* (London: Tavistock, 1965).

Chapter 4 is based on a public lecture entitled 'Decolonisation and the "Ethiopianisation" of Africa'. In the presence of the President of Portugal and the Portuguese cabinet, this was given at the Catholic University of Lisbon to inaugurate the establishment of a Centre of African Studies there on 19 May 1983.

Chapter 5 is based on a public lecture given at Wolfson College, Oxford, in 1985 in the series 'The Written Word' under the title 'Literacy and cultural identity in the Horn of Africa'.

Chapter 6 was first published as 'Spirit possession and psychotherapy in north east Africa', in Y. F. Hasan (ed.) *Sudan in Africa* (Khartoum

University Press, 1972). It is based on a paper delivered to the conference of the same name held in Khartoum.

A version of Chapter 7 was originally published as 'Identity and the political economy of Islamic conversion in Africa', *Approaches to African Identity*, Bayreuth African Studies Series no. 4, 1986.

Chapter 8 was written for the Fourth Conference of the International Society for Shamanic Research, Chantilly, September 1997.

Chapter 9 is an extensively revised version of the Hitchcock Lecture delivered at Berkeley University in 1977 under the title 'The myth of social anthropology'. Under this title it appeared in A. Marazi (ed.), *Antropologia Tendenze Contemporane* (Milan: Hoepli, 1989), but has not been previously published in English.

The jacket illustration is reproduced from a drawing by Romano Mastromattei.

CHAPTER I

HISTORY 'FUNCTIONALISED'

In this short and inevitably selective assessment of the emphasis placed on history and historical processes in social anthropology, I concentrate on the 'fieldwork mode of production' (and reproduction) and the many-stranded relationship between theory and empirical fieldwork. To open this discussion, I assume that theoretical directions in our subject reflect the complex interplay between at least three major sets of factors: current theoretical preoccupations (partly a matter of the wider intellectual *zeitgeist* and the anthropologist's own native ethnographic situation); the ethnographic 'facts' elicited and recorded in the course of fieldwork; and the ambient geographical and historical context in which field work is conducted (on the last theme, see also Fardon, 1990, p.3). These three factors obviously shade into each other reactively, and themselves comprise many important constituents.

Thus, the anthropologist's own ethnographic situation includes not only the intellectual fashions, local and cosmopolitan, to which he is subject and responds variously, but also his access to financial support for field research, and the strings, if any, attached to this. There is also the important question of the anthropologist's own ethnic identity, and whether his fieldwork is, as was conventionally the case, carried out in a foreign cultural setting. The increasing number of locally recruited social anthropologists working in Europe, North America, the Third World and elsewhere (e.g. in India, Japan and the Middle East), often practising a kind of 'auto-anthropology', makes this model more and more problematic. Likewise, as can never be too strongly emphasised, the ethnographic 'facts' are many stranded, ranging from 'objective' statistical data to concensus (as well as idiosyncratic) local models or theories of the culture and society concerned, such 'emic' material being by no means monolithic or unambiguously homogeneous. The culturally specific features of ethnographic regions (e.g. Indian caste) have a pervasive impact on the related theoretical as well as ethnographic literature. Hence, as we have seen, debates in anthropological theory frequently reflect regional ethnographic differences which, in effect, argue through the medium of their anthropological impresarios. This is not altogether surprising since 'theory', after all, is ultimately supposed to elucidate the ethnographic 'facts'. The *presence* (as well as *absence*) of a 'sense of history' in the ethnographic setting is thus something which has itself influenced attitudes towards history in British social anthropology.

Despite its anti-historical reputation – associated with the dominant structural-functionalist paradigm of Malinowski and Radcliffe-Brown – British social anthropology has often, in practice, included some reference to the historical dimension. Sometimes, this has amounted to little more than the provision of a historical backdrop to highlight the contemporary present. In other cases the anthropologist has found himself confronting a changing community and culture and has sought to capture this dynamism, inevitably grappling with the diachronic dimension. In its commonest and most extreme form, this has involved describing (and analysing) pre- and post-colonial European circumstances. Less frequently, anthropologists in this functionalist tradition have attempted to elucidate how contemporary customs and institutions have come to assume their current form – writing in the style of economic or social historians (as e.g. Isaac Schapera). Here social anthropologists have sought to write history in the sense of chronicling and examining the unfolding (or succession) of events over time. As with historians, the aim has been that of establishing particularistic causal chains of connectedness, ultimately explaining how the ethnographic 'present' has come to be what it is.

Some have gone further than this essentially particularistic enterprise. Despite the supposedly ahistorical constraints of functionalism, sometimes those working in this mode have explicitly attempted to test hypothetical correlations (or 'adhesions') between customs or institutions over time. Methodologically the temporal dimension has been seen here as an alternative or supplement to the spatial dimension for carrying out comparative analysis, offering a challenging laboratory situation. Naturally in this functionalist tradition, the emphasis and causal force assigned to historical factors is far from uniform. Yet this does not decrease its interest and significance as a persistent thread in the British structural-functionalist style. In seeking to identify and trace this filament, I appreciate that one risks succumbing to the dangers of what George Stocking rightly identifies as 'presentism' – rediscovering in the past the salient features of the present. All I can say in defence here is that historiography is indeed lamentably underdeveloped in British anthropology. The present tentative essay may, I hope, provoke other corrective (if not corroborative) research.

So if, as Schapera (1962) and others have demonstrated, attention to the diachronic aspects of cultures and social institutions is by no means novel, this historical emphasis in British functionalism seems more pronounced today than it was in 1966 when the annual meeting of the Association of Social Anthropologists of the Commonwealth discussed the relationship between the two subjects (see I.M. Lewis, 1968(a)). In a by-no-means simple fashion, this heightened interest in history in contemporary British social anthropology reflects shifts in the relative prominence of the ethnographic areas favoured for research, wider regional economic and political developments, the growth of cultural pluralism in Britain, and the varied influence of imported French and American anthropological vogues. This trend towards history (which he predicted) would please Evans-Pritchard (1950; 1961), the most persuasive (though not the most consistent) advocate of history in post-war British social anthropology. Maurice Freedman (1972), whose Sinological studies are markedly historical, summed up this trend (a shade optimistically) in his comprehensive 1970 stocktaking,

> two lines of development intersect, if not converge: historians grow more sociological and at the same time widen the range of their interests to include parts of the world in respect of which the documentary evidence is slight; anthropologists, on their side, increasingly gaze back into the dimmer time to which, in the case of many, they had been previously blinded by the dazzling brilliance of the present.

Yet, if the tide now seems to be generally flowing in this direction (and is often helped along by historians), British social anthropologists have by no means fully exploited the opportunities which an historical perspective offers for understanding contemporary social formations, far less for wider-ranging comparative analysis. Many are still prone to succumb to what M.G. Smith (1962; cf. Moore, 1994) aptly called 'the fallacy of the ethnographic present'. Hypnotised by the dazzling brilliance of the ethnographic present in all its splendid particularity, they tend to reify and concretise social processes, arbitrarily detaching these from their spatio-temporal settings and transforming them into rigid, timeless structures. This prompts assertions (usually unsubstantiated) that one set of social or cultural features, 'generates' (i.e. determines, or causes) some other set. At the very least, this encourages uncritical statements about the assumed interdependence of institutions or customs which happen to co-exist, but whose mutual necessity is not rigorously demonstrated.

Associated with this distorting ahistorical treatment is the equally misleading practice of comparing, holistically and without qualification, total 'societies' or 'social structures', rather than appropriately contextualised social institutions and processes. This methodological malpractice, or variants of it, has often been condemned (as for instance by Evans-Pritchard (1961) and by Leach (1961) who draws his own arbitrary boundaries). But the practice continues unabated. So, many of my colleagues blandly assume that, irrespective of scale or complexity, all 'societies' – whether small, loosely linked hunting bands or vast centralised empires – share the same operational and organisational requirements, producing the same degree of social cohesion, and can consequently be meaningfully compared with reference to variations in cosmology, concepts of time or whatever. This is like asserting that the architectural and engineering logistics of mud huts are the same as those of sky-scrapers and gothic cathedrals. This leads to such remarkable propositions as the claim advanced by M. Bloch (1977, p.288) that the hunting and gathering Hadza of Tanzania have as much 'society' as the Balinese, differing only in the extent to which 'their social theory [is] expressed in the language of ritual'.

An awareness of the rather obviously different ways in which time may be perceived in the same or different cultural settings, is not, in itself, evidently any guarantee that the pitfalls of the 'ethnographic present' have been overcome. Thus, if an enhanced emphasis on history opens the door to a more scholarly and systematic study of institutional correlates and causes, British social anthropology has still much ground to cover.

FUNCTIONALISM AND HISTORY

In addition to the 'presentism' which intense personal fieldwork in the style of Malinowski encourages, our difficulties are, of course, also rooted in the historical circumstances in which functionalism and later structural-functionalism developed. What has come to be known as 'British structural-functionalism' – associated with A.R. Radcliffe-Brown (1881–1955) and B. Malinowski (1884–1942) – grew up partly in reaction to the prevailing cultural history (or historical ethnology) tradition of the Continental diffusionists. It was also a reaction to the evolutionary school. Despite the different concepts of functionalism, in part reflecting their contrasting intellectual backgrounds, held by Malinowski and Radcliffe-Brown, they shared a holistic view of the interdependence of contemporary customs and institutions and of the role of the past as an anchor for the present. This fitted well with the circumstances of their major field research in remote, geographically discrete island communities, on the margins of world history. Since, in these exotic isolated cultures, the past was virtually unknown and seemed largely unknowable, the 'function' of stories and myths about this past lay primarily in the latters' contribution to the maintenance of the present social and political order. Hence, what Radcliffe-Brown dismissed as 'conjectural history' could (and should) be ignored as a source of *bona fide* history Their students (including Evans-Pritchard whose first degree was in History, and others with different formations) who constituted the next and formative generation of modern British social anthropology, carried out fieldwork in a wide range of geographical settings in the heyday of British colonial rule between the two world wars.

The relationship between British colonial rule and the anthropology practised in different places under its protection – rather than unequivocally in its service (as has so often been asserted: see e.g. Kuklich, 1991) is complex and would be distracting to examine here. However, one point is perhaps relevant. As is well known, the system of 'indirect rule', favoured by the British, involved delegating authority through 'traditional' indigenous political institutions. This entailed preserving and perpetuating 'traditional' structures (and sometimes inadvertently creating new ones in the process) as functioning enterprises, endowed with considerable local autonomy. As argued in Chapter 4, the conspicuousness and accessibility of such patently functioning communities seems likely to have reinforced, and perhaps promoted, the holistic, functionalist approach in British social anthropology. (French anthropology with its stress on *culture* may, correspondingly, reflect the French pattern of direct rule, with its emphasis on cultural assimilation.) Indirect rule did not, of course, exclude change, nor isolate the peoples studied by British anthropologists from wider external influences, political or other.

Although Gregory Bateson (1936), Raymond Firth (1936) and Reo Fortune (1935) followed closely in Malinowski's ethnographic footsteps, carrying out their research in Oceania, this 'desert island disc' style set by the two founding fathers was inevitably disturbed by the wider and historically more complex range of field experience encountered in other regions. While generally pursuing the functionalist analysis of interlocking customs and institutions within that arbitrarily defined isolate, a particular 'society', Malinowski's and Radcliffe-Brown's immediate successors showed to varying degrees, and in different ways at different times, that this approach did not necessarily make history, where it could be traced, irrelevant. Equally, although science as well as a certain romanticism encouraged the quest for 'authentic', pre-colonial customs and institutions, this did not inevitably exclude acknowledging and exploring the impact of colonial rule itself in the ethnographic context. In fact, this was often a prerequisite for discovering the 'traditional' pre-colonial situation. Hence the claim (which, ironically, is itself functionalist) that imperialism necessarily generated an unquestioning 'functionalism' incapable of considering the impact of colonial rule is not borne out by the facts. Of course, originating as it so often does ultimately in US sources, this assumption is not surprising – given the well-documented complicity between some American anthropologists and organisations such as the Central Intelligence Agency (CIA). But it is ethnocentric to project this imperialist view everywhere else.

Already in this formative period between the wars, sub-Saharan Africa bulked large as the major theatre for British fieldwork. Apart from European (and less pervasively Islamic) influence, this marginal zone was not central to one of the world's 'Great Traditions', and lacked a readily accessible written history and corpus of associated scholarship. The fact that even in these seemingly unencouraging circumstances, British functionalist anthropologists were prepared to dabble in history is at first sight all the more remarkable. However, when we examine this situation more closely we find significant local variations. Attention to historical forces and factors is most evident in the work of those social anthropologists (many of them South Africans) whose research was based in central and southern Africa, where internal as well as external historical forces – including migration and immigration, and industrialisation and urbanisation – were prominent features. These were naturally especially striking in pluralist South Africa (more closely linked to the Christian 'Great Tradition'), the home of Bantu studies and, later, Bantustans, where the historically oriented Afrikaans School (with its Continental connections) played a significant role in the development of the ideology of *apartheid*.[1]

Independently of this, the pre-apartheid tradition of writing tribal

histories, pioneered by missionaries, was taken up by social anthropologists like Isaac Schapera and continued within the functionalist
framework imported (or reinforced) by Radcliffe-Brown's presence
under General Smuts' aegis at Cape Town from 1920 to 1926. The
pre-apartheid era on the whole seems to have stressed the *cultural*
(rather than biological) differences between white and black – a gulf
which, if in some views exceedingly wide, could in theory be bridged
(eventually) by acculturation and assimilation. In this vein, the majority
of Anglophone South African anthropologists in this period, and later
those who opposed apartheid, stressed the obvious cultural, social and
political changes in which their subjects were immersed. So Monica
Wilson's exhaustive study of the Pondo was fittingly entitled *Reaction
to Conquest* (1936), and she and her left-wing husband, Godfrey,
the controversial first Director of the influential Rhodes-Livingstone
Institute, opend in 1937[2] in Northern Rhodesia (Zambia), produced
what is generally considered to be the first modern general social
anthropological analysis of social change – a subtle, sophisticated
work which retains its value (Wilson and Wilson, 1945). Schapera's
historical studies on the Tswana (1942; 1947; 1952; 1970) (which can
be described as 'social' or 'economic' history) continued throughout
this period. Moreover, having spent five years at the London School
of Economics (LSE) with Malinowski, returning to South Africa in
1930 (where he stayed until 1950), Schapera found no difficulty in
combining the latter's functionalism with his own interest in history
which he passed on to his students (who included such key figures as
Max Gluckman, Ellen Hellman, Eileen Krige and Hilda Kuper).

This early development of an historical emphasis in the work of those
British functionalist anthropologists (all directly or indirectly students
of Malinowski or Radcliffe-Brown and sometimes of both) in central
and southern Africa, where dramatic socio-economic change was so
prominent, thus *preceded* Evans-Pritchard's much-cited 'historical'
study of the Muslim Sanusi religious order in Cyrenaica. (Based on
war service in Libya and published in 1949, this was presented by
its author as 'one of the few genuinely historical books written by an
anthropologist *de carriere.*').

After the war, having succeeded Radcliffe-Brown as Professor of
Social Anthropology at Oxford in 1946, Evans-Pritchard's influence over
other anthropologists working from the Rhodes-Livingstone Institute in
central Africa (Max Gluckman, Elizabeth Colson, John Barnes, Ian
Cunnison and, somewhat differently, Clyde Mitchell, a pioneer – with
A.L. Epstein – of modern urban ethnic research) may have reinforced

this diachronic tendency. Thus, while in his celebrated Marett Lecture of 1950 Evans-Pritchard was proclaiming that social anthropology was a kind of historiography, an aesthetic or philosophical discipline, not a science (as he had earlier maintained), influenced by Schapera and others these younger colleagues were already publishing a number of explicitly historical studies.[3] Here oral and documentary sources were employed, not only to elucidate contemporary social structure and institutions, but also, if more rarely, to explore diachronic changes in co-related institutions over time. The historical method was thus being applied, as Evans-Pritchard urged (1961; 1970), to examine hypotheses on the functional interdependence of social institutions. Barnes, for example, found confirmation (albeit in my view erroneous) of Gluckman's hypothesis (relating patriliny, stable marriage and high marriage payments as opposed to bilaterality (and matriliny), unstable marriage and low marriage payments) in his diachronic comparison of 'traditional' and 'contemporary' (late 1940s) Ngoni society.

After leaving South and central Africa for England and becoming founder Professor of Social Anthropology at Manchester in 1949, Max Gluckman, whose historical concern had a Marxist edge, stressing conflict as well as consensus,[4] directed his colleagues and students to examine diachronic and processual themes. 'Process' and Custom' became battle cries mobilising this closely knit team. As well as others who carried out fieldwork in Europe, India and the Middle East, these included Ian Cunnison (another of Evans-Pritchard's many pupils) whose pioneering account (1959) of rural ethnicity and history in the pluralist Lunda state on the Luapula river in central Africa deserves wider attention than it has received.

In this 'British' Africanist anthropology (with its influential South African members), we thus see by the early 1950s research on social change and history (urban and rural), radiating out from industrial, multi-racial South and central Africa (the Rhodes-Livingstone Institute). These themes were thence widely rediffused via Gluckman's far-flung 'Manchester School' network and, especially in relation to history, intermittently reinforced by converging currents from Evans-Pritchard's prestigious 'Oxford School'.

In east Africa, particularly at the East African Institute for Social Research opened at Makerere College, Uganda, in 1950, ethnic pluralism focused on 'tribal' rather than racial divisions. Here a parallel emphasis on history was prominent, especially in Aidan Southall's imaginative analysis of the Alur 'segmentary state' (1956) (supervised by Schapera, now at LSE) and in that of the American Lloyd Fallers

(1964) in association with Audrey Richards – whose research on the Bemba was supervised by Malinowski. On the other side of the continent, in Nigeria and Ghana, emphasis on the history of contemporary social systems was clearly present in the work of other social anthropologists of the 'British School'. As in South Africa, this was obviously influenced by local traditions of tribal historical research by expatriate missionaries, officials and native historians. The earliest 'modern' social anthropological study embracing this tradition and explicitly discussing the nature and meaning of indigenous views of the past, was the comprehensive diachronic analysis of the Nupe Emirate of Bida in northern Nigeria (*A Black Byzantium*, 1942), made by another of Malnowski's students, S.F. Nadel. Colleagues who continued this tradition included the theorist of pluralism, M.G. Smith (1960), with his ambitious comparative political history of Hausa states; G.I. Jones (1963) on the history of trade and state formation in the Oil Rivers; and, in direct collaboration with historians, the work of R.E. Bradbury (1967) on the Kingdom of Benin. The strongly historical orientation of Smith's and Bradbury's work was certainly reinforced by their connection with Daryll Forde, at University College, London, who, despite the influence of Malinowski and Radcliffe-Brown, never fully embraced 'structural-functionalism', retaining an eclectic Africanist perspective which reflected his earlier work in geography and archaeology. Uncharacteristically in British anthropology at this time, Forde stressed the importance of ecology and by no means excluded cultural diffusion or historical ethnology.

In northern Ghana, although its full historical thrust was not so apparent until a little later, Jack Goody (1967; 1968; 1971) was conducting somewhat parallel research. His affiliation was with another of Malinowski's earliest protégés, Meyer Fortes (also South African), established as professor at Cambridge from 1950. Like his friend and contemporary Evans-Pritchard, Fortes (1970) was exploring the manner in which concepts of time related to (and in his functionalist view) reflected contemporary social structure (with memorable effects on his students).[5] In a sense his elaboration of the significant theme of the (generational) developmental cycle in family and domestic groups may be seen as a synthesis of diachronic and functionalist synchrony. With reference primarily to domestic groups, Fortes's terms 'production' and 'reproduction' have acquired a new lease of life, with a slightly different meaning, in the Marxist anthropological vogue of the 1970s. We shall return to further historical developments in Cambridge anthropology later.

Moving into the 1950s we thus reach the period when, in keeping with the growth of African nationalism and preparations for eventual independence, history departments in the mostly recently established African universities were busily engaged in reconstructing African history and exploring the vast potential resources disclosed by oral history. If still lacking the rigorous precision later developed for it by Vansina (1964; 1965) and his colleagues, this technique was now securely established in British Africanist anthropology. It would, perhaps, be too much to say that these anthropologists had 'discovered' or even 'rediscovered' Africa's heritage of oral history – but they certainly helped to make it better known and accessible to professional historians more familiar with documentary sources. They also played an important part in establishing that, contrary to the opinions of some historians, Africa did possess a pre-colonial history.

Although this trend was encouraged by African nationalism and impending independence, favouring an emphasis (à la Malinowski) on the past (as a base for the future) and on development and social change, social anthropology itself was at this time acquiring a negative connotation in local élite circles. Despite the pan-African fame of Malinowski's Kenyan student, Jomo Kenyatta (1938), anthropology had generally acquired the reputation of studying (and hence perpetuating) 'primitive tribal societies'. It was consequently associated with divisive tribalism (also allegedly fostered by colonialism) in a context where the goal was national solidarity. It is ironical to note, en passant, that anthropologists were frequently regarded by expatriate British colonial officials as romantic reactionaries, exploitatively dedicated to the preservation of archaic tribal institutions for academic reasons. 'History' and 'Sociology' were less offensive labels. It is scarcely surprising that a number of departments of social anthropology at African universities, with African as well as expatriate staff, found it prudent to adopt the title 'Sociology'. In any case, many social anthropologists had already discovered that the most readily intelligible, and least misleading, way of presenting themselves to their informants was as historians.

Of course, as African studies developed as an area specialisation, political scientists, historians and other specialists naturally sought to extend their research into terrain traditionally monopolised – often faute de mieux – by social anthropologists. In the immediate pre- and post-independence periods in Africa (950s–60s), social anthropologists thus tended to be under attack from all sides. This made 'historian' an even more attractive flag of convenience. Thus was the historian F.W. Maitland's prophecy about the historical destiny of anthropology curiously and partially fulfilled! It is surely not without significance that this hostile tendency seems to have been much less pronounced in countries such as the Sudan and Ethiopia where there were secure ethnic élites and social anthropology had, at least traditionally, mainly concentrated on 'subject' or marginal populations (e.g. the southern Sudanese Nuer, Dinka, etc.). (There is an intriguing resemblance here to the situation in India discussed below.) In other circumstances, where social anthropology was seen as linked positively with nationalism – as, for example, in my own case in Somalia, criticism was also limited (cf. Lewis, 1998a).

HISTORICAL TRENDS IN REGIONAL ETHNOGRAPHY

As suggested above, although particular local factors clearly encouraged local variations, the general absence of a 'Great' historical tradition in sub-Saharan Africa (which retained its position as the most popular zone for field research well into the 1960s) makes the (admittedly variable) attention paid to history in British social anthropology the more striking. We shall return to consider how this might be interpreted when we review developments in contrasting 'Great Tradition' regions (such as the Middle East and India) shortly. Before proceeding we must not, however, exaggerate the historical tendency we have been exploring in the works of these British Africanist anthropologists. None (with the partial exception perhaps of Evans-Pritchard, Isaac Schapera, Jack Goody and M.G. Smith) of the British-based anthropologists so far mentioned made history a major and enduring focus of his work, or could be described as a true hybrid of the two professions, having achieved a synthesis of both disciplines. Nor was the emphasis on history or the use to which it was put by any means uniform. Excluding the mere 'historical backdrop' approach, these ranged, as we have seen, from particularistic diachronic ethnographic accounts to (more rarely) serious attempts to employ historical data to test hypotheses on the postulated interdependence of institutions (e.g. Barnes on Gluckman's marriage stability hypothesis). It would be dangerous, too, as later comments will indicate, to overestimate the influence of Evans-Pritchard, whose name tends to be totemically linked with history in the lineages traced here.

With all these provisos, this African experience affords an instructive illustration of the flexibility of British structural-functionalism. In its capacity to include a considerable emphasis on diachrony (not to mention various other tendencies), this 'British School' turns out to be a rather broader church than it has sometimes been depicted. This is not altogether surprising when we recall the movement's history. After all, Durkheim, the main source (other than Herbert Spencer) for the British structural-functionalists' holistic approach at the theoretical level, also provided in this *Division of Labour* (1893) a programmatic (and to some extent evolutionary) model for the historical study of 'social facts' and of social change.

Moreover, Radcliffe-Brown, Durkheim's chief apostle in Britain, was at pains to distinguish between 'conjectural history' and solidly based authentic history. It was only the former that he condemned: the importance of the latter in understanding phenomena was not disputed. Indeed, history in the proper sense of the word was complementary to synchronic structural-functionalism. As Radcliffe-Brown put it in 1935:

> one explanation of a social system would be its history, where we know it – the detailed account of how it came to be what it is and where it is. Another explanation of the same system is obtained by showing that it is a special exemplification of laws of social physiology or social functioning. The two kinds of explanation do not conflict, but supplement one another.

(Virtually echoing this two-layered view a quarter of a century later, Evans-Pritchard pleads for integration: 'I believe an interpretation on functionalist lines (of the present in terms of the present) and on historical lines (of the present in terms of the past) must somehow be combined'.) A later essay (Radcliffe-Brown, 1952; see also Stocking, 1984, p.136; 1995, p.332) implies a closer if somewhat ambiguous, interdependence between the two approaches:

> In a *Synchronic* description we give an account of a form of social life as it exists at at certain time, abstracting as far as possible from changes that may be taking place in its features. A *diachronic* account, on the other hand, as an account of such changes over a period.

In striking and conscious contrast to Malinowski (1938) who saw social change and historical development as involving *cultural* change and exchange, Radcliffe-Brown (1952) held that such processes were essentially *social*, and should be understood in terms of the interaction of economic and political structures.

At the risk of oversimplifying and imparting an exaggerated consistency ot a period spanning thirty years, we could perhaps conclude that in

Radcliffe-Brown's version of functionalism, if history was by no means outlawed, those who ventured into diachronic pastures were cautioned to proceed with circumspection. The problem of how to deal with the temporal dimension and the ensuing dialogue with professional historians, linguists and other specialists, has inevitably become more acute and sustained as British social anthropologists have become more and more involved in the study of communities which are firmly embedded in the literate 'Great Traditions' of the world, whether in Europe, the Mediterranean, Islamic north Africa and the Middle East or south and south-east Asia. (This shift in ethnographic regional specialisation has become increasingly pronounced since African independence in the 1960s with, more recently, Papua New Guinea replacing sub-Saharan Africa as the European anthropologists' last exotic frontier – already within the reach of up-market package tourism.)

As is well known to his students, Evans-Pritchard used his Marett Lecture (1950) to distance himself from his predecessor at Oxford and past mentor, Radcliffe-Brown. Attacking the latter's sterile scientistic functionalism, Evans-Pritchard nailed his own colours to the mast with the new rallying cry 'history'. Social anthropology was, he proclaimed, a closely linked kindred discipline, and it was time his colleagues mended their fences and repaired the misguided functionalist breach with history. Malinowski's less theoretically orientated functionalism was simply a methodological guide and regularly dismissed by Evans-Pritchard as a mere 'literary device' . . . in rather poor aesthetic taste. This new orientation, or re-orientation, was in any case inevitable, he predicted, now that his colleagues and students were increasingly turning their attention to communities which belonged to the historical Great Traditions. In practice, however, this has turned out to be a more complex and protracted process than Evans-Pritchard seems to have envisaged. In sub-Saharan Africa, if linguists are excluded, social anthropologists enjoyed a virtual monopoly. But in these other more complex regions, anthropologists were the outsiders and novices venturing into charted and well-tilled territory, already subject to centuries of sophisticated research and scholarship in many languages – indigenous as well as European. This was a daunting prospect.

It is therefore perhaps not surprising that, as they sallied forth into these new areas under the banner of structural-functionalism, British social anthropologists were prone to emphasise the distinctive novelty (and superiority) of their work, rather than seeking to embed it firmly within the existing corpus of regional specialist scholarship – the price of entry to which, in terms of linguistic and historical competence, tended to be high. It was thus attractive to assume the confident posture that these older (and by implication 'old-fashioned') branches of Oriental scholarship concentrated on books and sacred literature, conveying an idealised view of life, whereas social anthropology focused squarely on real life as manifest in the actions and thought of living contemporary peoples in their everyday activities. Orientalists, to put it crudely, studied official religion: anthropologists popular religion. This increased rather than diminished the gap between social anthropology and history, and reinforced the reactive distinction between synchronic structural-functionalism and culture history. Thus, rather than encouraging convergence between history and modern social anthropology as Evans-Pritchard had assumed, the reverse tendency seemed more pronounced, at least initially, actually postponing the eventual and more recent amalgamation, if not synthesis, which appears more prominent today.

With the dearth of serious historiographical research on British social anthropology, it would be premature (and probably inaccurate) to assume that such convergence as has occurred has proceeded at a constant or regular pace in 'Great Tradition' regions such as south Asia or the Middle East. If our rough and ready model of the interaction between metropolitan developments in *zeitgeist*, anthropological theory and regional ethnography and setting has some validity, we would not in any case expect to find such simple chronological uniformities. The case of India, which as a non-specialist I can only raise superficially here, seems nevertheless instructive. An Indian appraisal in 1977 concluded that 'Indian anthropology, which had been born and brought up under the dominant influence of British anthropology, matured during its constructive phase also under a British influence' (Vidyarthi, 1977). In fact, of course, with intriguing analogies to the situation in South Africa, anthropology has a long history in India under the British Raj. It was taught in Indian universities by Indian scholars as early as 1920, and British and Indian officials had long carried out ethnographic research on castes and tribes, paralleling the early work of professional British anthropologists such as Rivers, the Seligmans and Hutton. This work accompanied the wider enterprise of Indology which concentrated on Hindu literature, history and religion in the culture-historical style of Oriental studies.

The magnitude of the challenge involved in mastering the requisite linguistic and historical expertise seems to be partly reflected in the otherwise surprising paucity of studies in India during the heyday of British social anthropology in the 1950s and 1960s. While many

Indian and some European scholars continued the older ethnographic tradition (especially among 'tribes'), the pioneering modern structural-functionalist work was, of course, Srinivas's study of village religion among the Coorgs (1952). This exemplary analysis of the social function of ritual and symbols followed the path advocated by his mentor, Radcliffe-Brown (as exemplified in *The Andaman Islanders*). But it also departed from this model, attempting to come to terms with the temporal and spatial setting through the in-effect diffusionist concept of 'Sanskritization', referring and relating village practice to the Great Tradition of the sacred texts.

Further afield, in 1954 Edmund Leach published his well-known *Political Systems of Highland Burma*. As Gluckman has pointed out, this can be seen as a kind of synthesis of the synchronic and diachronic approaches in the form of an oscillation between two essentially static states exemplified in the Shan and Kachin political formations (or 'ideal types'). A succession of subsequent British anthropologists pursued the microcosmic village study tradition pioneered by Srinivas, without much reference to the wider Hindu macrocosm. (In this period the originality of Kathleen Gough's (1952) detailed historical research on the formerly polyandrous Nayars doubtless partly reflects the fact that, in the changed circumstances of contemporary Nayar life, these exotic practices could only be treated retrospectively). The works of Bailey (1960) and A.L. Epstein (1973) (likewise students of Gluckman), in particular, however, can be seen as ushering in a new trend, concerned with the village-level response to change and modernisation, stressing class as well as caste, changes in the character of *jajmani* – relationships, the role of entrepreneurs and political factions, and social networks – all reaching outside the village.

This wider emphasis, looking outwards from the village microcosm, complemented the approach persuasively advocated in the late 1950s by Evans-Pritchard's Indianist colleagues at Oxford, Louis Dumont and David Pocock, insisting that what social anthropologists saw in villages, to be properly understood, had to be set in the wider context of the sacred texts and enduring principles of Hinduism. It is difficult for a non-Indianist to gauge the extent to which this renewed focus on the dynamic interplay between the Little and the Great Tradition may reflect the concurrent influence of the American cultural-historical approach on Indian ethnography – whose impact, at this point, L.P. Vidyarthi emphasises. The younger generation of Indianist anthropologists in Britain (including R. Burghart, C.J. Fuller (1979; 1992) and J. Parry (1980; 1994) among others) see themselves as taking Dumont and

Pocock's prescription a stage further. They focus attention on the practice of the 'Great Tradition' in such cardinal institutions as worship and pilgrimage at major shrines, temples and holy cities. Presumably it is against this background that one should evaluate Fuller's assertion that 'the anthropological analysis of Hinduism is still in its infancy'. Much the same could perhaps be said for Sri Lanka, where parallel work on Buddhism is proceeding and, according to some views, has already developed more fruitfully than its Indian counterpart.

Europe, the Mediterranean and the Middle East and Islamic north Africa are all areas to which, unlike India, British social anthropologists only began to pay serious attention in the 1950s. While in the case of Europe and the Mediterranean there are not the same formidable barriers to acquiring scholarly expertise in the culture history of the Great Tradition, it is interesting that the initial emphasis was, as in India, again mainly on microcosmic village studies.

John Davis's refreshingly stringent appraisal (1977) of Mediterranean studies (including his own) remarks on the contrast between Evans-Pritchard's confident pronouncements on the inevitability of historicising developments in this region and the paucity and weakness of historical analysis by British anthropologists working in the area. In the view of this specialist (whose training includes both disciplines):

> the tendencies have been, on the one hand, to indulge in rather patchy sketches of 'the historical background': on the other, to create methodological devices whereby the facts about the past can be drawn into an account of changing structures. No anthropologist has undertaken research into the past societies in quite the way Evans-Pritchard intended . . .

This severe judgement risks underestimating the creative exploration of such regional themes as honour, shame, kinship, *compadrazzo* and class, and the relationship between local and central power – themes which, in general, Davis himself discusses admirably. It is true that Evans-Pritchard advocated the inclusion of history by anthropologists in their ethnographic accounts of particular communities as deepening and enriching the anthropologists' cultural biography (a sort of diachronic 'thickening' of ethnography, to adopt Geertz's phrase). But he also saw the temporal as complementing the spatial dimension in the wider endeavour of comparative analysis, seeking the causal and other linkages between interlocking social institutions and customs.

The Mediterranean area extends into the Muslim world where

anthropologists of the British structural-functionalist mould have found themselves face to face with the competing 'Great Tradition' of Islam. Here again we find many diachronic studies of local communities (and sometimes ethnic groups) – a number of which have disclosed social processes of general theoretical significance. Thus, for example, Abner Cohen's (1965) theoretically unpretentious analysis of the changing significance of lineages in three separate periods in the history of Arab villages along the Israeli–Jordanian border demonstrates how lineages may, according to the wider politico-economic context, stress or disregard endogamy. More effectively in my opinion than his subsequent more explicitly theoretical works, this study with its simple tripartite historical dimension demonstrates how cultural principles (in this case agnatic ideology) can lie dormant over long periods of time, re-emerging into full activity when conditions are appropriate. One sees here in the long term a pattern of interaction between marriage and descent which one can find also in spatial comparative analysis. Widening their focus from their original concentration on the political institutions of Somali nomads in the 1950s, my own studies of the persistence of segmentary lineage organisation in a time perspective including the macrocosmic political dimension of the modern Somali state (1960–1990), and its collapse (in 1990/91) challenge received views on the preconditions for such organisation (I.M. Lewis, 1988, 1994; 1997c).

Particularly in sub-Saharan Africa, the spread of Islam offers special opportunities for testing general theories on the historical and ecological modalities of Islam, and for exploring a whole series of possible structural interdependencies in the context of this 'Great Tradition'. This setting is especially apt for examining the merits of rival theories of religious conversion. Here we confront the essentially diffusionist views of Islamicists such as J.S. Trimingham (1968) and historians such as H.J. Fisher (1973). Both adopt a tripartite model, distinguishing three stages in Islamicisation: germination/quarantine; crisis/mixing; and re-orientation/reform. Robin Horton (1975) counters with an 'intellectualist' argument, emphasising the analogies between indigenous theistic beliefs and those of Islam. These concepts are in turn held to correspond (in Durkheimian fashion) to the scale of social relations, increasing with trade. My own supplementary view, partly inspired by Parkin's (1970) observation that Giriama entrepreneurs are 'involuntarily' converted to Islam as a cure for illness, stresses the role of Islam as supplying a universalistic identity (cf. below, Ch. 7).

As I have also argued traditional main morality religions displaced by Islam frequently become 'peripheral possession cults', appealing particularly to women and men of marginal status (I.M. Lewis, 1971; 1996). Spirit-possession is thus cast in a context of conflict, and can be examined as a strategy of attack analogously to witchcraft accusations (see below, pp. 94-95). As with the study of the genesis of cargo-cults in Papua New Guinea (pioneered by Peter Worsley (1957)), a careful examination of the history of possession cults (cf. Chapter 6) provides important insights into the dynamics of religion and its social concomitants. This offers a useful vantage point from which to reconsider Ernest Gellner's 'Pendulum Swing' theory of Islamic modalities (itself oddly reminiscent of the political scientist and political commentator Robert MacKenzie's famous election swing-ometer). As may be recalled, this posits scripturalist puritans in towns, illiterate enthusiasts in the countryside, and is similar to the concept of Sanskritisation in south Asia, inviting the same kind of criticism. Thus women's possession cults in Islam, although represented locally by men (and by Islamicists) as 'primitive survivals' are, in reality, often a paradoxical response to Muslim embourgoisement and an increased emphasis on orthodoxy and respectability on the part of men (cf. I.M. Lewis, 1996, pp.139–54).

THE IMPACT OF MARXIST AND OTHER INFLUENCES

Our brief and inevitably selective regional survey suggests the complex, rather than as Evans-Pritchard seemed to envisage (perhaps ethnocentrically) direct and immediate relationship between the adoption of a historical approach and the presence or absence of a Great (historical) and literate Tradition. Yet it has to be admitted, or at least this is what our survey suggests, that *in the long run*, 'the *longue durée*', the historicity of 'Great Tradition' ethnographic regions catches up even with wayward British social anthropologists.

We have so far treated British anthropology in the style of a 'desert island disc' anthropology – as though it were itself a remote exotic flower, immune from external intellectual influences. How have other factors in our tripartite schema for the relations between data and theory in social anthropology affected these developments? Here we have to include American and French influence, particularly since the 1960s, and the changing socio-cultural home environment of British anthropology. This period was also one of marked expansion in the size and scale of the British anthropological profession. The small segmented clan of the 1950s has developed into a fractious tribe, or congeries of tribes, with opposing factions competing for monopoly control over new ideas, new directions, new fashions. The questing spirit of this phase is well conveyed by Adam Kuper's remark at the end of his 1973 (p. 236) survey of 'The British School': 'I do not know what the future of social anthropology will be. If I did, I would be there already'.

Prior to post-modernism (cf. Chapter 9), the most obvious foreign influences since the 1960s have, of course, been French structuralism and Marxism, with linked theoretical currents from America including the new (or renewed) cultural ecology. Since Marxism embraces history (indeed fetishises it) while Lévi-Straussian structuralism formally opposes it (but, naturally, not unequivocally), these rival French influences might be expected to cancel each other out – at least in aggregate – leaving the developing historicist trends in British anthropology to proceed under their own steam in their appointed directions. However, as usual with the diffusion of ideas and vogues, the resulting situation is clearly more complicated. The leading British apostles of structuralism – Rodney Needham and Edmund Leach and their followers – generally paid little attention to history in their latest work (although they might from time to time engage in historiographic forays). On the other hand, some of the recent work by British-based anthropologists of self-declared Marxist affiliation is certainly strongly historical in orientation. Efforts are made to reconstruct the past of contemporary social formations in the light of the evidence available and to interpret current processes of change historically. (This is done both with reference to new field data (e.g. Kahn, 1980) and in re-evaluations of 'classic material' (e.g. Friedman, 1975).) More generally, apart from, and in addition to, its 'radical chic' cachet, part of the attraction of 'Marxist anthropology' is surely that it offers an epistemologically appropriate paradigm for coping with manifestly diachronic data, especially in the post-colonial and post-functional era. This explicit (and continuously self-revised) Marxist thrust – assembling more and more 'pre-class' formations under the elusive umbrella of class conflict – has, I think, also contributed to a renewal of the ecological approach in British social anthropology, with emphasis on particular social formations as adaptations to specific environmental conditions.

These exotic influences appear to have reinforced our diffuse native Marxism (already noted in Gluckman's 'Manchester School') and confirmed Jack Goody's (1968; 1971; 1977a; 1977b; etc.) influential influence on history in Cambridge anthropology, with his long and close collaboration with the innovative social historian Peter Laslett.[6] More generally the resulting hybridisation between the two subjects is perfectly illustrated in the sustained and wide-ranging work of the well-known historian-anthropologist, Alan MacFarlane (1970), on English witchcraft, and on the roots of individualism in England (1978) and so on. The important intellectual feedback here is by no means restricted to British historians.

If diffuse Marxist influences and tendencies promote the diachronic vein in British social anthropology (which has rarely been completely suppressed) they also paradoxically risk encouraging a return to an unhistorical, circular holism which is characteristic of the most rigid, mechanical functionalism. Here, as in the writings of Maurice Godelier (1977) on hunters and gatherers (and other topics), which have been influential in Britain, effects are transmuted into causes in the most simplistic Radcliffe-Brownian style, and the genuine pursuit of historical, causal relations is evaded.

As some of its practitioners have openly acknowledged (e.g. Kahn, 1981; Bloch, 1986), though not so trenchantly as Marxist philosophers like G.A. Cohen (1978), this Marxist anthropology thus risks degenerating into what amounts to an ahistorical 'super-functionalism'. From this perspective, Marxist anthropology in the 1970s and 80s appears as the acceptable face of functionalism. Since this functional tendency is found in French Marxist sources as well as in Lévi-Strauss's own (anti-historical) structuralist analyses (where the 'function' of myths is to abolish time, and so on), it can hardly be attributed to the polluting influence of British empiricism in domesticating these exotic intellectual imports. Marxist anthropology is thus in practice, not unambiguously, historical, and the net impact of these external vogues is not as far-reaching as might appear at first sight. In conformity with Kuhn's model of the development of science in terms of an uneven series of paradigm shifts, like their colleagues in other fields British social anthropologists tend to exaggerate the discontinuities and to underplay the continuities in the history of the discipline which, appropriately, remains largely unwritten.[7]

Finally, here, we should note the (as I see it) reinforcing influence of the development of ethnic pluralism in Britain itself. The growth of interest in and of research on ethnicity in the 1960s and 70s (following the first flutter of concern with 'race relations', linked to the early wave of West Indian immigration in the early 1950s), surely obviously reflects increasing ethnic pluralism – and self-conscious awareness of this – at home. In the heyday of the subject, 'desert island disc' British anthropology was a 'tele-anthropology' carried out at a safe distance from home. Now, against all expectations, the exotic quarry of the British anthropologist has suddenly appeared on his own doorstep. As argued (p.130), this has clearly reinforced (if not created) the growing interest in British anthropology in 'ethnicity', both in urban contexts in Europe and the Third World. More to the point in this chronicle of diachrony, this pluralist development has also fostered a more historically sensitive interest in those processes that contribute to ethnic identity (ethnogenesis). Although this has prompted protracted debate on the problematic ethnic identity off such sacred cows of British anthropology as 'the Nuer', the vital and complex issue of the relationship between 'culture' and 'society' is still neglected, with all the unfortunate implications for reification noted above.

THE INEVITABILITY OF HISTORY

Thus if, as I believe, British anthropologists are increasingly tending to emphasise historical factors in their collection of data and analyses, this is above all a belated reflection of the contemporary settings from which anthropologists come and where they work. Market forces of a different kind are also working in the same direction. With dwindling financial resources available for 'pure' research, it is easier to find support for 'applied' research on 'relevant' problems in the field of development, and these almost inevitably include 'social change' and a diachronic time-base. Obviously this has its dangers. For anthropologists may, in a desperate bid to attract funds for research, oversell themselves, offering remedies which they are not necessarily much better equipped to provide than other social scientists. On the other hand, I suspect that the hostility which some display towards applied and development anthropology partly reflects theoretical insecurity and concern to avoid exposing theories to the testing laboratory of social change. This seems regrettable since, if subsequent developments cast doubt on the accuracy of an earlier interpretation, the latter clearly requires revision.

Surely, then, we should applaud our colleagues when they candidly acknowledge that, in the retrospective light of history, they feel it necessary to revise earlier analyses. So, for instance, Raymond Firth (1959) has recorded how, after an interval of thirty years, he found changes in Tikopian society which led him to revise his analysis of, *inter alia*, the nature of chiefly authority. Similarly, Emrys Peters (1972) has explained in detail how the unexpected results of an election in a Shiite village in south Lebanon jolted him into realising that he had been beguiled by the local folk-model of the power structure and had failed to perceive possibilities which existed for change and manipulation: of course, and this is the whole point of comparative analysis which treats the spatial and temporal dimensions as equivalently relevant, the same insights may become apparent through the accumulation of (spatially distinct) comparative data. Thus, for instance, the treatment of Somali spirit-possession, which at first appeared to be exorcism (I.M. Lewis, 1969a), when subsequently examined in relation to a wider spatial and temporal range of comparative data could be seen to be more aptly described as initiation (I.M. Lewis, 1971; 1996). I have attempted to use a similar mixture of spatial and historical data to explore the changing correlations between lineage cohesion and marriage preferences associated – as it seems – with the settlement of nomads, the transition to cultivation and the expansion of political solidarity in southern Somalia (I.M. Lewis, 1969c).

In fact, as studies of the decline (say among the Tiv) or development (in a Canadian Eskimo community studied by Riches (1975)) or expansion in the Mount Hagen Highlands (Strathern, 1971) of spheres of exchange show, it is precisely such changing circumstances that give us the best insight into their basic characteristics. The same might be said equally of kinship – partilineal, matrilineal and bilateral – that its multiplex capacities and resilience become fully apparent in situations that a diachronic perspective exposes.

These are particular instances of the continuing value of Evans-Pritchard's insistence on what might be called the 'dust-settling' role of history in illuminating the salience and permanence of institutions. As he trenchantly put it, 'those who ignore history condemn themselves to not knowing the present, because historical development alone permits us to weigh and to evaluate in their respective relations the elements of the present.' So, for instance, many highly stratified and apparently rigidly ascribed political systems (such as, for example, that of the Ethiopian Amharas) appear differently (at least in their *de facto* tolerance of status mobility) when viewed in historical perspective. Equally, 'highly egalitarian' political systems – amongst pastoral nomads, for example – may exhibit patterns of *de facto* differentiation over time and in contrast to dominant political ideology. Much debate in anthropology about the 'nature' of a particular cultural system often seems an artefact of studies of the same 'system' at different points in time. Again, we simply do not know what such local political history 'means', unless we know what actually happened. Claims by African Muslims (such as the Somali) that their founding ancestors sailed across the Red Sea on prayer mats from the Arabian holy land are not likely to be taken at face value by cynical anthropologists (see e.g. I.M. Lewis, 1994, pp.95–112), but other aspects of genealogies may be less self-evidently 'true' or 'untrue'. The dynastic traditions of the Soli of Zambia are instructive here. A recurrent theme is that the origins of Soli dynasties are traced to legitimate foundlings who, for one reason or another, were abandoned and then rediscovered and reinstated. John Argyle (1971) has been able to demonstrate that this is in fact a myth for political usurpation. This has suggestive analogies with a host of other similar dynastic myths of origin of this 'Moses in the bullrushes' type, including the Oedipus myth, Romulus and Remus, and many other heroic 'legends' (or myths) from classical antiquity. One could obviously not begin to know that these were essentially rationalisations for contemporary political legitimacy, unless one was able to establish that they were not historically accurate and, indeed, deliberate distortions of historical truth. So the encapsulation of the past in the present can only be elucidated by reference to valid knowledge of the past.

I would go further and urge that to identify and understand the 'present', and to trace true functional interdependencies over time, we need also to take proper account of the spatial setting of our data. This, presumably, is what M.G. Smith had in mind when he referred to the 'spatio-temporal' dimension of the cultures or societies we study. This, naturally, opens the door to consideration of the spatial or geographical diffusion of cultural and social facts – a prospect astonishingly neglected by contemporary British social anthropologists, which is all the more remarkable in view of the rapid diffusion of 'theories' and fashions in contemporary anthropology in Britain as elsewhere. Marxism is well known for refusing to apply to itself its own canons of the relativity of truth-value. Here we see a kind of reverse phenomenon in which anthropologists happily participate in the diffusion and rediffusion of ideas amongst themselves while tacitly maintaining that, despite globalisation, their subjects of study are immune from such processes.

By sensitively situating our data in their geographical and temporal context, we more readily appreciate the arbitrary criteria we use to register cultural and social continuities and discontinuities (think, for example, of the problematic distinction between a 'language' and a 'dialect'). As discussed in Chapter 9, it is difficult to overestimate the importance of this, since so much hangs on the ambiguous concepts 'society' (privileged in the British tradition) and 'culture' (privileged in the American anthropological tradition).

Structural-functionalism is, as most people nowadays recognise, primarily a method. This is true. But we need to add that actualised as it is in the characteristic British 'fieldwork mode of production' it promotes a synchronic perspective in which the fieldworker focuses in great depth on a small and arbitrarily isolated range of phenomena – bracketing off much that may be relevant in the wider spatio-temporal setting. This is a major source of perennial tension between the particular and the general. Blinded by the extraordinarily intense nature of the fieldwork experience, British anthropologists tend to invest their data with a permanence and multifold concreteness which this evidence does not necessarily possess. As we have seen, although all anthropology is in some sense comparative (implicit if not explicit), this intensely subjective initiation rite promotes secondary ethnocentricity in the sense that the anthropologist is apt to believe that all the data he or she collected can explain themselves. In this spirit, particular rituals are regularly claimed to 'generate' particular ideologies, without any effort being made to explore whether other extraneous factors might not be involved. Such particularistic fieldwork is encouraged by vague, general, overarching, theoretical orientations – rather than informed by clearly stated hypotheses based on comparative analysis of existing data. Such crude determinism is also profoundly ahistorical.

To conclude: this inevitably far from exhaustive review of historical trends in British social anthropology will, I trust, at least serve to demonstrate that 'functionalism' is a very broad methodological category which, despite appearances and ancient dogmas, does not intrinsically exclude history. Even Radcliffe-Brown, as we have seen, envisaged complementarity between explanations which traced interdependencies in the way institutions worked (such praxis constituting 'functionalism'), and how they had developed over time in the past ('history'). It is only when functionalist interpretations are pushed to the limit, to explain completely why particular institutions exist, rather than how they operate at a particular time, that history is made to seem redundant.

NOTES

1 An important role here was played by Dr Verwoerd's associate in Afrikaans, anthropologist W.M. Eiselen. See e.g. Gluckman (1975). This tradition continues in the work of contemporary Afrikaans anthropologists such as P.J. Goertze who are much preoccupied with such concepts as '*ethnos*' and '*volkekunde*' (cf. German *volkekunde*). Historically and today, the division between ('liberal') English-speaking and ('racist') Afrikaans-speaking South

African anthropologists is by no means clear-cut. The former *'verlichte'* Afrikaans-speaking Minister of Plural Affairs (formerly 'Bantu Affairs'), Pete Koornhoff, is an Oxford-trained social anthropologist whom I knew as a fellow student in the early 1950s. For an interesting, if tantalisingly brief sketch of recent developments in South African anthropology, see Sharp (1980); see also Schmidt (1996) and A. Kuper (1999).

2 G. Wilson, *The Constitution of Ngonde* (1939) and G. and M. Wilson, *The Analysis of Social Change* (1945). For a perceptive account of Godfrey Wilson's politics, his relations with the Northern Rhodesian colonial government, and the ethos of the Rhodes-Livingstone Institute, see Brown (1973).

3 J.A. Barnes, *history in a Changing Society* (1951a); *Marriage in a Changing Society* (1951b); *Politics in a Changing Society* (1954).

4 See e.g. Gluckman (1957). On this strain in Gluckman's work and influence, see Firth (1975); Brown (1979); Frankenberg (1981).

5 See e.g. Bloch (1977).

6 An interesting example of work in this mode, which seeks to combine history and anthropology to reach general theoretical conclusions, is Maurice Bloch's analysis of the persistence, over several centuries, of particular circumcision rituals among the Merina of Madagascar – despite striking socio-economic and ideological change. Based on this historical and ethnographic data, Bloch concludes that: 'rituals . . . have, because of their nature, a much greater fixity than other aspects of culture' (Bloch, 1986, p.194).

7 Obviously, A. Kuper's lively and often anecdotal *Anthropology and Anthropologists: The British School 1922–72* (1973), which is a useful textbook, does not pretend to be a major contribution to historiography. The crucial figure here is, of course, George Stocking. Goody (1995) provides valuable reflections, not least his deservedly severe assessment of the inadequacies of Kuklick (1991).

CHAPTER 2

A HISTORICO-FUNCTIONALIST DEBATE

(ERNESTO DE MARTINO, MICHEL LEIRIS &
E.E. EVANS-PRITCHARD)

METHODOLOGICAL CONTRASTS

My theme here is the problem of establishing what people in other
cultures and other traditions – past and present – who have ostensibly
rather colourful beliefs, actually believe, and how seriously they take
their beliefs: how they are enacted in practice, how they are defended.
Even at the individual level, where there is more scope for the
exploration of 'mind-sets', as psychiatrists routinely discover, this is
a complex matter, and one which seems to have been of central concern
to De Martino, the inspirational founder of modern Italian ethnology and
what has become 'ethno-sociology', the distinctive Italian style of social
anthropology, linked historically to folklore and comparative religion.

In this context I want to re-examine the sophisticated and insightful
interpretation De Martino offers of the symbolism of the tarantula
spider in the tarantist cult of southern Italy. This, of course, is a
topic to which Professor Clara Gallini has herself also contributed.
Methodologically, as I hope to demonstrate, despite shortcomings in
the empirical aspects of the research, there are still important lessons
to be learnt from De Martino's analysis. I also take this example of
his work because I believe that it is probably the best illustration of
De Martino experimenting with actual ethnographic research. This,
naturally, appeals especially to me as an empiricist British social
anthropologist. I wish to compare De Martino's approach with that
of the French surrealist poet and ethnographer, Michel Leiris, in the
context of the latter's work on the symbolic meaning of Ethiopian
possession cults.

Although Leiris (1958) employs a Continental teamwork method of
research which is not dissimilar to De Martino's, he is concerned with a
more exotic, alien culture whose representatives (his informants) did not

speak this language. Leiris was also working in the strongly developed French Africanist tradition.

I shall then confront these attempts to understand and assess exotic religious beliefs with Evans-Pritchard's (1937) famous study of Zande witchcraft. Evans-Pritchard's work was, of course, carried out after, and in the spirit of, the Malinowskian 'revolution' in British social anthropology inaugurated by the publication of Malinowski's *Argonauts of the Western Pacific* in 1922, and involved his pioneering style of prolonged fieldwork with the anthropologist speaking the local, vernacular language.

This study of Zande mystical ideas, conducted and published in the 1930s, was, as we shall see, to a large extent an extended, if implicit, dialogue with the French sociological philosopher, Lévy-Bruhl, whose work Evans-Pritchard considered carefully and critically, reaching conclusions which are not, I think, too dissimilar from those of De Martino (in *Mondo Magico*: cf. also, Clara Gallini's lucid intro-duction to *La Fine del Mondo*, lviiiff.). Evans-Pritchard, like De Martino and Leiris, was also concerned to establish the interplay between conscious and unconscious factors in the mobilisation of mystical beliefs. These common interests and aims make all the more intriguing the question which I want to pose in conclusion. Why, with such similar interests and attitudes towards exotic reli-gious phenomena, did De Martino neglect Evans-Pritchard's brilliant discoveries about African thought? Evans-Pritchard, who had studied the subject before he became an anthropologist, also shared De Martino's concern with history – although from a rather different point of view perhaps. (One might also ask why did the English anthropologist, who read Italian, ignore De Martino?) De Martino's books show that he read Anglophone anthropological literature, quite widely as far as I can tell, although mainly, it seems, from American sources. There was therefore no linguistic barrier. But there may have been a formidable epistemological barrier, as well as very different traditions of area specialisation and fieldwork methodology – despite the research of Africanist anthropologists like Grottanelli and Bernardo Bernardi, whose careers overlapped in time with De Martino's and who (especially in the case of the latter) champi-oned the Malinowskian style of prolonged, intensive fieldwork. My Italian colleagues may be able to elucidate these questions, and so help to situate the distinctive character of an Italian ethnology and ethno-sociology tracing its roots to De Martino (see Gallini and Massenzio, 1997).[1]

DE MARTINO & TARANTISM

Although I may be wrong in thinking this, since I am not equally familiar with all De Martino's works, *La Terra del Rimorso* (1961) seems to me the best example of his subtle interpretative powers applied to a concrete exotic phenomenon: tarantism in the 'south' (cf. Hauschild, 1986; 1993).

As is well known, this study by De Martino and his multi-disciplinary team focuses on the actual practice and symbolic meaning of the tarantist cult as it survived in Salente (Apulia) in the 1950s. The research investigates the cult 'in the field', and contextualises it in its wider historical setting. This latter process of contextualisation is conducted in a manner which will be familiar to those who know well De Martino's voluminous philosophical writings on history and historiography. In his account, De Martino presents individual case studies as documentary evidence and also gives a generally convincing description of events which he presumably witnessed, or was told about. Although employing a teamwork research procedure of the type common in social surveys, he thus conducted his admittedly brief period of field research in ways which, at least to some extent, are not totally different from the Malinowskian empirical tradition.

The tarantist cult, of course, typically involves women, who are recruited by being symbolically bitten by the tarantula spider-spirit, and seek a cure in musically accompanied domestic rituals, or at church shrines such as the famous chapel dedicated to St Paul at Galatina in Salente. The symptoms of the affliction that in its acute phase may include dizziness, weakness, feelings of anguish, psychomotor agitation, stomach and muscular pains, nausea and increased erotic appetite, are attributed to the bite of the spider.

In Apulia, there are two varieties of actual tarantula: *Lycosa* and *Latrodectus*. Although it inflicts a savage bite, the first spider is essentially harmless. *Latrodectus*, on the other hand, although not very aggressive in its behaviour and usually only attacking human beings when they come into contact with it, is small and slow-moving: but it is much more dangerous. Although not immediately painful, the toxins injected by its bite have a powerful psychotropic effect, and are capable of actually producing all the symptoms listed above, causing the victim to feel severely ill for several days (De Martino, 1961, p.78; Gallini, 1967 , pp.278 sqq.). Intriguingly, although the behaviour and symptoms thus actually produced by *Latrodectus* are similar to those in the acute phases of tarantism, this spider is not directly implicated in the cult. As De Martino shows, the 'bite' here is a symbolic construct which can recur at different points in an afflicted person's life, and can even be inherited over the generations. Its initial occurrence is usually in a context in which the victim experiences exceptional stress, or personal difficulty, and it can occur again in the same or similar circumstances. Initiation into what, in common with Victor Turner, I have called a 'cult of affliction' assumes the form of symptoms of illness and distress which are interpreted as evidence of a tarantula spirit's attack.

While men out working in the fields are actually more at risk from the bite of the real *Latrodectus*, it is the less physically exposed women who are most likely to succumb to the attentions of the spirit-spider in Apulia. The main treatment involves a form of exorcism that is carried out at St Paul's Chapel in Galatina where, when De Martino's team visited it, they found that 32 out of 37 of those seeking a cure were women. The victim is believed to be possessed by the spider (which assumes various human names and personalities) and finds relief in dancing the dance 'of the little spider' (the tarantella) and pays homage to St Paul. This saint is credited with causing what he can cure, and indeed merges with the spider to form a spirit hybrid which appears in the course of the exorcistic rites and in women's dreams and visions, often with an erotic content. The tarantist victims are commonly considered to be married to the spider-saint. Despite the fact that the toxic bite of *Latrodectus* can actually produce symptoms similar to those associated with the bite of the spider-spirit, it is the other *Lycosa* spider, with its harmless bite, that is identified with the spider-spirit.

This corresponds with the appearance of *Lycosa* which is particularly active at night, moving rapidly to pursue its prey aggressively: unlike *Latrodectus* and most other spiders, it does not weave a web to trap its prey. But, apparently, because of its menacing size, its fierce manner, and painful – if harmless – bite, it is *Lycosa* that is primarily identified with the symbolic spirit-spider. In fact, it seems very likely, as De Martino argues, that the spirit-spider is historically a hybrid construct based on features taken from each of these two varieties of spider. As he puts it: 'tarantism was not reducible to latrodectism but was also not independent of it, since latrodectism must be considered as an important historical and existential condition for the genesis of tarantism.'

De Martino, thus, presents a subtle, multi-causal analysis of the tarantist spirit-spider that takes full account of the characteristics of the two animal species with which it is linked. Although he does not refer to it (and was probably unaware of its existence), this has significant resonance with Mary Douglas's (1957) treatment of the symbolic significance of the scaly ant-eater, or pangolin, in the Congo. Douglas's analysis of pangolin power rests on her theory of classificatory anomalies. Her interpretation, however, disregards the fact that in her ethnographic material there are again two varies of the same animal – in this case two species of pangolin – only one of which, she claims, is invested with mystical power. Unlike De Martino, her treatment, does not present a careful examination of the features of both varieties of animal that are potentially available for symbolic attention. Hence, as I have argued elsewhere (I.M. Lewis, 1991), De Martino's analysis enables us to see how Douglas's argument is seriously flawed.

With the presentation of a few illustrative case histories, De Martino establishes the epidemiology of tarantist possession quite convincingly. What, however, despite the intuitive subtlety of his analysis, he does not do is to present these exotic southern Italian spirit beliefs and practices in their full local folk-religious context. He does not really provide sufficiently detailed documentation on living popular religion, and the wider mystical beliefs of the local peasantry. Here, of course, what is needed, rather than a mere catalogue, is a multi-dimensional picture of the interweaving texture of local beliefs. This lacuna may result from an assumption that the wider background of popular Italian Catholicism (which he to some extent describes in *Sud e Magia* (1959)) can be taken for granted. But a more significant factor is probably his research methodology which is, after all, a long way from the participant-observation techniques pioneered by Malinowski in his famous Trobriand Islands study. However imaginative and sympathetic, De Martino's ethnographic account is actually not at all in the mode of what might today be called 'thick description' (which was not invented by Geertz, although he gave it a name).

In attempting to characterise and assess De Martino's work, it is surely also important to note that the domestic location of his major research must have played a powerful role in the development of subsequent Italian social anthropology (and ethno-sociology) where European regional studies are especially prominent. One can only speculate how different things might have been if, like Lanternari and his successors, De Martino had carried out major fieldwork in Africa, rather than 'at home'.

MICHEL LEIRIS AND ETHIOPIAN SPIRIT-POSSESSION

With Michel Leiris's study of spirit-possession in Ethiopia, carried out in 1932, much earlier than De Martino's tarantism research, we confront a much more detailed field study, yielding a correspondingly fuller cultural account of exotic mystical beliefs. Methodologically, his was again the work of a small team which spent less than six months in the field, but which included a talented Ethiopian religious specialist. The results produced a pioneering and admirably comprehensive portrait of the famous Ethiopian *zar* spirit cult, presented essentially as a complex syncretic religious phenomenon with significant links to Ethiopian Christianity and to Islam. Although not especially focused on sociological aspects, the broad social features of this cult, practised by women, and by men of marginal social groups, are clearly delineated. But the particular strength of Leiris's material lies in the sophistication of his analysis of the drama of possession and the intriguing question of the states of mind (conscious or unconscious) of the 'possessed'.

These are issues which, not only in relation to tarantism but also more generally, fascinated De Martino (as in *La Fine del Mondo*), making it all the more surprising that he does not make more explicit reference to Leiris's analysis of the *zar* cult. (Leiris is cited in a footnote as an ethnographic source on *zar* in the long, concluding third part of *Terra del Rimorso*, entitled significantly 'Historical commentary'.) Certainly, as a specialist on possession, I know of no more subtle analysis of the seance as drama and its devotees as ritual actors. *Zar*, according to Leiris, is a 'lived theatre' in which there is a 'formal, but not absolute belief in a substitution of personality during possession'. The possessed are unanimously said to be unconscious of what they do and say during their crises, many disclaim knowledge of their actions while they are in this state. But the shaman priestesses of the cult sometimes hold possessed people partially responsible for their actions. The *zar* spirits themselves 'resemble personages in a theatre since they only exist as a function of the scenic events that they condition and in which their character finds its illustration' (Leiris, 1958, p. 101).

With this ambiguity regarding the state of consciousness of the enthusiasts, the ritual is fundamentally theatrical, so that it is easy, as Leiris observes, to imagine how with the decline of faith and the impact of modernity, this 'lived theatre' could develop (or degenerate) into a play theatre, with a reduction in seriousness and a rise in frivolity and pretence (Leiris, 1958, p.129). This is a prophetic assessment since, with increasing secularisation, in common with other similar cults, *zar* has indeed become more and more a recreation, or folkloric entertainment-theatre in the modern sense (see e.g. Last 1991). Despite the many striking parallels (to some of which he refers), Leiris's account clearly achieves a more comprehensive cultural contextualisation than De Martino's chronologically much later work on tarantism.

EVANS-PRITCHARD AND ZANDE WITCHCRAFT

For all their brilliant insights into symbolism and the multi-layered and often even contradictory character of the beliefs people officially hold, these studies are inevitably constrained (and limited) by the brief and rather superficial nature of the field research methodology employed. This becomes obvious when we compare these descriptions with Evans-Pritchard's truly path-breaking study of the mystical beliefs of the central African Azande, based on intensive, prolonged participant observation using the vernacular language. This was research in the living Malinowskian fieldwork tradition and, although it was done a long time ago in the late 1920s and early 1930s (about the same time as Leiris's work), it is widely recognised that Evans-Pritchard's richly documented study remains unsurpassed as the most illuminating analysis of exotic mystical beliefs ever written.

Evans-Pritchard demonstrated convincingly how Zande beliefs in mystical power constituted, in the way in which they were deployed, a self-sustaining system that successfully confronted the contradictions and problems of everyday existence. More sharply than many other people with similar beliefs, the Zande distinguish between two types of malign mystical power. One, which Evans-Pritchard translated into English as 'sorcery', involved this use of magical spells, rites and medicines – tangible and visible techniques which could, actually, be observed. What he translated as 'witchcraft' (*mangu*) was a power potentially possessed by everyone. According to the Zande, this had an organic basis in the small intestine in the human body. This power was weak in children, but strong in the elderly.

The distinction between the two evil forces corresponds neatly with class distinctions in the Zande political system: sorcery is more powerful than witchcraft and practised by chiefs and traditional aristocrats. Witchcraft, in contrast, occurs amongst the mass of the population, being associated with men as much as women. Either force, according to context, is invoked to explain misfortune and illness, particularly unexpected difficulties and problems, for example, crop failure, bad luck in hunting game, marital problems, and so on.

Contrary, however, to what Lévy-Bruhl (with whom Evans-Pritchard conducted an implicit dialogue) supposed, these beliefs in mystical causation do not exclude a parallel understanding of empirically based, non-mystical causation. Thus, if a man sustains an injury in the course of hunting, this is not in itself due to witchcraft. But if the injury refuses to heal and becomes life-threatening, witchcraft may be suspected to be involved. The agency of the initial injury is understood perfectly, but its unusually refractory nature requires further, mystical explanation. Similarly, with everyday technology, if things do not work, they must have been done imperfectly. But if some otherwise technically perfect process goes wrong, witchcraft may be implicated. This dual, causal philosophy comes out clearly in the case of death. Death in general is considered to be unnatural and due to witchcraft. But when an old person dies, only his close relatives would look to witchcraft as the cause. Others, less involved, would see death here as an inevitable consequence of old age. Witchcraft, thus, essentially explains *why* particular disasters happen to particular people. It does not necessarily explain how they happen, which is usually understood in empirical terms. Thus, witchcraft (or sorcery) answers the 'Why me?' question naturally posed by the victim when misfortune strikes. Zande do not simply accept that 'life is unfair'.

But, what we have here is not only a mystical theory of misfortune, existing alongside non-mystical causation, but also a social psychology of interpersonal relations. The victim of misfortune characteristically traces his plight to the malice of his enemies and rivals, assuming that those whom he hates or envies also hate him. Hence witchcraft is really a pseudonym for spite, malice and fear: something Zande recognise consciously. To capture this, we might paraphrase Marx's famous aphorism about religion to read: 'witchcraft is the odium of the people'.

At the same time, Zande declare that witchcraft is an unconscious force, and Evans-Pritchard takes this as a distinction between witchcraft and sorcery, and proposes a more general theory of mystical aggression based on this difference. However, I think he was misled here, since those accused of witchcraft routinely disclaim evil intentions, while those making the accusation assume that the witch acts with deliberate malice. Thus consciousness or unconsciousness is not a defining characteristic of the malevolent agency itself. Witchcraft is both deliberate and accidental; which view is taken depends on the situation of the parties involved.

To pursue this further would take me beyond my present purpose which is simply to show how close and profound study of the actual operation of a set of mystical beliefs enables us to understand their ideological force and vigour, without invoking the misleading ideas of Lévy-Bruhl. Evans-Pritchard demonstrates conclusively the multiplicity of causal agency in Zande thought, with overlapping and interpenetration between empirical and non-empirical causal forces and their situational mobilisation. He speaks of Zande 'faith' in mystical power tempered by scepticism. Overall, when events contradict mystical predictions, and magic proves inadequate, deficiencies are explained away without leading to the collapse of these mutually sustaining beliefs and practices. Although Zande do not see these beliefs as forming a system in the way they appear to a foreign observer, it is nevertheless their interdependence which explains their persistence.

Subsequent research on the Zande has revealed a number of short-comings in Evans-Pritchard's pioneering study (see e.g. I.M. Lewis, 1976, p.73; 1993, p.107). But this way of analysing ideology holistically (functionally), in terms of self-sustaining and self-confirming sets of interrelated assumptions, has immense possibilities in enabling us to understand the power of beliefs that we do not share and may regard as profoundly erroneous.

Ernest Gellner used this methodology with devastating effect in his famous examination of the key concepts of the Oxford Linguistic Philosophers (*Words and Things*, 1956) and subsequently applied the same style of analysis to the leading ideas of the 'church' of psychoanalysis (Gellner, 1985) and, more recently to 'post-modernist anthropology' which he wittily and wisely castigated as 'meta-twaddle'. De Martino at least escaped having to contemplate these decadent anthropological absurdities. If, as Dr Saunders (1997) argues, De Martino missed his appointment with contemporary American anthropology, perhaps he was fortunate to do so!

EVANS-PRITCHARD AND DE MARTINO

It seems to me more unfortunate that Evans-Pritchard's Zande study and its significance, especially in relation to the debate on so-called 'primitive mentality', seems to have escaped De Martino. Evans-Pritchard's Zande material could have provided useful ammunition to De Martino. This poses intriguing questions for an outsider such as myself. Why did De Martino ignore Evans-Pritchard's work? Since *La Fine del Mondo* and *Il Mondo Magico* contain many references to the works of American anthropologists, this is clearly not simply a matter of linguistic boundaries: and one might note that his close colleague

Vittorio Lanternari, in his writing, refers extensively to the works of the British functionalist school.

This omission of Evans-Pritchard's work seems all the more striking in view of the frequency with which De Martino refers to Lévi-Strauss who could never claim to have carried out in-depth field research on exotic mystical beliefs at this level of profundity or sophistication. Most of Lévi-Strauss's inspired writing is based on secondary sources. But then as far as I can see, there are few references in *Fine del Mondo* to the great master and protagonist of first-hand observation, Malinowski, whose functionalist analysis De Martino does, however, summarise succinctly and accurately. Here it seems that De Martino's adherence to history led him to adopt a negative attitude towards Malinowski's positivism. This, surely, can be seen clearly in *Terra del Rimorso* where De Martino draws attention to numerous ecstatic north African cults as constituting historical and geographically contiguous 'parallels' to tarantism. Here, although he also notes what he calls 'functional' parallels with Haitian vodu (citing Metraux and Herskovits), he evidently prefers to work within a cultural and historical diffusionist paradigm. (And of course, this is the same tradition out of which Lévi-Strauss has fashioned structuralism – despite its ahistoricism, so his appeal to De Martino is not entirely surprising. Other factors are obviously also involved.) This European historical tradition was also conserved in American cultural anthropology (via Boas) which was itself closer to psychiatry and psychoanalysis, and these subjects, as Romano Mastromattei (1997) has argued, represented De Martino's abiding preoccupation (cf. Lanternari, 1997).

Though, as I have argued here, Evans-Pritchard's Zande witchcraft material would have provided useful ammunition for De Martino, the latter might have been surprised to discover that the English anthropologist was also an historian under the skin! On the other hand, if in his turn Evans-Pritchard had been familiar with De Martino's analysis, he might have been encouraged to import an enhancing historical dimension to his study of Zande mystical beliefs and practices which, as he was well aware, were indeed subject to historical processes. (The 'de-historicisation' which his treatment of Zande magic and witchcraft implied, was thus tactical and provisional, rather than absolute.) But perhaps ultimately, what we see at work here, in both these cases, is once again the power of hermeneutic frontiers, and the hegemonic force of a particular intellectual tradition.

NOTES

1 For further information on the development of modern Italian anthropology, see Bernardi (1973); Grottanelli (1977); Saunders (1984). The crucial role of De Martino, as a disciple of Gramsci, is discussed in Lanternari (1997). For a short account from a British perspective, see I.M. Lewis (1987, pp.9–12).

CHAPTER 3

DECONSTRUCTING DESCENT

This chapter seeks to examine some of the problems involved in comparing unilineal descent in different societies, problems which even if they cannot yet be fully resolved have to be considered if the study of unilineal descent is to proceed further. There is now, of course, an already considerable and indeed ever-increasing volume of writing, both regional and comparative, on segmentary lineage systems in particular and on unilineal descent in general, and some of the problems to which I wish to draw attention have been raised before, though not, I think, sufficiently systematically. What I wish to deal with principally is the question of how unilineal descent varies in different unilineal descent systems, and how such variations can be assessed, or measured (if indeed this is possible), and also to focus attention on the implications of such variation. The sort of question which this chapter seeks to enquire into is therefore: are some societies more or less 'strongly' patrilineal or matrilineal than others; and, if so, in what respects; and, further, by what criteria can such differences be objectively established.' What, in short, are the implications of saying that one society is 'more, or less, strongly patrilineal (or matrilineal)' than another?

Traditionally, of course, patrilineal and matrilineal descent are opposed categories used for distinguishing tribal societies. And since Radcliffe-Brown's classic paper on patrilineal and matrilineal succession (Radcliffe-Brown, 1935b), the range of types of descent system has been widened to include double unilineal systems, different types of bilateral system, and other variations with a plethora of barbaric titles. Double and bilateral descent systems have been exhaustively discussed previously (Freeman, 1961; Goody, 1961; Leach, 1962) and I hasten to say that the object of this chapter is not to add to that debate, although some of my points have perhaps some bearing on it. My concern, then, is with differences and variations in systems of unilineal descent which cannot be described or accounted for in terms of the parallel recognition of both patrilineal and matrilineal descent, however combined. For convenience I shall deal almost entirely with patrilineal descent, although the issues apply, I think, equally to descent traced matrilineally.[1] Finally, although the variations in the value given to descent discussed here do not depend upon the recognition of any form of bilateral or dual descent, the functional implications may, as I hope to show, be similar.

DESCENT IN SEGMENTARY LINEAGE SOCIETIES

The role of descent as an organisational principle in different societies naturally varies widely, but it is generally agreed that there are certain broad categories of rights and obligations which tend, in varying degrees and with varying emphasis, to be attached to and transmitted by descent. These are usually taken to relate to property, jural and political status, religion, and social status in the widest sense. And it is assumed, I think, that the most thorough-going kinship definition of a person's general social status and property rights is provided for in lineage organisation. This is often simply taken for granted. Radcliffe-Brown (1950, p. 78), however, makes the point quite explicitly when he states that what 'mother-right' and 'father-right' have in common is extreme emphasis on lineage; and this is surely also the reason for the title of Professor Fortes's fundamental survey of descent systems (Fortes, 1953). Indeed, all this is so obvious that it hardly needs saying. And yet, there are immediate implications which, though often noticed, have not hitherto been explored adequately. These derive from the significance attached to lineage organisation in different types of society.

Let me first take the case of those unilineal organisations usually called segmentary lineage systems, for here the unilineal principle is all-pervasive, or almost so, and defines the individual's social status in the widest possible sense. As Freedman (1958, p. 138) puts it: 'The purest form of unilineal descent group is to be found in a society which is a segmentary system in its totality'. Let us examine the extent to which segmentary lineage organisation varies among the Nuer (Evans-Pritchard, 1940a, and b), the Tiv (L. Bohannan, 1952; Bohannan and Bohannan, 1953; L. Bohannan, 1958), the Cyrenaican Bedouin (Evans-Pritchard, 1949; Peters, 1960), and the northern Somali (I.M. Lewis, 1961; 1962a).

In all four societies a person's position in his community at large is defined first by his affiliation in the patrilineage to which he belongs by birth. There is moreover no doubt that these four peoples all possess an extremely highly developed patrilineal ideology, although there are differences in the extent to which each has a specific lineage terminology. What we seek to examine is the degree to which patrilineally defined segmentary lineage status determines the jural, political and religious status of the individual in as absolute terms as possible. How exclusive, in other words, is the patrilineal principle, and to what extent is it aided or reinforced by other principles of association and status ascription? And, of course, we have to remember that the unit of comparative analysis is the whole society in each case. We are, after all, comparing the Nuer, Tiv, Bedouin and Somali as separate entities, and what we say must be modified if it applies only to a limited area of the society, or is restricted to certain levels of activity in it.

THE RANGE OF GENEALOGICAL ASCRIPTION

First, consider the range of socially significant genealogical articulation. The Tiv, Bedouin and Somali have a single national or 'total' genealogy which embraces the whole society or culture in each case. Tiv genealogies go back to 'Tiv' (indeed they go back to 'Adam'), Bedouin pedigrees go back to an ancestress Sa'ada,[2] and Somali genealogies go back to 'Samaale' and beyond to Arabian lineages. To reach their eponym Tiv count back about fifteen named generations, the Bedouin about a dozen, and the Somali sometimes thirty generations or more.

But although genealogical span has often been taken as an index of unilineality, it is not a very effective criterion, and certainly not an unambiguous one. Generational span has first to be set in relation both to the size of population and to the extent to which, at this level, there exists genealogically based corporate activity. The Tiv number about 800,000; the Cyrenaican Bedouin about 200,000; and the northern Somali at least two and a half million. Yet unfortunately there are difficulties even with this sort of assessment, for there is no straight and invariable relationship between genealogical depth and population size because of the different manipulative processes which operate in different segmentary lineage societies (cf. L. Bohannan, 1952; Peters, 1960, pp. 32 ff; I.M. Lewis, 1961, pp. 144–52). The way in which genealogies relate to actual social and political process and the procedures of adjustment to which they are subject are by no means the same among the Tiv, Bedouin and Somali. Hence we must conclude that genealogical depth, even in relation to size of population, is not in itself an unequivocal and cross-culturally valid measure of unilinearity.

Let us now consider the question of what the genealogies actually represent in social and political terms at this 'national' level. Do the three societies ever mobilise as effective political entities on a national scale; or is there any jural identity which has a national, all-embracing character?

Tiv fight their neighbours and indeed are engaged in a general movement of expansion, but apparently the whole society is never mobilised on a genealogical basis. The Tiv do not constitute a corporate political group, even transiently. Neither apparently do the Bedouin or the Somali. Indeed the Somali when inspired by diffuse general hostility (as, for example, towards the Amharas) do not express their unity in genealogical terms, but in terms of their national cultural identity.

As far as jural identity is concerned, each of the three societies would seem to possess a common code and means for the settlement of disputes on a society-wide basis. Moreover, legal issues are evaluated according to the segmentary lineage context in which they occur. As the Bohannans put it for the Tiv: 'The moral attitude to homicide – both in peacetime and time of war - is on a scale of values determined by the social distance (in lineage terms) between the people involved' (Bohannan and Bohannan, 1953, p. 26). For the Tiv, murder involves several magical consequences; for the Bedouin and Somali, it raises the question of blood-money and vengeance. And all Somali, as all Bedouin, recognise the tariffs of compensation embodied in Muslim law.

In contrast to the Tiv, Bedouin and Somali, the Nuer do not have a single national genealogy. But like the former they do not apparently combine on a national basis against their traditional enemies, the Dinka. Their genealogically based politico-jural solidarity stops short at the 'tribe' and does not embrace the whole ethnic group.

Despite these differences in lineage coverage between the Nuer, on the one hand, and the Bedouin, Tiv and Somali, on the other, the truth of course is that all four societies are essentially cultural entities rather than corporate political units. Yet there is a sense in which the genealogical placement of the individual within a national framework in the case of the Tiv, Bedouin and Somali is more complete and pervasive than it is among the Nuer. To this extent, and to the degree that jural identity is also involved, unilineal descent could be said to be more important, because more inclusive, among the Tiv, Bedouin and Somali than amongst the Nuer.

THE MAXIMUM CORPORATE GROUPING

Let us now consider the largest corporate politico-jural unit in each case. This among the Nuer is the 'tribe', which because of the association between 'dominant' clans and tribes has a genealogical structure. This unit Evans-Pritchard defines as the largest group within which there is both a means and a moral obligation to settle disputes. The external implications are that tribes may be divided by fighting and warfare, whereas, internally, among their segments fighting is institutionalised in terms of the blood-feud. In comparing the Tiv, Bedouin, Somali and Nuer it is on the former criterion – that of political unity as manifest in war – that we have to fasten. For, as has already been pointed out, the latter jural criterion used by Evans-Pritchard to define the Nuer tribe in the case of the Tiv, Bedouin and Somali applies to the whole community – at least in principle. With this qualification we can now examine Nuer tribes and the corresponding units in the other three cases.

Among the Nuer, a tribe has a maximum strength of about 4,000 souls, and the lineage unit associated with it a genealogical span of ten generations. The equivalent Tiv unit has a genealogical span of about eight generations. Among the Bedouin, the corresponding unit seems to contain about 20,000 souls with a genealogical depth of again about eight generations. With the Somali the comparable unit may contain as many as 150,000 persons and the length of pedigree in this case is of the order of twenty generations. We can conclude, therefore, that of the four societies the Somali can boast the largest maximum politico-jural unit with the correspondingly longest genealogy. The implications of this conclusion are that among the Somali unilineal descent provides a basis for more extended corporate politico-jural solidarity than in the other three cases. In this respect, and in this respect alone, the Somali might be said to be the most patrilineal of the four societies.

Let us now consider the related problem of the degree to which, within the maximum politico-jural unit, lineage segmentation is politically significant. In other words, within his unit, to what extent are ancestors in the genealogies points of corporate cleavage or aggregation. With the Nuer it seems that every level of genealogical differentiation in a tribe's associated 'dominant' clan is, in principle at least, structurally significant. There are, however, four main levels of corporate action within the tribe-clan and outside the family. Indeed, this pattern is so well known that it has become a kind of paradigm applied, somewhat holistically, to very many lineage societies. The Tiv, similarly, seem to have universal genealogical group differentiation, although four levels are apparently most significant. With the Bedouin the position is similar, although there is only a threefold differentiation within the 'tribe' and this exhausts the possibilities of genealogical division. There are three levels of division and three connecting ancestors between the founder of the tertiary section and the tribal eponym. The Somali, on the other hand, resemble the Nuer and Tiv, every ancestor being potentially at least a point of lineage division, but within the unit we are discussing there are two main levels of corporate action outside the family.

This discussion tells us little more than that there is a more flexible and potentially wider range of socially significant segmentation within the largest political unit in the case of the Tiv, Somali and Nuer, than with the Bedouin. Because of the variable relationship between structural relations and genealogical organisation, however, we cannot, I think, in this case draw any valid conclusions bearing on the general significance of descent in this area of grouping.

The next consideration is that of the cultic significance of segmentation. Do these societies have religious cults which are consistently organised on a genealogical basis? Is a person's religious status defined by his lineage affiliation. To answer these questions we have to note first that none of the four societies practises ancestor worship in terms of Fortes's characterisation of this form of religion (Fortes, 1960). The Nuer, Bedouin and Somali worship a single deity. Among the Nuer, this deity or Spirit who is unique to them is seen as refracted into subsidiary spirit-entities by reference to the hierarchy of lineage segmentation. The Bedouin and Somali, by contrast, both venerate ancestors as part of the Sufistic cult of saints and, although different levels of lineage grouping evoke different ancestors, this cult cannot, I believe, be described in terms of 'refractions' of God or Spirit in a manner analogous to Evans-Pritchard's description of Nuer religion. Moreover, lineage ancestors constitute only one class of the general category of saints, charismatic individuals who may be alive or dead, and who are regarded as intermediaries in the believer's relationship with God. Indeed, as I have argued elsewhere (I.M. Lewis, 1998(b)), Muslim saints play a very similar role to saints in Catholicism and their existence, and the faith men place in their powers of mediation, arguably enhance rather than detract from the lofty omnipotence of God. Thus it would seem correct to say that Nuer religion is more closely related to their segmentary lineage organisation than is the case with the Bedouin or Somali. With the two latter, and certainly in the case of the Somali, the significance of the ancestor cult increases as the degree of politico-jural cohesion decreases. There is a more vital cult of lineage ancestors at segmentary levels where politico-jural solidarity is weak than at levels of grouping where people share strong bonds of collaboration.

The Tiv have certainly a very different religious system, although again there is no comprehensive segmentary lineage ancestor cult. Thus, of the four societies, only in the case of the Nuer is the religious cult uniformly tied to lineage organisation; and this, of course, is a very simplified (and perhaps distorting) way of referring to the realities of Nuer religion. Yet if we are to assess the significance of patrilineal descent in these four cases in relation to religion, we must, I think, conclude that the Nuer make more use of the unilineal principle for religious purposes than do the Bedouin, Tiv or Somali.

To sum up our discussion so far: we can say that, although among the Somali the maximum genealogically defined politico-jural community (and the range of politically significant agnation) is greater than with the Nuer, Tiv or Bedouin, lineage status has, apparently, more importance in religion for the Nuer than in the other three cases. Thus we might legitimately argue that, from the point of view of political and jural corporateness, descent is most important among the Somali. But from the point of view of religion, agnation is most significant among the Nuer. Before we can go beyond this to conclude that some of our four societies are in an overall sense more 'strongly' patrilineal than the others we must bring other criteria into the discussion.

THE UNIQUENESS OF DESCENT AS AN ORGANISING PRINCIPLE

The fundamental test of the importance of unilineal descent in a particular society must surely be the extent to which it is empirically the organisational basis for social activities in the widest sense. We have to enquire, therefore, to what extent the uniqueness of descent as a basis for social action is mitigated by the existence of other principles performing similar functions. Let us again consider the question of politico-jural collaboration.

Evans-Pritchard makes it very clear that among the Nuer the fundamental principle of grouping has a territorial basis and is in fact what Maine referred to as 'local contiguity'. Nuer politico-jural units are basically territorial entities, and descent is an aiding principle of social cohesion. Nevertheless, agnation is very important for, following a discussion of ecology and territorial grouping, Evans-Pritchard can say that: 'Tribal unity cannot be accounted for by any of the facts we have so far mentioned, taken alone, or in aggregate, but only by reference to the lineage system' (Evans-Pritchard, 1940b, p. 284). And the system of lineages of a 'dominant' clan enables Nuer to think of their tribe in the highly consistent form of clan structure. There is, moreover, a 'straight relationship' between political structure and the clan system of segments. Yet the Nuer themselves, Evans-Pritchard makes plain, conceive of their politico-jural cohesion primarily in territorial terms and the clan and lineage system comes into play to support the former.

These facts seem to indicate that here unilineal descent is a supplementary principle of aggregation, albeit one of great importance. With the Tiv, the position is, apparently very similar. Here territorially defined divisions of society are associated with lineage divisions and there is an 'almost one-to-one correlation between the territorial position of *utar* (territorial segments) and the genealogically defined order of segments' (Bohannan and Bohannan, 1953, p. 21). Moreover, agnates tend, more than among the Nuer where they are often dispersed, to reside together and there thus seems to be the regular consistency between territorial units and lineage segments which exists among the Nuer only in relation to 'dominant' clans and lineages. Again, it seems to me that we must conclude that descent amongst the Tiv is an aiding principle giving consistency and cohesion to what are essentially territorially defined groups. Territory (*tar*) is the primary referent of politico-jural cohesion.

The position with the semi-nomadic or transhumant Cyrenaican Bedouin is very similar. There is a general co-ordination between spatially defined territorial groupings and genealogical ties: 'The Cyrenaican genealogy is a conceptualization of a hierarchy of ordered territorial segments' (Peters, 1960, p. 31). Thus what Dr Peters calls the 'tertiary segment' of a tribe – the smallest political group whose members are bound by blood and the payment and receipt of blood-money – has its own homeland, water-supplies, pastures and ploughland. In Bedouin society this is the vengeance group, a lineage unit with a span of five generations most of whose members live in their own homeland. Here again the fundamental bonds are surely those springing from common residence and association in their cultivable land-holdings and also in their summer grazing camps. Territorially based sentiments of loyalty are reinforced and given structural definition in lineage terms.

Thus in all three societies (Nuer, Tiv and Bedouin) the basic politico-jural aggregates are primarily territorially defined, and the lineage organisation, although existing to a variable extent as a system in its own right, serves to substantiate territorially founded relationships and provides the dominant idiom in which these are stated. The fundamentally territorial character of social and political association in general is indeed usually taken for granted, and has been assumed to apply as much to segmentary lineage societies as to other types of society (cf. Middleton and Tait, 1958, p. 5; Fortes and Evans-Pritchard, 1940, p. 10; Schapera, 1956, *passim*).

The position amongst the nomadic Somali, however, is very different. Here there are no fixed local groups, no permanent grazing areas, and no firm assertion of territorial ties. And although rights to water resources provide some limitation to the loci of pastoral movements, which are primarily dictated by the distribution of grazing, there are no stable territorial units. Local contiguity is not a principle of social collaboration. In these circumstances, the fundamental principle of association, the first 'given' as it were, is not territorial attachment but agnatic descent. Thus for the nomadic Somali descent has a primacy which it does not seem to possess among the Nuer, Tiv and Bedouin. To this extent, I would argue that more is expected of descent as an organisational principle among the Somali than with the other three cases. Descent is therefore operationally more important in Somali society.

And yet, from another point of view it might be argued that the contrary is true. For the Nuer (Evans-Pritchard, 1940a, pp. 198 ff), Tiv (L. Bohannan, 1952), and Bedouin (Peters, 1960) exemplify the classical principles of segmentary lineage organisation where genealogies are, by different processes, adjusted to accord with political realities. The politico-jural ideology is uncompromisingly one of descent and 'co-ordinate segments which have come into existence as a result of segmentation are regarded as complementary and as formally equal' (Middleton and Tait, 1958, p. 7). So that even if social cohesion derives fundamentally from co-residence, the genealogical idiom is consistently maintained and genealogies are adjusted in step with changes in the balance of power (cf. I.M. Lewis, 1961, pp. 298–9). Among the Somali, however, where the rule of self-help places a premium on numerical supremacy, a specifically contractual principle is employed to achieve a balance of power in segmentary relations without resort to genealogical manipulation.[3] Small genealogically defined groups seek strength by alliance with stronger lineages by means of formal contractual agreements. Some contractual alliances do not always follow the principle of segmentary opposition, and sometimes indeed are in direct defiance of genealogical proximity.

Now, the Muslim Bedouin also employ a similar contractual principle, but this seems to be restricted in application to the level of the tertiary tribal segment whose agnatic members 'have agreed on the blood' (i.e. to the common obligation to pay and receive blood-compensation in concert). Notwithstanding this limited similarity between Somali and Bedouin, however, the latter manipulate their genealogies in order to maintain a consistent relationship between lineage and political solidarity. It could therefore be argued that, although agnation is perhaps a less fundamental principle among the Nuer, Tiv and Bedouin than with the Somali, it nevertheless more consistently represents political identity and is consequently a more thorough-going basis for politico-jural relations.

There are however other facts to be considered. Both the Nuer and Tiv have an age-set system, a feature lacking amongst the Bedouin and Somali. What social functions, we must ask, are served by this organisation in Nuer and Tiv society? While it is clear that in neither case are 'political relations between local groups controlled by the holders of statuses in age-set or age-grade systems' (Middleton and Tait, 1958, p. 3; cf. Bernardi, 1952, p. 331), as among the Nilo-Hamites, yet age-sets do have some political functions. For the Nuer, Evans-Pritchard records that: 'the age-set system may, however, be regarded as a political institution, since it is, to a large extent, segmented tribally and since it divides a tribe – as far as its male members are concerned – into groups based on age, which stand in a definite relation to each other' (Evans-Pritchard, 1940b, p. 290). We are also told that the politico-territorial system and the age-set system are both consistent in themselves and to some extent overlap, but they are not interdependent (as the lineage and territorial systems are).

Tiv age-sets similarly seem to have a political dimension, being associated with territorial segments. It thus appears that the existence of an age-set organisation amongst the Nuer and Tiv and its partial investment with political functions to some extent reduces the uniqueness of descent as a political principle in these societies. In this respect it might be argued that the role of descent as an exclusive organisational principle is weakened among the Nuer and Tiv in comparison with the Bedouin and Somali. And if we note a further Tiv principle, that of *ikul* treaties and market pacts which have some political functions, we have again to make a new assessment of the strength and importance of patriliny in the four cases.

THE FACTORISATION OF DESCENT

In what must seem an excessively rambling discussion, I have so far sought to show that if social function is the criterion, then in some respects unilineal descent is more important among the Bedouin and Somali than among the Nuer and Tiv, while in other respects this is not so. Perhaps for many it is labouring the obvious to say that it is in fact extremely difficult to establish that in any overall sense descent in one of a number of segmentary lineage societies is 'more important' than in others. The difficulty in making such statements arises of course because of the wide range of variables which cannot be held constant to set against the single criterion of unilinearity, and questions of judgement are involved which are not readily susceptible to simple measurement or enumeration.

But at least the facts so far surveyed indicate the extent of the problem and serve to underline the validity of Peters's statement (with reference to the Bedouin) that in such societies descent 'is not one thing, but many: it includes in its scope succession, status, inheritance, bride-wealth, blood-money, domestic and political behaviour, etc., and these can in turn be factorised into a number of components' (Peters, 1960, p. 49). The trouble – for comparative estimates of the extent or 'strength' of descent – is of course that the various components have different values and different operational importance in different societies. In some areas of social action the weighting is important and highly significant; in other respects it may be less so: yet how is one to arrive at an objective summation which gives a total evaluation characteristic of a particular society?

LINEAGE ORGANISATION IN STATES

So far, taking lineage as the epitome of unilineal descent, and segmentary lineage societies as the most thorough-going form of lineage organisation, we have considered this type of system only. I want now to widen the frame of reference by examining the significance of descent in politically hierarchical societies which have, nevertheless, a lineage organisation.

As has often been observed, such peoples as the Southern Bantu generally, the Ashanti and the Yoruba provide examples of tribal states in which there is a lineage organisation but where unilineal descent is relevant to property inheritance, status and local organisation, rather than to the political structure in a wider sense. In political contexts, at least in those above the minimal local level, the lineage system as a means of controlling external corporate relations is replaced by an hierarchical organisation of political statuses, which may, of course, have a kinship pattern. Here we often have to distinguish between the presence or absence of politically corporate unilineal descent groups and such a principle of political kinship as perpetual succession (Cunnison, 1956). What is significant in this context is that in states of this kind unilineal descent has only limited political functions.

Take the Zulu (Gluckman, 1940; 1950), for example. Here there is a patrilineal organisation, and lineages of up to nine generations in depth are, partially at least, residential units. Lineage segments provide the core organisation of villages, and a number of villages so based in one neighbourhood form a recognised group in opposition to other similar groups. Segments are arranged in a genealogical structure, yet this does not pervade the whole social system, and contributes, consequently, to social cohesion only at a limited level of grouping. The political superstructure of Zulu society is not an extension of this segmentary lineage organisation. Hence with systems such as that of the Zulu it can be argued that in relation to political solidarity unilineal descent is less important than it is among the Nuer and Tiv, and so on. In this functional respect we might say that the Zulu are 'less' patrilineal than the Nuer. It would be more accurate, however, merely to say that patrilineal descent among the Zulu and Nuer has in some important respects different functions in each society.

Consider now lineage organisation in south-east China. Here, as Freedman (1958) has shown, we have a system where local units have a segmentary lineage structure; but where, although genealogies may be reckoned back for twenty-five generations, and higher orders of lineage grouping emerge in ancestor worship, the whole society is not pervaded by the lineage principle. As with the Zulu and the other tribal states referred to above, there is here a political superstructure based on principles other than that of unilineal descent. As with the BaSoga (Fallers, 1954), as Freedman points out, in south-east China lineage and bureaucratic organisational principles are to some extent opposed. Here, then, is another example of a politically hierarchical system with a unilineal descent organisation of limited political functions. In this respect south-east Chinese society, like that of the BaSoga, or the rather different Zulu system, is less unilineal than truly segmentary lineage societies.

With unilineally articulated 'segmentary states' such as the Alur (Southall, 1954), we have something closer to the true or 'pure' segmentary lineage system and to that extent a more strongly unilineal type of organisation.

THE CONSISTENCY OF THE DESCENT PRINCIPLE AND THE LOYALTIES CREATED BY IT

In the preceding sections we have been considering what, I suppose, might be called the operational exclusiveness of unilineal descent as a principle of social organisation with special reference to politico-jural corporateness. It is now time to consider unilinearity from another, though not entirely unrelated, point of view, that of internal exclusiveness and self-consistency. We now have to ask the question: to what extent is the unilineal principle rigidly adhered to and traced through *real* blood ties; and further, how absolute are the loyalties of members of the unilineal group?

Where in patrilineally organised societies some of the links in descent are actually through women, it can be argued that the consistency of descent, and therefore the strength of patriliny in this sense, are weakened. Thus where, as sometimes happens with the Nuer, Zulu and Tiv, links through women are converted into patrilineal ties, this detracts from the exclusiveness and absoluteness of the patrilineal principle (cf. Schneider, 1961, p. 11). Differentiation by matrilateral or uterine ties in a patrilineally based system, does not, however, diminish the power of patriliny, for the recognition of such links follows from polygyny and merely takes advantage of what Fortes calls 'complementary filiation'. Is fictional agnation in patrilineal societies also to be regarded as abrogating the patrilineal principle?

It seems not generally regarded as having this effect: and yet, if a person can exchange one lineage status and loyalty for another, this surely implies a less exclusive system of descent than where this is impossible or very uncommon. And this raises the very important issue of the relative loyalties of unilineal kin and of affines. From what is generally assumed to be the Roman model of *patria potestas*, Radcliffe-Brown (in Radcliffe-Brown and Forde, 1950, p. 78) argues that the extreme form of patrilineal descent requires that in marriage a woman is transferred completely from her father's *potestas* to that of her husband, the jural bonds between a woman and her siblings (and agnates) being finally severed by marriage.

Fortes takes the same position: 'In the limiting case, at the patrilineal pole, marriage may entail the almost complete severance of a woman from her natal family and the virtual extinction of her sisterhood and daughterhood' (Fortes, 1959, p. 20). Gluckman, likewise, in his stimulating discussion of descent and affinity among the Zulu and Lozi, argues that the strength of Zulu patriliny is to be seen in the severance of a woman's ties with her own natal kin when she marries, and her absorption (in a legal sense) into her husband's agnatic group (Gluckman, 1950, p. 182). And this, with the practice of the levirate, ghost marriage, and 'woman-to-woman marriage', as with the Nuer, for Gluckman demonstrates the power of Zulu patriliny. The same point of view is expressed by Freedman (1958, p. 134) in his analysis of lineage organisation in south-east China where women, though never completely assimilated in their husband's group – for they retain their own surname – are very strongly identified by marriage with their husband's lineage. Here Freedman argues that the strength of Chinese patriliny can be seen in the relinquishing of female agnates and their incorporation in their husband's group; and again widow-inheritance is taken as an index of strong patriliny.

These evaluations of empirical data seem to stem largely from the acceptance of the Roman *gens* organisation and *patria potestas* as the paradigm of patrilineal descent. In his discussion of the nature of matriliny, Schneider (1961, p. 11) has sought to give this interpretation a theoretical gloss. Schneider holds that, although in principle the strongest kind of descent group is that whose members are in no way assimilated into their affinal groups, the patrilineal group can dispense with its female members in exogamous marriage, acquiring in return wives from other groups, without in any way challenging the essential strength of patriliny. Woman are only required for procreation, not, as with men in both patrilineal and matrilineal systems, for authority.

Without in any way attempting to dispute that what Fortes (1960) calls 'jural authority' is always predominantly vested in men, whatever the system of descent, there is another point of view which can, I think, be put with equal cogency. This proceeds form the assumption that unilineal descent (whether patrilineal or matrilineal) *may* define the status of all members of the descent group irrespective of sex. Thus in patrilineal systems sisters and daughters are, potentially at least, as much agnates as brothers and sons, although as women their overall social status is usually considerably inferior to that of men. Woman then, may be members of their lineage, with their political and jural status firmly tied to it, even if they are perhaps only second-class citizens.

Thus, to refer to actual ethnographic data, in the case of the BaSoga (Fallers, 1957), although citizenship is not invariably tied to agnation and clientship is an important ascriptive principle, women are not strongly absorbed into their husband's groups by marriage but retain their natal patrilineal affiliation. Fallers argues that in this respect the Soga are more patrilineal than the Nuer or Zulu. Similarly Leach (1957) holds that a similar situation amongst the Lakher makes them no less patrilineal than the Jinghpaw whose marital institutions conform to those of the Zulu and Nuer. Likewise I consider that where, among the Somali, a woman is not fully absorbed into her husband's lineage but retains much of her pre-marital natal politico-jural status, this indicates strong patriliny rather than the reverse (I.M. Lewis, 1962b, pp. 39–43). And this is true of both the northern nomadic Somali and of the southern part-cultivating Somali who have quite different patterns of marriage. The former tend to marry widely outside the group, whereas the latter most frequently marry patrilateral parallel cousins, or matrilateral cross-cousins.

In both cases, there is a high divorce rate, marriage is unstable, and a woman's life is *always* (before and after marriage) primarily the responsibility of her own natal kin. This is evident in the fact that when a married woman is killed, her bloodwealth is due not to the husband but to her own patrilineage. With the Cyrenaican Bedouin similarly a woman's patrilineal affiliation is never fully extinguished by marriage, and responsibility for her life rests ultimately with her own kin. Since among the Bedouin not all marriages correspond to the preferential cousin pattern, these data, like those for the northern Somali, show that, contrary to Leach's suggestion (Leach, 1957, p. 550, this type of descent is not invariably associated with preferential marriage. Indeed the Tswana (Schapera, 1950) provide an excellent example of the converse: they have a system of preferential cousin marriage like the Bedouin, and yet their system of descent follows the pattern of the Nuer and Zulu where marriage does incorporate women in their husband's group.

Thus in certain patrilineal societies, some with hierarchical political institutions and others without them, marriage does not incorporate a woman fully in the group of her husband. Among hierarchical systems, examples are provided by the Amba, Soga, Ruanda, Lakher and Fulani; and, in uncentralised segmentary lineage societies, in the Tiv, Bedouin, Somali and Tallensi. Since, as I have argued elsewhere (I.M. Lewis, 1962b, pp. 41–3), these societies all have fairly high divorce rates , there seems to be a general correlation between unstable marriage and the extent to which a woman, after marriage, still retains strong legal ties with her own kin.

From the point of view of this discussion, however, what is significant is that in some patrilineal societies, whether the unilineal principle permeates the political structure or not, and is therefore 'functionally strong' in this sense, descent links men and women in a different way from the Roman paradigm. We have therefore to recognise that, whereas in some societies women are little more than pawns in a patrilineal system, in other strongly patrilineal societies their patrilineal affiliation is little less binding than that of men.

Thus while it seems often to be assumed that the patrilineal group does not include women, indeed Radcliffe-Brown (in Radcliffe-Brown and Forde, 1950, p. 41) states this quite explicitly, there are other patrilineal societies where women, although of markedly inferior status to men, have yet strong patrilineal rights and obligations. Such cases resemble matrilineal societies in that the sibling bond is strong between the sexes to the corresponding detriment of the marriage tie. A correlate of this type of patriliny, is, I suggest, the existence of strong matrilateral ties. And since these depend for their validity and force upon the attachment of women to their patrilineages of birth, I do not see how this can be regarded as detracting from the absoluteness and exclusiveness of patrilineal descent *per se*.

Here again we touch on the wider issue to which I have already referred: that the strength of patriliny cannot simply be assessed in relation to the extent to which matrilineal principles of grouping are, or are not, recognised. Nor, I believe, will a distinction between patriliny as a unilineal phenomenon, and 'father-right' as a jural principle, make the point of distinction adequately.[4] Institutional complexes (e.g. local contiguity, contract, age-sets, hierarchical political organisation, etc.) separately, or in conjunction, may detract from the exclusiveness of patriliny just as effectively and significantly as the parallel recognition of matrilineal descent. In other word, patriliny cannot be weighed against matriliny in a functional vacuum. From this functional point of view some bilaterally organised societies or systems of dual descent may be just as strongly patrilineal, or matrilineal, as other societies where only one principle of descent is followed, but where other institutional principles are an important basis for the ascription of status.

A brief comparison of the Plateau Tonga (Colson, 1953) and the west African Yako (Forde, 1950) will show very well what I mean. Matrilineal descent among both Tonga (who are classified as matrilineal) and among the Yako (regarded as having double descent) seems to have a similar importance. In both societies matrilineal kin have corporate interests in cattle and movable goods; in marriage, for they are exogamous and pay and receive bridewealth in concert; and in the payment and receipt of damages. Moreover, matrilineal kin have common ritual duties. Among the Yako recognition of the complementary principle of patrilineal descent is the basis for territorial allegiance and land-holding. But with the Tonga these interests are based on the principle of local contiguity, and social cohesion is maintained by the interaction of this principle with that of matrilineal descent. From this functional stand-point, therefore, matrilineal descent is no more important among the 'matrilineal' Tonga than it is among the Yako characterised as having double descent. Nor are the Yako any less matrilineal than the Tonga.

This example will perhaps suffice to indicate, in relation to what was said previously, how, if social function is the criterion, organisational principles other than descent have to be considered on the same plane of relevance as descent in characterising a social system. To this extent the labels 'matrilineal' and 'patrilineal', and so on, are only fully meaningful when other principles of organisation are taken into account in establishing the 'type' of a particular society or system.

CONCLUSIONS

In discussing some of the problems which are encountered in the study of unilineal descent, I have followed Fortes and Evans-Pritchard's dictum (1940, p. 3) that 'comparative study . . . has to be on an abstract plane where social processes are stripped of their cultural idiom and are reduced to functional terms'. From this point of view, the sort of taxonomic exercise performed by Fried (1957) where descent groups are classified in terms of matriliny or patriliny, corporateness, the presence or absence of ranking and stratification, and the character of exogamic proscriptions, seems to me of limited utility. For such criteria may have little direct relation to the operational realities of social organisation. Moreover, in such a scheme of classification quite different functional situations may be lumped together and important underlying differences obscured. We need to know what unilineal descent entails in a society, in all its manifold implications, before we can attempt to characterise social systems in terms of 'strong' or 'weak' patriliny (or matriliny) and before we can draw meaningful analogies. Otherwise the criteria of our classification are little more than superficial cultural features which may have very limited practical significance.

Thus while many traditional social systems contain as one of their organisational principles the recognition of unilineal descent, the functional significance of this varies widely. Even in patrilineal segmentary lineage societies there are considerable differences in the importance assigned to descent as a principle of social cohesion and status ascription. Thus, as I have shown, in some respects patrilineal descent has a greater primacy among the Somali than with the Nuer, Tiv or Bedouin, while in other respects the reverse is true. Similarly, if we examine the nature of social ties based on descent in relation to women as well as men, and compare descent with affinity, we find that some patrilineal systems resemble the Roman paradigm while others do not. And this, as it seems to me, quite fundamental difference in the character of agnation is not dependent upon whether a unilineal system is or is not of the segmentary lineage type. Patrilineal systems where men and women share similarly strong agnatic ties are found in both centralised and uncentralised political organisations. And the same is true of patrilineal descent systems of the Roman type.

Thus, if we focus attention on the character of the sibling bond, some kinds of patrilineal system have more in common with matrilineal systems than with other patrilineal organisations, and the difference cannot be accounted for in terms of bilateral or dual descent. Moreover, if we take into account the contributions made to social cohesion and status ascription of institutional complexes other than descent, we have to acknowledge that to type some societies as patrilineal, or matrilineal, or as possessing bilateral or dual descent, without paying equal regard to the other operative principles of organisation, may be highly misleading. Certainly at best it tells us surprisingly little. And here I feel we must recognise the validity of Leach's contention that: 'It may be that to create a class labelled matrilineal societies is as irrelevant for our understanding of social structures as the creation of a class of blue butterflies is irrelevant for the understanding of the anatomical structure of lepidoptera' (Leach, 1961, p. 4).

Finally, since descent has multiple characteristics in most societies, to say that one society is 'strongly' patrilineal or matrilineal, or is more patrilineal or matrilineal, than another, has in itself little meaning, except perhaps as an evaluation of native sentiment. From some points of view, as we have seen, the Tonga are no more matrilineal than the Yako. Comparison of the strength of descent in different societies must, therefore, be with respect to specific functions or areas of status ascription. The degree of variation which is evident with even as few societies as have been discussed here is striking. To emphasise this, significant points of difference for six of the patrilineal peoples discussed in this paper (the Tiv, Bedouin, Somali, Nuer, Zulu and Chinese) are shown in the accompanying table.

Can one now simply add up the positive entries under each aspect of descent in order to reach a characteristic score of patrilineal 'strength' for each society? Few people, I imagine, would accept

	Society					
	Tiv	Bedouin	Somali	Nuer	Zulu	Chinese
Inherent properties of descent:						
Unilineally consistent[1]	0	0	+	0	+	0
Binds men and women equally[2]	+	+	+	0	0	0
Functional aspects of descent:						
Embraces whole society[3]	+	+	+	0	0	0
Political cohesion	+	+	+	+	0	0
Jural cohesion	+	+	+	+	+	+
Religious cohesion[4]	0	0	0	+	+	+
Non-occurrence of other structural principles:						
Nil local contiguity	0	0	+	0	0	0
Nil age-set organisation	0	+	+	0	0	+
Nil contractual collaboration	0	0	0	+	+	+
Nil centralised government	+	+	+	+	0	0

NOTES:
1. A positive entry here means that descent is exclusively (or virtually exclusively) traced through real agnatic kin; links through women are not made a basis for fictional agnatic ties.
2. A positive entry here indicates that women do *not* surrender their agnatic affiliation when they marry; men and women, more or less equally, retain their agnatic statuses of birth throughout life.
3. A positive entry here indicates that genealogical ascription embraces the entire society and culture; there is a single 'national' genealogy.
4. A positive entry here is meant to imply that religious beliefs and practice are to a significant extent organised on a lineage basis.

this, for it would assume that all the criteria accounted for are of equal significance. Thus when all the aspects into which descent can be factorised are considered, I see no simple way of making any total evaluation of the significance of descent in a particular case, unless, perhaps, we adopt the typological procedures of archaeology and speak of Nuer-type segmentary lineage societies, and so on. And yet even here we are likely to be in difficulties, for the facts reviewed in this paper, if they do nothing else, at least illustrate abundantly that a system which is 'strongly' patrilineal or matrilineal in one respect is not necessarily so in another. Thus it is obvious that any comparative study of societies from the point of view of unilinearity must compare the specific respects in which unilineal descent is significant in each case. The lumping together of societies on the basis of patriliny or matriliny alone can only lead to confusion. The socio-political implications of descent are often much more significant than whether descent is traced in the patri- or matri-line.[5]

NOTES

1 I realise, of course, that patrilineal descent and matrilineal descent are not 'mirror images' (to use Southall's expression), or logical opposites, although I do not accept all the points of difference made by Schneider in his theoretical discussion of matriliny (Schneider, 1961).

2 This is not an indication of matriliny, but arises from the common practice of distinguishing segments within a patrilineage along the lines of uterine differentiation ('complementary filiation' in Fortes's terminology). All the patrilineal societies mentioned in this chapter make use of this principle which, of course, follows from polygyny. (for the Bedouin, see Peters 1960, p.29.)

3 This is not to be taken as implying that Somali genealogies are accurate historical records. There is a general correlation between the numerical strength of a lineage and the number of generations in its pedigree. Since quite wide differences occur in the span of collateral lineages it seems that the genealogies of small groups are telescoped, while those of large groups ramify with increasing numbers and population strength. Thus names which are not significant points of ramification but merely serve to continue a single unilineal line tend to drop out of the genealogical record. Hence the genealogies of large groups are probably more accurate historically than those of smaller lineages. At the apex of Somali genealogies, where descent is traced from Arabia, a strongly mythical element enters, and at this level genealogies have an altogether different character (cf. I.M. Lewis, 1995, ch. 4).

4 As Leach (1957), p.51) has pointed out, some matrilineal societies evince a certain degree of 'father-right, if by this term is meant the degree of jural authority which a father has over his children. In his discussion of Lozi and Zulu kinship and affinity, Gluckman (1950) uses the terms patriliny and 'father-right' more or less interchangeably, but seems to indicate that a valid distinction might be made between them. While granting that there are contexts in which a distinction could usefully be drawn, I do not see how the sorts of difference in patrilineal descent discussed here could be expressed in this way.

5 While arguing that functional criteria are of extreme importance in establishing the nature of descent in different societies, I do not believe that simple and invariable correlations can be drawn between descent systems and socio-ecological conditions in an adaptive sense, as for example by Stewart (1955) or Sahlins (1961). Sahlins's contention, based on an apparently rather cursory survey of the literature, for instance, that segmentary lineage systems develop in tribes expanding into an already occupied ecological niche seems to have little general validity. One of the greatest intrusive movements in north-east Africa was that of the Galla (who now call themselves Oromo) who employed an age-set organisation of

warriors in their movement of conquest. And although the Somali similarly expanded in their wake with a segmentary lineage organisation, they later adopted an age-set warrior organisation in their wars with the Oromo. When their main movements of expansion ceased they abandoned the age-set organisation which they had adopted and retained their segmentary lineage organisation. For more general discussion on segmentary lineage systems and their politico-jural significance in modern as well as 'traditional' contexts, see Southall (1976); Kuper (1982); Karp and Maynard (1983); Schlee (1985); Gellner (1995); Munson (1995); Helander (forthcoming); I.M. Lewis (1998a).

CHAPTER 4

FRONTIER FETISHISM
& THE 'ETHIOPIANISATION' OF AFRICA

The explorers dispatched by Prince Henry the Navigator along the African coast to seek a sea-route from Portugal to the Indies brought back reports of a great Christian king who ruled in the far interior. These accounts confirmed earlier rumours of a Christian African country, called Ethiopia, ruled by a monarch named Prester John, to whose court a regular Portuguese embassy was dispatched in 1520. (The name of the reigning Emperor then was Lebna Dengel.)

With its biblical associations, Ethiopia was shown on maps of Africa of this period as a vast Christian kingdom, including most of Africa south of Egypt and east of Angola. This, of course, was an exaggeration, reflecting ignorance and Eurocentric Christian bias. It was actually in the closing decades of the nineteenth century, with imported European arms, that Ethiopia assumed her greatest expansion under the redoubtable Emperor Menelik II. Bearing the name of the founder of the dynasty resulting from the legendary union of the Queen of Ethiopia and King Solomon, Menelik astonished the European colonial powers by defeating an Italian army in 1896 and establishing Ethiopia as a formidable local super-power in the 'Scramble for Africa'. Since Haile Selassie's deposition in 1974 and the ensuing revolution, Ethiopia is now, of course, a socialist republic – not an empire. However, it retains much of its traditional political anatomy, deriving from its history as an ethnically heterogenous conquest state.

This is one form of traditional African political organisation. It is not the only traditional African form. By an accident of history, the European partition of sub-Saharan Africa produced similar, ethnically heterogenous states. Decolonisation left this pluralist type of state as the dominant form in contemporary independent Africa. As I shall endeavour to argue, European colonisation and decolonisation have thus led to a process which, from the point of view of comparative political anatomy, might aptly be called the '*Ethiopianisation*' of Africa. As I hope will be clear, I do not mean by this that all independent African states share the policies or formal political organisation of the present Ethiopian regime. I refer to a deeper and more basic level of political structure.

To present my argument I shall have to examine the political anatomy of African political units in *pre-colonial* Africa. Before embarking on this, let me say a few words on the terms 'nation' and 'tribe' since they are also part of African political terminology.

NATIONS AND TRIBES

As is well known, especially in relation to the Third World, the terms 'nation' and 'tribe' regularly convey a political judgement, the first usually positive, the second usually negative. 'Nation' is associated with civilisation, literacy, progress and development generally; 'tribe', in contrast, has the reverse associations, being intimately linked with parochialism, backwardness and primitiveness.

This is an interesting transformation of the original etymological sense of these two terms. Originally, the Latin *tribus* referred to the three (possibly legendary) founding tribes (Titii, Ramnes and Luceres) whose members were collectively citizens of the Roman city-state. Notwithstanding these impeccable origins and the cachet associated with such expressions as the 'Twelve Tribes of Israel', in the eighteenth and nineteenth centuries colonising Europeans applied the word 'tribe' indiscriminately to describe the supposedly 'uncivilised' archaic communities into which the indigenous peoples of Africa, America and parts of Asia were divided before the imperial partition.[1] The term was thus applied ot distinctive cultural entities, whose members spoke the same language or dialect, generally occupied a common territory, and might or might not acknowledge the authority of a single chief or political leader and so form a more or less clearly demarcated *political* as well as social *unit*.

While nineteenth-century Europeans rarely dignified the peoples of the 'Dark Continent' with the title 'nation', it is interesting to note that this, as it were, suppressed term should have reappeared in the religious vocabulary of vodu and other similar syncretic Latin American religions where the various gods and spirits, transported with slavery to the new world, are grouped in 'nations'. So, those whom Europeans disparaged as primitive tribes were resurrected as 'nations' (Hausa, Ibo, Guinea, Dahomey, etc.) in this syncretic cosmology.

The concept 'tribe', which the nineteenth- and twentieth-century European administrators employed in Africa, was used to designate a range of traditional socio-political units varying enormously in culture, constitution and size. While individual administrators, *especially if they were British*, might admire independent-spirited pastoralists and wild nomadic warriors without kings or chiefs, it was usually found easier to recognise and rule centralised states such as those of the Bakong, BaGanda, Ashanti and the like – even if they had first to be conquered or 'pacified'. Hierarchical political institutions were familiar to the imperial mind and, particularly in the systems of 'indirect rule' invented by the British proconsul, Lord Lugard, could be conveniently accommodated within the overarching imperial superstructure. The general assumption of hierarchical government encouraged expatriate European officials to recognise and appoint 'traditional' leaders, even sometimes where they did not actually previously exist. Such innovations, often unrecognised and unintended, had the effect of social engineering, leading to the re-grouping or even creation of entirely novel political units. Thus British colonial rule particularly, often rigidified traditional tribal divisions as well as introducing new ones, although this was not always a direct or deliberate policy. Under the *pax colonica*, whole new ethnic groups sometimes formed, modelling themselves on 'traditional tribes'. The case of the *Nubis*, powerbase of the notorious Field Marshal Amin, is instructive here. Taking its name from the Nuba area of the Sudan, and claiming to speak a distinct language 'Ki-Nubi', this Muslim military caste in Uganda developed out of a largely Nilotic diaspora (Shilluk, Dinka, Bari and Kakwa, etc.) of soldiery left behind in the area when the Turko-Egyptian regime in the Sudan collapsed.[2] British administration in Uganda required a local militia and the Nubis were gradually able to monopolise this crucial role and turn it to their advantage. They were not exactly created ex-nihilo by the European administration for this purpose: rather they saw their opportunity and produced a synthetic ethnic identity to safeguard it. As one anthropologist justly observes:

> Critics have often accused the colonial governments of a deliberate policy of 'divide and rule', and of suppressing wider African loyalties and individual group development. That this was commonly the *effect* of colonial rule is evident, but there is limited evidence to demonstrate that such policy was deliberate throughout and put into practise. The process was more subtle and complex than that. But probably most administrators, of both high and low rank, merely took it for granted that the tribe was a readily

identifiable, time-honoured unit, indigenous to African perceptions and activities.

Anthropologists have been aware of this for a long time. Many indeed have analysed the delicate interplay between European administrators' *stereotypes* of tribal identity and the *reality* of the colonial power-structure in which tribes and tribalism flourished. To recognise this does not, of course, mean that 'tribal conflicts are explainable primarily by reference to colonial domination' (Godelier, 1977, p. 96). The well-informed Soviet Africanist R. M. Ismagilova (1978, p. 10) provides a more realistic assessment:

> The specific features of African society in our day are often explained simply as the effect of colonialism. That view has led to both foreign political scientists and African politicians having an attitude to the traditional structures and surviving institutions of tribal-clan society that is not always correct. Yet many of these phenomena are strong and exert considerable influence on the social development of African peoples.

PRE-COLONIAL NATIONS AND STATES

Although it was recognised that different African tribes had different customs and different forms of political organisation, few colonial administrators had the time or specialist training to study systematically the range of types of African polity. It was consequently in the main left to the first generation of modern social anthropologists conducting intensive field research in the 1930s and 1940s to attempt to chart the spectrum of indigenous African political formations. If there is some truth, and it is certainly limited, in the charge that these anthropologists sometimes failed to emphasise the impact of the colonial superstructure, this was largely because they sought as far as possible to recover the *authentic* African traditional structures – untainted by Western influence. Hierarchically organised states such as those of the Kong, Zulu, Bemba, Ganda, and so on, were displayed in all their complex intricacy. More enigmatic were those uncentralised political formations without chiefs which, at first sight, lacked government in the conventional sense and had no specific political institutions to organise their affairs. Politically uncentralised pastoralists like the *Nuer* of the southern Sudan challenged the anthropologist to discover how anarchy was averted in such cultures whose constituent political units were so much larger than the small, familistic 'bands' characteristic of hunting and gathering peoples. The English anthropologist Evans-Pritchard (1940) was able to demonstrate convincingly now amongst such pastoralists, in the absence of any chiefly or bureaucratic administrative hierarchy, a minimum degree of order could be effectively maintained through the mobilisation of loyalties based on a combination of kinship and neighbourhood. The key lay in the intimate entwining of ties of descent and of locality. In a circle radiating outwards from the level of the village, each local community was identified with a corresponding lineage segment. Hence genealogies were political charters, describing how people came together in unity or divided in hostility according to their closeness in kinship on the model of the Arab proverb: 'Myself against my brother; my brother and I against my cousin; my cousin and I against the outsider'. Political cohesion was expressed in the idiom of kinship, the 'segmentary lineage system'; of balanced kinship divisions, corresponding to that of territorial divisions on the ground – villages and groups of villages.

Within this *segmentary* structure, political decisions were made democratically in general assemblies of all the adult men of the community involved, this group expanding and contracting along kinship (and neighbourhood) lines according to the political context. So, in such 'segmentary lineage societies', closely related local groups would temporarily unite against a distant enemy, and dissolve in mutual antagonism when this common threat disappeared. In the absence of chiefs or other official political figures, the strength and limits of such elastic and fluctuating political cohesion could be measured by examining the procedures followed in ventilating and resolving disputes at the various levels of grouping. The point at which the moral duty to resolve conflicts by *peaceful* mediation became completely attenuated marked the limits of the political community. This division of the people or nation, united internally by the ideal of peace and harmony and externally by war, was identified as the 'tribe'. Nuer society thus consisted of a series of independent and mutually hostile political divisions ('tribes'), loosely inter-connected by culture, language, mode of production and diffuse potential sentiments of pan-Nuer identity.

In the wake of this pioneering discovery, other anthropologists soon found that this system of 'minimal government' based on segmentary lineage organisation was not unique to the Nuer but played a crucial political role in many other traditional African societies as well as elsewhere. This wider recognition of the general currency of what has passed into political science terminology as the '*non-state*' (MacKenzie, 1967) encouraged anthropologists to devise ever more elaborate and comprehensive political typologies. Political anthropology thus became pre-occupied, some would say obsessed, with the presence or absence of formal political institutions and hierarchy and with isolating variables associated with the transition from 'non-states' to states and vice versa.

This concentration on the presence or absence (qualitatively and quantitatively) of centralised authority (chiefs and kings) deflected attention from the intriguing question of the relationship between political cohesion and cultural identity. Indeed, these Africanist political anthropologists were accused of assuming that *cultural* and *social* boundaries necessarily coincided. The most obvious exception to this criticism is the famous 'conquest' theory of state-formation according to which states arise from the collision of peoples of different cultures, one group gaining political ascendancy over the other developing a centralised state organisation to maintain control in the face of cultural differences. In endorsing this ancient theory, the British founders of modern political anthropology also suggested the collarary that cultural homogeneity was likely to be associated with uncentralised, segmentary political systems such as that found among the Nuer. Other anthropologists contributed splendidly detailed analyses of the power structure of complex, culturally heterogeneous traditional states. It is, however, only relatively recently and largely due to the application of the concept 'plural society' to Africa's traditional polities that we can trace the beginnings of a more systematic examination of the relationship between *political* and *cultural* identity in pre-colonial Africa. For J. S. Furnivall[4] who coined the term in the ethnically heterogeneous context of Dutch Indonesia (in 1934), the 'plural society' was one of colonial domination with a medley of peoples who 'mix but do not combine'. In the pre-colonial *African* context, we can identify culturally plural states and heterogeneous 'empires' such as Ethiopia, Mali, Songhay and Dahomey. We can contrast these with *homogeneous* states such as Kongo, Ashanti, Benin, Yoruba and Ganda, while a third category of 'homogenising' states are transitional between the two extremes. There are clearly at least two possibilities in the *transitional situation.* One is that what today would be described, as 'nation-building' is in progress, as a dominant caste or ethnic group seeks to consolidate its position by extending its culture in melting-pot fashion to embrace the entire population.[5] The other is that the politically dominant group is engaged in the reverse process, of making itself as culturally distinct as possible from those it governs and so transforming power into an ethnic monopoly. Here the trend is towards pluralism, rather than towards ethnic homogeneity.

These comparative studies by anthropologists of pre-colonial African political structures tend to follow the nineteenth-century English radical political philosopher, John Stuart Mill, in seeing a connexion between *cultural homogeneity* and *democracy* on the one hand, and *cultural pluralism*, hierarchy and autocracy on the other. However, this is obviously not necessarily the case since, as we have just seen, some centralised and far from democratic societies possess a homogeneous common culture, for example, the Kongo. Indeed democracy and despotism flourish in both culturally homogeneous and heterogeneous societies.[6] Thus the association of pluralism with despotism which derives originally from Furnivall's work in Indonesia seems accidental. In fact, I would suggest that, over the last decade, the term 'pluralism' has acquired an increasingly favourable connotation – suggesting harmonious tolerance of a variety of life-styles. Thus it is probably significant that in the 1970s South Africa adopted the idiom of 'pluralism' (to the extent of restyling its former Minister of Bantu Affairs 'Minister of Plural Affairs') in its quest for more favourable publicity for its modified 'new version' of apartheid.

My concern here, however, is not to attempt to assess the currency of democratic political structures in Africa before the imperial partition of the continent. All I seek to demonstrate is the co-existence, both in hierarchical state systems like the Kongo and Ganda and in uncentralised polities like the Nuer or Somali or Tonga, of culturally homogeneous as well as heterogeneous political formations. Thus the pre-colonial 'map of Africa' included true (culturally homogeneous) nation-states, 'non-state' (i.e. uncentralised) nations, and pluralistic heterogeneous Hapsburg-empire-style states like Ethiopia. Particularly in view of homogenising trends, it would, I believe, serve little purpose to speculate on the relative preponderance of culturally homogeneous or culturally heterogeneous political formations in pre-colonial Africa. I have simply sought to demonstrate that here 'traditional' Africa enjoyed a mixed political economy.

COLONIAL AND POST-COLONIAL AFRICA

It is a remarkable irony that the European powers who partitioned Africa in the late nineteenth century when the idea of the nation-state was paramount in Europe should have created in Africa a whole series of Hapsburg-style states, comprising a medley of peoples and ethnic groups lumped together within frontiers which paid no respect to traditional cultural contours. This general process of 'balkanisation' in which divisions of the same people were parcelled out amongst different colonial territories is well-illustrated by the fate of the BaKongo. Even more extreme is the case of the Somali who were fragmented into five parts: one (in Jibuti) under the French, one (the Ogaden) under Ethiopia, another (Somalia) under the Italians, and two under British rule (British Somaliland and the northern-frontier district of Kenya). This is no doubt an extreme case, but it illustrates the general process which gave an entirely new complexion to sub-Saharan Africa. Pluralism was in the ascendant and the pluralist Hapsburg-style states which had formerly represented *one* style of African polity became the prevailing mode for the whole continent (especially south of the Sahara).

It was perhaps fortunate for African nationalists, although this can hardly have been foreseen, that the European powers who thus enshrined pluralism as the dominant political strain in the continent referred to their colonial subjects as 'tribes' rather than 'nations'. Thus, in the struggle to achieve independence from the European colonisers, African political leaders appealed to the transcendant 'nationalism' which colonisation kindled amongst subject populations irrespective of their tribal identity. Tribalism, which had developed considerably under the *pax colonica*, particularly in urban contexts where competition for resources and power was acute, was inevitably cast in the role of a negative atavistic force impeding the growth of national solidarity. 'Tribalism' like 'nationalism' in common with other forms of group identity is notoriously reactive. So in pluralistic African colonies, 'tribalism' developed in much the same way and with almost all the same characteristics as 'nationalism' in nineteenth-century Europe.[7] In Angola, Mozambique and elsewhere such divisive, particularistic forces had to be thrust into the background in the urgent nationalist campaign to gain independence.

The achievement of independence by Europe's ex-colonies perpetuated the pluralist multi-ethnic state or 'state-nation' whose virtual monopoly is readily seen by contrast with the few exceptions: Botswana, Lesotho, Somalia. Whereas metropolitan connexions had helped to differentiate African states in the colonial period, in the post-colonial era there were fewer distinguishing features, and states tended to become identified with their heads of state. The other obvious basis of demarcation lay in the boundaries separating one state form another. So the colonial boundaries, which balkanised Africa and provided the foundation for its modern independent states, are today appropriately enough the subject of what amounts to religious veneration. This I refer to as 'frontier fetishism'.[8]

To conclude, I have argued here that there are two pre-colonial styles of African polity, one based on ethnic identity, the other culturally pluralist. In the widest African perspective, both can claim equal legitimacy and 'authenticity'. Colonisation and decolonisation, however, have changed this traditional pattern in favour of pluralism. This process might be called the 'Ethiopianisation' of Africa, making it not inappropriate that the Organisation of African Unity should have its headquarters in Addis Ababa. The price of the monopoly held by this form of 'state-nation' (rather than 'nation-state') is the inevitable boost it gives to its internal erstwhile 'tribal', but now increasingly canonised as 'national' or 'ethnic', divisions. Confounding all the highly artificial and tendentious distinctions drawn by political sociologists and others, 'tribes' have literally become 'nations' (or 'nationalities') almost overnight. Nowhere in Africa is this better understood than in contemporary Ethiopia.

Developments in Ethiopia since the overthrow of Haile Selassie's *ancien regime* in September 1974[9] further illustrated this trend. The 'creeping revolution', as it was generally known, which spread slowly through all public services and eventually unseated Haile Selassie, was conducted under the slogan 'Ethiopia First'. But, after Colonel Mengistu had seized power from the more liberal leaders of the Provisional Military Government, he and his Marxist clique soon came to recognise the problem posed by Ethiopia's multiple 'nationalities' and established an Institute, which included Ethiopian anthropologists, to study and enumerate the different groups. Following the Soviet model, they received limited recognition, and there was no question of granting autonomy to Eritrea where the secessionist struggle gathered momentum (cf. I.M. Lewis, 1983).

It was, of course, the success of the Eritrean secessionist war which led to the downfall of Mengistu's oppressive rule and its replacement (with Western encouragement) by the allies of the Eritreans, the present Tigrean-based regime. The new government, with Marxist (indeed Stalinist) ideological roots, had a more widely representative powerbase and pursued policies which, it was claimed, would suit Ethiopia's pluralist political circumstances.

Although there were many significant opposition groups which reflected these ethnic divisions and some of which sought an equivalent degree of autonomy to that enjoyed by Eritrea, in many ways the most acute threat was that posed by the conservative Amhara pressure groups associated with the *ancien regime*. It needs to be recalled here that, in the dynastic history of the Ethiopian state, the empire was founded and first ruled by Semitic-speaking northern highlanders – originally the Tigreans, and after them by the Amhara. Hence, the latter's overthrow by the former was, in terms of their ancient ethnic rivalry, simply another twist in the long history of their competition for dominance. The Amharas, whose nationalism had previously been identified with their control of modern Ethiopia (in the period of Haile Selassie and then Mengistu), was now expressed as the shrill voice of a marginalised and oppressed ethnic category. In the wider context of types of nationalism, the political identity and consciousness of both these historically dominant ethnic groups corresponds to that associated with literacy – which Gellner erroneously takes to be universal (see Chapter 5 below).

Outside the charmed circle of Semitic power in Ethiopia, the most pressing local nationalisms are those associated with the Cushitic-speaking lowlanders – the largely pastoral Afar, Somali and agro-pastoral Oromo. With the existence of the state of Somalia – based on Somali ethnic identity – from 1960, and the claim that rights of Somali self-determination extended across its borders into the Somali areas of Ethiopia, Jibuti and Kenya, it was clear where the most immediate threat lay. When the Somali campaign to restore the independence of their kinsmen in the Ethiopian Ogaden (named after the main local Somali clan) was defeated in the 1978 war,[10] this movement largely collapsed – although Somalian support, at various levels, for their Muslim Oromo allies still continued.[11] The new Ethiopian regime which came to power in 1991 divided the state a year later into fourteen regions and autonomous towns: these include region 5 for the Ogaden Somalis (and other local Somali clans); region 2 for the Afar; and region 4 for the Oromo (by far the largest single ethnic group) – a huge area, enclaving the capital, Addis Ababa, and running across the whole country.[12]

Thus, in contemporary Ethiopia we confront two sometimes over-lapping ancient nationalisms, associated with literacy and bureaucracy, and two mutually reactive 'traditional' nationalisms in which literacy is a secondary factor as the following chapter argues. Hence, in contrast to the views of A. Smith (1971), Hinsley (1973) and Gellner (1983), I conclude that nationalism is not a modern invention, nor necessarily connected with literacy, nor is it a monopoly of the oppressed creature – it may be exactly the opposite (as was historically the case with the Amhara and other imperialist groups): an ideology of domination. Above all, it is a highly sensitive, inter-active expression of cultural identity which thrives in confrontation and contestation.[13] Its pervasive force is a testimony to the universal appeal of the myth of the naturally created and ideally autonomous community, with its special claims to a unique heritage. Pluralism is a formula which seeks to contain these fractious forces but may, paradoxically, only succeed in inflaming them.

NOTES

1 Cf. P.H. Gulliver (ed.) (1969, p.8).
2 For an intereseting account, see Southall (1973).
3 Leach (1954).
4 *Netherlands India; Study of a Plural Economy*, 1934.
5 See Cohen and Middleton (eds) (1970).
6 See P.L. van der Berghe, 'Pluralism and the polity' in Kuper and Smith (1971, pp.67–84).
7 For an excellent treatment of this theme, see Argyle (1969, pp.41–58).
8 This term is inspired by the memorable defence of the inviolability of the ex-colonial frontiers made by President Julius Nyerere of Tanzania at one of the first meetings of the Organisation of African Unity. The frontiers of African states, Nyerere proclaimed, are so irrational they must be sacred!
9 On the invitation of friends at the University who were involved in some of the civilian movements which brought about the revolution, I was in Addis Ababa on the day the military publicly seized control. This event had been carefully orchestrated with the screening, the night before, on Ethiopian television of a skilfully edited version of the grim BBC film on the 1972 famine in Wollo. This version included shots of the birthday banquet staged for the Emperor's grandson during the Wollo famine. (See I.M. Lewis, 1982, pp.1–22; Clapham, 1988, pp.32ff.; Gascon, 1995, pp.111ff.; Markakis and Ayele, 1978, pp.102ff; Tubiana, 1980.)
10 See I.M. Lewis (1988, pp.231ff).
11 See I.M. Lewis (1998b, ch. 8).
12 This reflected the ethnic demography of Ethiopia whose largest and most widely scattered ethnic group, over 20 million strong, are indisputably the Oromo. The Tigreans were assigned region 1 in the extreme north, with the Amharas to their south in region 3.
13 On the reactive nature of such identities in east Africa, see I.M. Lewis (1968b), and in southern Africa, Vail (1989), whose analysis of nationalism and ethnicity is very close to that advocated here.

CHAPTER 5

WRITING NATIONALISM IN THE HORN OF AFRICA

LITERACY AND NATIONALISM

Languages, Samuel Johnson remarked, are the 'pedigrees of nations'. This view of the political significance of language is endorsed by those modern political scientists who define a nation as those people 'who speak the same language' (Minogue, 1967, p. 154). Other students of nationalism go further and add literacy as an indispensable qualification for the development of effective national identity (Gellner, 1983). This of course is in line with Professor Ong's bold claim, that writing 'heightens consciousness' (Ong, 1982).

The validity of this thesis would seem, at first sight, to be demonstrated all too graphically by the case of the Horn of Africa, which we examine here, where three of the world's great literate traditions have contended and interpenetrated for over a thousand years, producing extreme nationalist conflicts. I would like to suggest, however, by considering the very recent introduction of widespread mother-tongue literacy among the previously oral Somali, that the relationship between nationalism and literacy is rather more equivocal. Even in the case of core Christian nationalism, which since the conversion of their rulers in the fourth century has constituted the central dynamic of the Ethiopian state, élite, court, and restricted religious literacy have arguably been more an expression and instrument of national consciousness than its source.

HORN OF AFRICA CULTURE HISTORY

The three Great Traditions represented in the Horn of Africa are of course Judaism, Christianity and Islam. Although the first is most directly associated with the so-called 'black Jews' – the indigenous

Falashas – the Judaic tradition also strongly colours the politically dominant Christian tradition of the Semitic-speaking Tigreans and Amharas
who have controlled Ethiopia since its foundation at Axum (see
Ullendorff, 1968; Jones and Monroe, 1935). Commanding the Ethiopian
highlands where they live as settled farmers, these two ethnic groups
are hierarchically organised into ruling military stratum, clergy and lay
peasantry. Christianity has been firmly appropriated and indigenised in
this dominant, local, *literate* tradition; first in the liturgical language
Ge'ez, and later in the related Tigrinya and Amharic languages. Since
the Amharas succeeded in installing themselves as the ruling ethnic
group in this expanding Christian-conquest state some five hundred
years ago, Amharic has been known officially as 'the language of the
king', and as the medium in which the extremely important Minister of
the Pen recorded royal decisions and court history. The historic mandate
of the Amhara ethnic élite to conquer and convert neighbouring peoples
in the name of the Lion of Judah was conveyed and enshrined in the famous national epic *The Glory of Kings* (or, 'the pride of kings'), written
but not composed in the fourteenth century. This unique charter, which
traces the origins of Ethiopian kingship to Menelik I, issue of Solomon
and Sheba, like the Old Testament for the Hebrews, or the Qoran for the
Arabs, is the repository of national and religious feelings (Ullendorff,
1960, p. 144). It is, as Donald Levine (1974, p. 92) aptly describes it, 'a
national script' for the Christian Ethiopian state, which by this time (the
fourteenth century) was already locked in protracted religious wars with
the surrounding Muslim principalities and peoples, including illiterate
Cushitic-speaking lowland pastoralists, such as the Somali.

Although the oral tradition of the Somalis lays claim to the sixteenth-
century Muslim conqueror Ahmed Gran (1506–43), under whose fierce
attacks the Amhara Kingdom almost collapsed, there was little direct
contact between the two ethnic groups until the closing decades
of the nineteenth century and the colonial partition of the Somali
nation, in which Ethiopia, with its new European guns and rifles,
participated under Menelik II, the founder of the modern empire-state.
In this scramble for new possessions Menelik was as emphatic as his
European competitors (the French, British and Italians) in stressing
his God-given civilising mission to share the benefits of Christianity
with new 'heathen' subjects. This long history of isolation,[1] religious
animosity and sometimes accommodation with Islam, and in the modern
era, military conflict with European powers, has naturally sharpened
Ethiopian nationalism.

Just as it had appropriated and indigenised Christianity, the Amhara core national culture of this expanding African 'Hapsburg empire' absorbed new subject groups, offering the possibility of assimilation and upward mobility with conversion and Amharaisation – the key, for both Menelik and Haile Selassie, to integrating Ethiopia's ethnic mosaic. Ethiopia thus pioneered the 'nation-building' process characteristic of most post-colonial African states, with literacy in the mother tongue of the Amhara élite being the final signature of full citizenship. The surge of ethnic consciousness aroused by modernisation under Haile Selassie led, after the 1974 revolution (to which it contributed), to literacy campaigns which utilised the Amharic script to write several of the other languages of the 85 officially recognised Ethiopian 'nationalities'. Before the revolution only Amharic could be written;[2] after the revolution only Amharic could be written in. Ethiopia had now, literally, a national script.

LANGUAGE AND RELIGION AMONG THE SOMALI

Despite their early conversion to Islam, reflecting their proximity to Arabia and peripheral involvement in the ephemeral Islamic states which encircled Ethiopia in the Middle Ages, the Somalis, so far as we know, had not previously translated their strong sense of *cultural* nationalism into political terms. They had never constituted a state. It was characteristic also of their mixed Islamic literary and Somali oral heritage that this first manifestation of nationalism, coinciding with Ethiopian, British and Italian colonial penetration, was couched in the classic Muslim form of a *jihad*. But, led by a sophisticated Somali sheikh well versed in Arabic literacy, the success of the 'holy war' depended crucially on this man's power of oratory and genius – still widely recognised – as a major *oral* poet. I refer, of course, to the fiery Somali crusader Sayyid Mohammad 'Abdille Hassan, whose guerrilla forces defied the Christian colonisers of his people from 1900 to 1920. His banner was the banner of Islam, his book the Holy Qoran; but his battle cry was delivered in oral Somali, not written Arabic. (His oral legacy has provided, retrospectively, an oral charter for modern Somali nationalism, including literacy in the mother tongue.)

Arabic is the language of the Qoran, which must be transmitted in Arabic. From the time of their adoption of the faith, centuries ago, the Somalis have had access to Arabic, the language of Islam. But despite a vernacular tradition of Arabic instruction going back to the twelfth century (see I.M. Lewis, 1969b, pp. 75–82), Arabic has remained the prisoner of its exalted status as the Word of God, the magical language of religion, known, orally and to some extent written, only by religious specialists and a few merchants and sailors. Indeed the distinction between these religious specialists and the warrior laity, who form the majority, constitutes the most pervasive division (after that of gender) in the strongly egalitarian social system of the Somalis. The two roles are complementary, since the warriors need holy mediators to regulate their internal problems and to negotiate on their behalf with God. Thus, traditionally, these exponents of Islam, with limited literacy in Arabic, teach the Qoran in itinerant religious schools; solemnise marriage, divorce and death; assess damages in disputes; mediate and dispense blessings and therapeutic potions. The subordination of their restricted literacy tradition to the priorities of this primary oral culture is epitomised by the regular oral treatment which they provided for illness. This digestion of holy writ was effected by drinking a decoction made by washing into a cup powerful passages from the Qoran, from a piece of paper onto which they had been transcribed.

Despite (and because of) its unique religious significance, Arabic remained marginal, restricted to ritual contexts and external trade. It was not indigenised and the Arabic script was similarly little used to transcribe the vigorous, dominant-medium oral Somali (for which it is in any case not linguistically a perfect vehicle). The men of God who controlled this prestigious, if minority, literate tradition clearly had vested interests in maintaining its exclusiveness, and they were not necessarily anxious to extend its use to promote written Somali. Equally, some Somalis have suggested that, as a people proudly tracing their origins (through painstakingly constructed *written* genealogies) to the family of the Prophet Mohammed, they were reluctant to advertise to the literate Arab world that Arabic was not actually their mother tongue.

Undersigned or underwritten in this fashion, the language of the faith, oral Somali, well served the needs of a highly articulate and linguistically self-conscious people. Language was primarily for communication and complicated messages were regularly encoded in poetic form for rapid word-of-mouth transmission among these nomads, in what B. W. Andrzejewski (1982, p. 75) has called 'the oral postal service'. In this populist oral culture, oratory, and poetry in many different genres, occupied the centre of the stage. Opinion within one's own clan and outside it was influenced and formed by poems and oratory which captured the imagination of the listener. Reputations depended crucially on skill in these arts, which also entailed possessing a good command of the seemingly endless store of Somali proverbs. As the Somali historian Said Samatar points out, the Somali term for an orator means, literally, 'capable of speech', implying that those who lack oratorial skill are, virtually, incapable of speech. Without going into details, let me simply say here that thousands of poems, going back well over a hundred years, survive into the present, remembered for their artistic perfection and eloquence, a heritage endlessly replenished by new compositions (Andrzejewski and Lewis, 1964, p. 130). Seldom exceeding one hundred lines, and frequently containing archaic expressions, poems were composed and recited verbatim either by their authors or by readers, aided by the alliteration and scansion principles of the different genres. Modern poets and poetry reciters regularly possess a memorised repertoire extending up to fifteen hours of 'playback' time.

In this highly articulate oral culture, words are viewed as things – not in the magical vein associated with orality by Professor Ong, but rather as instruments, capable of inflicting deadly wounds which entail claims for compensation for defamation (*haal*), paralleling those applicable in cases of physical assault (*haq*). As a line from a famous poem by Salan 'Arrabey' (d.1940) on ingratitude puts it, 'The tongue is like a sword cutting off life'. The two systems of aggression, 'speech feud' and 'blood feud', are apt to intersect and reinforce one another. As a traditional Somali elder reflects:

Camels are looted and men killed because of poetry. The more camels a clan owns, the greater their resources. Camels bring men together. If a clan loots camels and kills men from another clan, the injured clan may bide their time and not rise in immediate revenge. But if the victorious clan attempt, as they often do, to immortalise their victory in verse, then the looted clan feels humiliated and immediately seeks to remedy their honour and avenge their wrongs. Thus revenge follows revenge, and feud, feud. (Samatar, 1982, p. 27)

TOWARDS SOMALI LITERACY

The first significant initiative towards literacy arose out of this oral culture itself, when in the wake of the expansion of colonial rule following the defeat of Sayyid Mohammad in 1920, a prominent elder of one of the major north-eastern clans (then under Italian jurisdiction) invented the first phonetically perfect script for Somali. The Osmaniya script, as it became known after its inventor's name, is written from left to right, unlike Arabic, and some of its characters are reminiscent of Amharic. When, twenty years later, the first modern Somali nationalist organisation was launched in what was then British-occupied (Italian) Somalia, this 'Somali writing' acquired a new and wider impetus as a vehicle for nationalism. This was in line with the motives which had inspired the script's inventor, who felt that national pride required his mother tongue to become a written language. This would also facilitate communication between widely separated cells of the new nationalist organisation in a script which would be indecipherable by European and Ethiopian administrative officials.

By 1947, when the Somali Youth League had become firmly established as the main nationalist party, the promotion of this script was one of its four major policy aims. However, changes in the leadership of the League soon led to a fierce debate between Osmaniya supporters and advocates of Arabic - viewed as the natural medium for a Muslim nation. The possibility of using Latin characters to write Somali also began to be examined by some nationalists. In 1957, three years before Somalia attained independence, the Somali Youth League Government printed a page of the official newspaper in Somali transcribed into Roman characters. This bold experiment produced such violent reaction, particularly on the part of traditional religious leaders, that it was not repeated. The pro-Arabic lobby denounced the use of the Latin script with the derogatory, punning slogan, *'Laatiin waa laa diin'* ('Latin is irreligion').

At independence in 1960, the Somali Republic (comprising the former British and Italian Somalilands) thus found itself with three written languages, Arabic, English and Italian. This confusing situation made it all the more urgent to solve the problem of finding an acceptable script for Somali. In 1966 a distinguished UNESCO Commission of Linguists, led by B. W. Andrzejewski, added its weight to the choice of Latin. But public opinion remained divided and volatile and the Somali government hesitated.

WRITTEN SOMALI

It was left to the military who seized power in 1969 to resolve the issue. In 1972, following what had for some years been the informal practice in the police and the army, General Siyad's regime adopted a very practical, Roman script for the national language.[3] What has been hailed as the 'Somali miracle of instant literacy' was achieved with the launching in 1973 of a concerted urban literacy campaign. Government officials were enlisted in 'crash courses' in the new script, with the prospect of losing their positions if they failed to master it.

Adult literacy classes drew large and enthusiastic attendances from the most educationally deprived sectors of the urban population, including women. The next step in this 'cultural revolution', as it was proclaimed by the then Minister of Information and National Guidance, General Ismail Ali Abokor (later imprisoned), was to extend literacy to the neglected nomads who form the majority of the population. Accordingly in the late summer of 1974 a task force of 30,000 secondary school students and teachers was dispatched in truckloads to the interior, to teach the nomads to read and write and to impart the basic principles of 'Scientific Socialism', now the official policy of the state. These privileged urban students were thus to share the fruits of the 'Glorious Revolution', as the *coup* was retrospectively named, with their nomadic 'comrades'. The guiding slogan, provided by President Siyad himself, was: 'If you know, teach. If you don't, learn.' As the general explained, in a major public speech:

> The key . . . is to give everybody the opportunity to learn reading and writing. . . . It is imperative that we give our people modern, revolutionary education . . . to restructure their social existence. . . . This will be the weapon to eradicate social balkanisation and fragmentation into tribes and sects. It will bring about an absolute unity and there will be no room for any negative foreign cultural influences.

The goals of modernisation, nationalism and independence are all fused here: a modern, integrated nation, consisting of those who not only speak the same language , but who also read and write it. (All this, of course, is very much in the spirit of Professor Ernest Gellner's theories of nationalism; although I have no reason to think that General Siyad's ideas emanated from this source.)

As it happened I was in Somalia in the summer of 1974 and saw the beginnings of the acute drought which was to cause the 'Rural Prosperity Campaign', as the programme was originally called, to be turned into a humane and well-organised famine relief operation. The emphasis of the campaign quickly shifted to an endeavour to meet the survival needs of the drought-stricken nomads – who, once grouped in relief camps, became enthusiastic recruits to the literacy classes.

Since 1974 however, with a substantial drift back to the nomadic economy, after several years of good rains, it has obviously been difficult, despite considerable effort, to sustain high levels of rural literacy. It is officially claimed that over 1 million people participated in the two literacy campaigns and that 400,000 of the urban population were literate by 1982, in addition to the half-million children enrolled in schools, where written Somali had also been established. These generous figures may also include some of the refugees who poured into Somalia after the Somali–Ethiopian conflict of 1977–8. More accessible statistics of Somali literacy can be gleaned from the records kept at the BBC Somali Programme of listeners' letters received from the Horn of Africa. These increased from a figure of 2,500 in 1973 to over 6,500 in 1983, the proportion of letters written in Somali in the same period rising from 12 per cent to 90 per cent.[4] However, difficult as it is to gauge the true numerical strength of the new literacy, there is no gainsaying its popularity or its genuinely populist character. Many people, with no experience of 'modern education', have achieved a greater mastery of the Somali vernacular, their own mother tongue, than those brought up in towns and given literacy training in foreign languages such as Arabic, Italian and English, which previously favoured the educated élite. The new mother-tongue literacy also corrects the sex bias of previous forms of formal education, such as Arabic, which gave men a great advantage over women. It is not surprising that this genuinely populist measure should be widely acknowledged as the most popular of all those introduced by the dictator Mohamad Siyad Barre.

The revolution in Somali literacy has created, nationally, corresponding demands for reading material and for stimulating new forms of literary production. In addition to the news stories and other material published in the daily *October Star*, the ideological bureau of the Somali Socialist Revolutionary Party produced a flood of propagandist pamphlets and manuals, as well as its monthly organ *Halgan* ('Struggle'). Hundreds of school textbooks as well as primers for adult literacy have been prepared by the curriculum department of the Ministry of Education. Over 6 million copies of books had been printed on the national press by the later 1970s, including the first Somali novels and written plays, scholarly dictionaries, collections of poetry and traditional folklore, and history books edited by the Somali Academy of Science and Culture. There were also translations of works by foreign authors as diverse as Brecht and G. A. Henty, as well as by less celebrated writers (as I discovered when, purely by chance, I stumbled upon a group of keen translators, busily rendering some of my own accounts of Somali history into Somali!). More novel, in a culture which, unlike Christian Ethiopia, has no tradition of visual art, are the propagandist posters, and shop and office signs, which literacy has encouraged. During the era of 'scientific socialism' these included posters at Orientation Centres displaying the revolutionary trinity of

Jaalle (Comrade) Markis (Marx), Jaalle Lenin and Jaalle Siyad. At a less elevated level one noticed various new names for restaurants and shops – including, in Mogadishu, a shop (*daas*) called 'Daaski Dallas'!

This remarkable development in mother-tongue literacy, producing a unique 'orally written literature' (Andrzejewski, 1984, pp. 227–9), has with little doubt been the most popular and effective of a package of modernising measures that included, in the lofty name of Scientific Socialism, the official abolition of the clan loyalties which had traditionally divided the nation, and the replacement of kinship by 'comradeship' (see I.M. Lewis, 1988, pp. 209–25). These secular innovations once again brought to the fore the complex issue of Somalis' Islamic identity. To reassure the local guardians of the faith, and for other strategic reasons, Somalia prudently joined the Arab League in 1974.

THE CONSEQUENCES OF LITERACY

In the historical context we have briefly sketched, it is clear, I think, that, having experienced for centuries the rivalry between the Amharic Christian and Arabic Muslim literate traditions, swelling sentiments of national pride fired the Somali quest for a national script. But has literacy actually increased national consciousness, as would be argued by Ong and other students of literacy? This, as we have seen, was according to President Siyad one of the major objectives in introducing Somali writing. That it has been achieved is the conclusion of H. M. Adam, the Somali political scientist and government official who has made the closest study of the problems of writing his native tongue. 'The writing . . . of the language', he says, 'has facilitated national integration and . . . strengthened Somali identity' (1983, p. 41). Although I cannot cite other than random personal impressions, in the wake of the national literacy campaigns, at least in urban centres in Somalia, there did seem to me to be a discernible increase in Somali linguistic self-consciousness and national pride. Certainly such nationalist sentiment found enthusiastic expression in 1977 in the campaign, initially intoxicatingly successful but ultimately disastrous, to liberate the Ogaden region of eastern Ethiopia (ethnically western Somalia). By this time, following the Ethiopian revolution of September 1974 and the ensuing power struggle in Addis Ababa, Ethiopia had become extremely vulnerable and the Western Somali Liberation Front (WSLF) guerrilla forces were able to drive out the Ethiopian garrisons with remarkable ease. As they liberated each settlement the WSLF proudly replaced all the Amharic signs and notices with announcements in the new Somali script, and opened schools to teach Somali writing. To the bitter dismay of Somali ambitions, however, all this was quickly swept away when, a few months after the super-power somersault which brought the Soviet Union to Ethiopia's side, Russian- and Cuban-supported Ethiopian forces reconquered the Ogaden (for fuller information, see I.M. Lewis, 1988). If they wished to write in their own language, those Somalis who remained in the region had now to do so in Amharic characters. This restoration of Amhara linguistic hegemony encouraged other ethnic nationalist movements, such as that of the vast Oromo nation, to follow the Somali initiative in using Latin characters to write their own national language.

LITERACY AND SECONDARY ORALITY

Events in the bitter years since the Ogaden débâcle indicate that while the 'instant literacy' we have examined may superficially have fuelled nationalistic feeling inside the Somali Republic, and in the adjacent Ogaden prior to the 1977–8 Somalia–Ethiopia conflict, it did not produce a radical and sustained transformation of nationalism into a modernist mode of the type associated with literacy by Gellner and others. In defeat, patriotism has been replaced by rancorous clan strife, which, far from being eradicated by the regime of Scientific Socialism, in fact became the latter's primary recipe for survival until it fell apart in 1990.

The resurgence of this powerful oral political tradition at the disposition of those who control state literacy may seem a little paradoxical. But written, or unwritten, language is after all a means of expression and not an end in itself. And it is not only written Somali that is involved here. We have in fact so far quite ignored, and now touch on in conclusion, what in the short term seems much more significant in its general social and political implications than Somali writing, impressive though that is. I refer, of course, to what Ong has called 'secondary orality'. By the time literacy had made its dramatic entry onto the Somali stage, the transistor revolution was already firmly entrenched, reinforcing, extending and amplifying Somali oral culture.

The highly articulate Somalis, as might be anticipated, took to radio, telephone, loudspeaker and tape-recorder with marked enthusiasm. When cheap transistor radios and cassette recorders became readily available, in the late 1960s and early 1970s, they were immediately extremely popular, sweeping Somali culture into the exciting world of secondary orality. Today it would scarcely be an exaggeration to say that every nomadic family has a radio, and from being a nation of bards the Somalis have rapidly also become a nation of radio buffs, listening avidly to Somati broadcasts from local stations and from places as distant as London, Moscow and Beijing. As they produced new works, poets now frequently used tape-recorders to supplement their memories. New 'pop' radio songs (*heello*), with musical accompaniments (Johnson, 1974; 1996; Banti and Giannattasio, 1996) relentlessly beat out the party line. Opponents of the regime both inside and outside the country composed stinging attacks on its leaders, sometimes in the form of opaque love songs. As in traditional Somali politics, the President's poets exchanged vitriolic verse with his opponents outside Somalia, and the same practice continued with the 'warlord' faction-leaders of the 1990s after the collapse of the Somali state. These vigorous poetical polemics constitute oral chain letters, stored in cassettes which circulate round Somali communities scattered all over the world.

In this surge of electronic rhetoric, Somali politics retains its overwhelmingly oral character, by-passing the written word. Somali writing, though indispensable in certain contexts, falls into second place, as an ancillary medium for communication – a written extension of an oral culture with its tendency towards fixed forms. Thus literacy, which symbolically as well as literally is so central to the Ethiopian (Amhara) national consciousness (as well as to the Tigrean), remains, I believe, peripheral to Somali identity. Yet across the border, within the Ethiopian pluralist mosaic, the extension of literacy in Amharic characters inflamed reactive sentiments of ethnic nationalism amongst those subject peoples who, like the Somalis, would write their language in their own way. In this case, by a kind of poetic justice, the rejection of unacceptable literacy heightened national consciousness.

NOTES

1 This theme is familiar from Gibbon's (1957, vol 5, p.69) rotund reference; 'Encompassed on all sides by the enemies of their religion, the Æthiopians slept near a thousand years, forgetful of this world, by whom they were forgotten.'

2 In Eritrea, more currency was allowed to Tigrinya, and of course Ge'ez remained as a specialised archaic religious medium. Arabic was also used as a written medium by literate Muslims.

3 This had been developed by one of the first presidents of the Somali National Academy of Culture, Shirre Jamam Ahmad, founder of the first Somali literary magazine, *'The Light of Knowledge and Education'*.

4 Figures kindly supplied by the BBC Somali Programme, London, which conducts extensive listener research in the Horn of Africa.

CHAPTER 6

PRESENT & PAST IN NORTH-EAST AFRICAN SPIRIT-POSSESSION

The Sudan Republic has been the scene of some of the most important and theoretically far-reaching discoveries in social anthropology.
Evans-Pritchard's classic studies of segmentary politics amongst the
uncentralised Nuer, and of witchcraft among the Azande, have not
merely revolutionised the sociological understanding of tribal societies,
but have also contributed much to a deeper understanding of the
institutional basis of conflict and cohesion in human society generally.
Thus political scientists today are gradually ridding themselves of the
old European stereotype in which politics is seen only in the context of
the centralised state and appreciating the implications of the segmentary
principle of political group formation as well as of Gluckman's derived
notion of 'cross-cutting ties' (see e.g. MacKenzie, 1967). Equally,
Zande witchcraft has become a model, shedding direct light in modern
studies by historians of witchcraft in sixteenth- and seventeenth-century
Europe, and even illuminating the operation of the apartheid philosophy
in South Africa (see e.g. van den Berghe, 1964, and I.M. Lewis, 1965c).
Of more practical interest perhaps, psychologists are beginning to see
the relevance of such witchcraft ideas as those of the Zande to what
might be called the study of the socialisation of guilt, a subject which
is obviously of universal significance (see e.g. Field, 1960; Leighton,
Lambo and Hughes, 1963 ; Loudon, 1959).

Psychologists are also becoming increasingly interested in the phenomenon of spirit-possession, which is the subject of this chapter,
and one of the earliest studies pointing out the mental health aspects
in this field was Nadel's paper on shamanism in the Nuba Hills
written over fifty years ago (Nadel, 1946). Despite a steady flow of
publications on the religious life of Sudan peoples since that date,
there has been very little explicit discussion of possession, so little
in fact that the cursory reader would be forced to conclude that this

is an unimportant phenomenon in the area as a whole. In contrast to this, the recent sociological literature on Ethiopia and the Somali Republic is increasingly emphasising the importance of shamanism and spirit-possession as cultural themes, even when these phenomena exist unofficially, or even clandestinely, on the fringes of Christianity or Islam. In this chapter, in which I shall discuss comparatively material from the two areas, I shall argue that this contrast is more apparent than real. In fact, as I hope to show, the material on spirit-possession in the two areas taken as a whole is so rich that it offers an important field for developing our understanding of the sociological and psychological functions of possession in general.

As I have argued elsewhere (I.M. Lewis, 1966a), studies of shamanism and spirit-possession have in the past been bedevilled by an understandable, but nonetheless excessive concentration on all the dramatic and 'expressive' aspects of possession to the exclusion of sustained enquiry into its significance in terms of social function. They have also, as have studies of religion by structural anthropologists generally, all too often neglected the time dimension, tending to treat particular religious phenomena as permanent and unchanging rather than viewing them in a context of historical change. The point here, of course, is that as with other institutions, the extent to which particular cults or beliefs represent responses to particular circumstances is often not fully apparent until they are viewed in time perspective. It is also very easy for synchronic analysis to over-rate the functional significance of institutions which when studied diachronically turn out to be ephemeral (cf. Firth, 1959; I.M. Lewis, 1968a). In the following discussion I shall try to take account of historical factors; I shall also attempt to deal with both the sociological incidence, or epidemiology, of possession, and its relation to wider religious phenomena.

My first distinction is between what I shall call main morality and peripheral cults. By the first term I mean those cults whose concern is the maintenance of general morality in a society, and by the second those which are not directly involved in this process. Cults venerating ancestors, or other mystical powers, who are believed to reward the just with prosperity and success, and visit sickness and affliction on the unjust and sinful, fall squarely within the first category. Cults addressed to disaffiliated spirits, or other powers, which are credited with bringing disease and affliction capriciously and without reference to the victim's moral condition, belong to the second.

The cult of *eqo* ancestor spirits among the Kafa of south-west Ethiopia provides a good example of the former, while the women's cult of *zar* spirits in Omdurman exemplifies the latter. In the case of the Kafa, society is divided into a number of clans and lineages, and the segments of lineages are usually led by a shaman (*alamo*) who acts as a medium for the spirits of his patrilineal ancestors. In this capacity he functions as an oracle diagnosing the causes of sickness and misfortune within his group in terms of the ancestors' displeasure over the immoral and sinful actions of its members. The ancestors who are approached and appeased through the lineage elder medium are primarily concerned with the maintenance of lineage morality and with the solidarity and cohesion of their groups. The position of chief shaman for Kafa as a whole is vested in a particular clan, and the incumbent of this office who has a special relationship with the traditional kingship consecrates all the 'officially' recognised shamans in other clans and lineages. There is thus, in fact, a shamanistic hierarchy within the Kafa kingdom (Orent, 1967). In contrast to this, the peripheral *zar* cult in such Northern Sudan towns as Omdurman is not directly concerned with the official public cult of Islam, nor does it perform any central role in the maintenance of general morality. As is well known, it primarily involves women and appears to function as a compensation for their partial exclusion from full participation in the men's world of Islam. The spirits involved here may be loosely equated with *jinn*, are often of foreign origin, and strike their victims haphazardly and mischievously without direct reference to moral infringements or misdemeanours.

MAIN AND MARGINAL CULTS

These two types of possession cult, the one directly concerned with public morality and the other not, may co-exist in the same society. This, for example, seems to be the position amongst some of the Nuba peoples studied by Nadel (1946; 1947, pp.440–58), although in this case the evidence is not very clear (which is perhaps why Nadel has adopted a psychological rather than sociological approach to his data). Thus Nadel describes chieftaincy in Koalib as connected with spirit-possession in such a way as to suggest that chiefs are shamans (1947, p.447). In Nyima, however, although shamans are the 'nearest approach to institutionalised political leadership' (Nadel, 1946, p.25), they exist alongside hereditary rain-making and hill priests, and are connected with a supreme deity who is regarded as the source of health and rain. In Nyima, particularly, Nadel stresses the recent rite of spirit-possession and its connexion with social change, a point to which we shall return later.

Again, frequently a peripheral spirit-possession cult exists side by side with a main morality cult which lays little or no stress on possession. If we ignore the presence of *Sufism* which stresses divine inspiration, if not possession, this might be said to be the position in the Muslim Sudan and Somali Republic. However, whether possession does or does not feature in the main morality cult, such peripheral possession cults seem to be important if not essential adjuncts acting either alongside or in place of witchcraft and sorcery[1] to explain malign disorder and chaos in a morally ordered universe. They provide what might be described as an 'escape clause function', explaining the existence of morally unmerited misfortune and disaster which cannot be accounted for in terms of punishment by an ideally just god. This saves the notion of the just deity from self-contradiction in the face of the general affliction and distress which man inevitably experiences (cf. Nadel, 1946, p.34; Lienhardt, 1961, p.81).

In an earlier article (I.M. Lewis, 1966a) I suggested that these fringe cults are also peripheral in another sense. Here I am referring to the fact that the incidence of possession afflictions is not purely arbitrary but tends to run in defined social grooves, those particularly subject to such possession belonging to marginal social categories. Thus in societies where their jural position is weak and other means of effectively pressing their interests and demands are absent, women loom large in the epidemiology of possession. This is also true of jurally deprived categories of men who, in such circumstances, provide the main sociologically distinct category of possessed males. Of course, I am not claiming that these peripheral possession cults appeal only to the socially dispossessed: clearly they also attract an element of psychologically disturbed individuals which cuts across social distinctions. All I am arguing is that notwithstanding this there is a higher incidence of possession affliction amongst those sections of society which are most strongly subject to social discrimination and subordination. Here the attention and special consideration which the state of possession brings enables members of these social categories to enjoy, for a limited time, or at special occasions in the calendrical cycle, a status transcending that normally accorded to them. The situation of the rebellious Omdurman *zar*-possessed housewives (Barclay, 1964) is a good illustration of what I have in mind here.

Where, however, the locus of possession is a main morality cult (as in Kafa, or to some extent among some Nuba groups), although it may be regarded ambivalently, possession is not so much an affliction as the overt manifestation of spiritual inspiration, often in fact the *sine qua non* for achieving political leadership. Here one would expect, almost by definition, that men rather than women would figure predominantly in the epidemiology of possession. I shall seek to demonstrate that this is in fact the case: and that where central and peripheral cults co-exist, as we have seen they may, the possession of men belongs in the first category and that of women in the latter. Of course where, as in some of the examples I shall cite, possession does not figure prominently, if at all, in the main morality cult, only women (or submerged classes of men) and psychologically disturbed individuals (of either sex) are subject to it. Where both types of possession occur together clearly some means must exist to differentiate and clarify possession status according to the sex and circumstances of those involved. This usually seems to take the form of classifying peripheral possession as inherently evil (cf. witchcraft and sorcery), and of prescribing exorcism as a standard treatment for those afflicted. (In the Catholic Church today, the situation seems to be that those cases of possession which cannot be interpreted by current psychology, or by recognised Catholic psychiatrists, are accepted as genuine.) Frequently indeed the spirits concerned in peripheral possession are sharply distinguished from those of the main morality cult. Characteristically they are conceived of as coming in from an outside foreign source, rather like German measles, or Asian 'flu.

This brings me to the question of historical factors and social change. In most cases where peripheral possession is reported it seems to be a relatively recent development associated with cultural diffusion and social change, and even sometimes a mediator of change expressing through the changing galaxy of foreign 'outsider' spirits new contacts and new experience; hence, in the colonial phase, the common invocation of 'European' spirits and possession by new imported elements of technology such as motor car or telephone spirits as in the case of the Nuba. Frequently, of course, satisfactory historical data are simply not available; but in some cases which I shall mention there is evidence that possession not merely at the periphery, but as part of the central morality, has developed from other types of religious system through the action of extensive economic and social change.

POSSESSION AND SOCIAL CHANGE

I begin my discussion with societies where spirit-possession is central to public morality, and consider first the Macha Galla who live as cultivators to the west of Addis Ababa in Ethiopia. Today the Macha have a thriving possession cult centring on God (*waka*) and his various refractions or subsidiary spirits known as *ayanas*. God is the guardian of morality and punishes wrongs and misdemeanours,which are considered sins, by allowing sickness and misfortune to afflict those who have committed these offences. Sacrifice and prayer for forgiveness and blessing are made to God through shamans (*kallus*) who hold specific priestly offices at all levels of social grouping from that of the extended patrilineal family to the clan. The spirits summoned at each level of grouping are considered refractions of *waka* who appears as a unity at the level of the Macha as a whole, and at that of the several million strong Oromo nation of which the Macha are a part (Knutsson, 1967, pp.50ff). Shamans, who in the regularly recurring ceremonies in honour of their spirits are often possessed, hold offices which are vested in the senior segments of lineages. These positions are hereditary and thus ascribed, and yet an element of achievement also enters the picture since shamans vie with each other for leadership of local congregations built round agnatic clusters, and some shamans attain positions of ritual leadership which extend far outside their own descent group. Here competition for power is couched in the idiom of possession. If, for example, the family head becomes regularly possessed in a dramatic fashion he is likely to acquire renown at a wider local and lineage level. Characteristically those striving for power experience much more violent possessions than those who have already acquired it.

While possessed, these shamans act as diviners and intercessors with their attendant spirits who are conceived of as manifestations of the central deity. They hear confessions and receive sacrifices and votive offerings in expiation of sins and in expectation of future benefits. They also exercise politico-legal power since they are also frequently asked to settle cases which secular courts have failed to dispose of (Knutsson, 1967, pp.109ff; H. S. Lewis, 1965). It need scarcely be added that these shamans are always men.

Women, however, are also subject to possession which in their case functions as a subsidiary explanation of illness[2] attributed to the action of malevolent peripheral spirits or demons (*zar, saytana*) which male shamans treat by exorcism. As with other peripheral cults, the treatment of such female possession provides women with a means of status enhancement, and also of putting pressure on their husbands and male kin who meet the expenses involved. It may also be used by them to extort gifts, ostensibly for the possessing familiar, from their husbands (Woldetsadik, 1967).

Thus here we seem to have amongst the Macha Oromo today a fairly clear polarity between the male-dominated main morality cult in which possession is an institutionalised mode of signifying divine inspiration, and female possession associated with illness caused by capricious spirits. At the cosmological level, however, the boundary between these is not absolute. For although the malign demons are thought to be quite distinct from God (*waka*) and his benign spirit refractions, they are regarded as subordinate to him and can thus be used by him to punish sin (Knutsson, 1967, p.54). This has implications to which I shall return later.

There is abundant evidence that the main morality cult of the Macha Galla* in its present shamanistic form is a cultural innovation of only a few generations' standing (Knutsson, 1967, pp.135ff.). Before this development, the Macha participated in the pan-Oromo cult of God (*waka*) who was represented on earth not by an array of possessed shamans at each order of grouping, but by a handful of divinely inspired high priests (also called *kallus*) of whom there was usually at least one each for the main Galla tribal groups. This pattern persists today amongst the southern branches of the Oromo nation: the Guji and Borana who remain those most attached to pastoral nomadism and least given to cultivation.Here this office of tribal priest (which is hereditary and apparently devoid of shamanistic features) is closely associated with the generation-set organisation (*gada*) which is traditionally the main integrating and governmental principle of Galla society. In fact, however, the Macha who are one of those groups which reached their present geographical position following the great northern expansion of the Oromo in the sixteenth century, did not ever succeed in establishing their own local *kallu*ship on the traditional pattern. Instead they had to depend upon the great *kallus* of the southern Galla tribes to which, before the final imposition of Amhara rule in the late nineteenth and early twentieth century, they used regularly to go on pilgrimage.

Thus traditionally they participated in the non-shamanistic *kallu* system, but did not have such an office of their own. In their new highland home they adopted cultivation and become subject to pressures of social change which were sweeping through all northern Galla society in the late eighteenth and early nineteenth centuries (Luling, 1965). In the case of the Macha, these led to the breakdown of the traditional and highly democratic political system based on the generation-set organisation (*gada*) which was sanctioned and hallowed by the *kallu*

---

* Galla is the name formerly applied to the Oromo people by the politcally dominant Semitic-speaking ethnic groups of Ethiopia.

priests. Pressure on the land increased, and although lineages were previously land-holding units, the development of markets and trade led to the growth of a new landed aristocracy of merchant adventurers and military leaders who came to control the land. In some northern Galla areas the emergence of these 'big-men' led to a general development of social stratification,with power based primarily on achievement, and the formation of Galla monarchies whose rulers adopted Islam (cf. H.S, Lewis, 1965), But amongst the Macha discussed here this process had not proceeded to this point before the Amhara incorporation.

This situation of social change with the rise of 'big-men' competing for secular power seems to underlie the religious changes we have discussed. As in other conditions of change and dislocation in which possession phenomena seem to flourish, so here achieved shamanistic positions, legitimised by possession, replaced for the Macha their former attachment to the divinely ordained high priests of the south. The *kallu* shaman took over from the *kallu* priest. And clanship, which although it had lost some of its significance in land-holding retained other social functions with the decline of the *gada*-system. Thus, shamanistic positions developed at various levels of clan segmentation, paralleling the refraction of God into constituent spirits, and the resulting *kallu* institution has come to include ascribed as well as achieved aspects. There seem in fact to be the makings of a new *kallu* religious establishment, rather similar to that of the Kafa *alamo*, amongst whose officiants possession is less dramatic and important a feature than it is for those aspiring to carve out new *kallu* positions for themselves.

This somewhat speculative sketch of the rise of shamanism in Macha Galla is written against the background of the situation represented by the Boran today who, as pastoral Galla, I am assuming represent, at least in broad essentials, the former condition of the Macha prior to their wholesale adoption of cultivation. Amongst the Boran the main integrative mechanism is the *gada*-system which is ritualised by the traditional non-shamanistic *kallu* priests (Baxter, 1965; 1966). God (*waka*) is not particularised into a series of refractions, and this is consistent with the fact that here lineages have little or no corporate identity and there are no other clear-cut lines of cleavage or factionalism in Boran society. Rather such ties of kinship as exist are cut across both by local ties, and by membership of generation sets. The effect is to greatly limit possible bases for group conflict within Boran society, and the importance of the resultant unity is further strengthened by the fact that the idea of internal harmony, the 'peace of the Boran', is constantly stressed in rituals associated with the *kallus* and with God. Disease and affliction are attributed to God, and interpreted as punishments for sin (breach of the Boran peace) and there is apparently no subsidiary escape clause such as witchcraft or peripheral possession. The latter indeed does not occur at all, even although there are some submerged social classes, and women appear, at least in some respects, to be in much the same jurally weak position as they are amongst the other Oromo.

Several considerations seem to be important here. First and most general, the Boran are the most conservative of the Galla, the least subject to external influence or social change. Second, their nomadic social system which involves the spatial separation of married siblings, each with a separate stock-herding unit (cattle, camels, sheep, goats, etc.), seems designed to promote cross-cutting ties and to minimise conflict. Third, although marriage is traditionally indissoluble and there is no formal divorce, separation is common, and women appear to enjoy considerable informal influence. Finally, it appears from Baxter's extended account (Baxter, 1954) that while the Boran do have an aetiology of disease which connects it with moral infringements punished by God, they also regard it, perhaps to an unusual degree, as an independent empirical fact unconnected with social relations or mystical causation. It is difficult to be sure of the relative significance of these factors. My own guess is that probably the most significant is the conservatism of the Boran and their isolation from external influences. Thus, there is some evidence of the development of a peripheral spirit-possession cult in the townships of northern Kenya where new cultural contacts are experienced most strongly (Baxter, personal communication).

BRINGING THE NUER AND DINKA INTO THE DEBATE

These data on the Galla seem to me to invite immediate comparison with those on the Dinka and Nuer. Although neither of these peoples' chief interpreters uses the term 'shamanism' both Lienhardt (1961) and Evans-Pritchard (1956) describe possession sufficiently frequently to warrant its being considered as a phenomenon of considerable significance. Amongst both there exists a traditional priestly organisation : the Dinka masters of the fishing spear, and the Nuer leopard-skin priests. Both these categories of priest are held to be divinely inspired by ascription rather than achievement, and neither require possession to validate their authority. However, there are other categories of ritual agent who owe their influence to spirit-possession, where achievement rather than ascription is involved, and who in both cases are said to be on the increase. In the case of the Nuer, such persons described by Evans-Pritchard as 'prophets' are possessed by spirits of the air, these being particularly captious and capricious and often of foreign origin. This is equally true of the Dinka spirits which Lienhardt calls 'free-divinities' and which again are often of foreign origin and generally feared. Thus it seems clear that here we have a new basis of religious authority developing in a similar way to that in Macha, and since both Evans-Pritchard and Lienhardt connect these developments, although they do not treat them in this way, with social change and culture contact, we seem to have a further parallel.

What I am suggesting then is that here we see the rise of a new main morality cult within the framework of the traditional religion in much the same fashion as amongst the Macha Galla. There is, however, another point of significance. Amongst the Dinka (the position amongst the Nuer does not seem so clear) the malign spirit Macardit is described by Lienhardt (1961, p.81) as 'the final explanation of sufferings and misfortune which cannot be traced to other causes more consonant with Dinka notions of Divinity as just'. And Macardit is particularly connected with women. This suggests that in relation to this spirit who frequently possesses women and whose sinister actions provide an escape clause for the Dinka main morality, there is in fact a peripheral cult of the kind we have seen elsewhere. It is not, however, clear from Lienhardt's account whether or not women use possession by this spirit (or by the female spirit Abuk) to advance their aims and interests in the way in which we would expect. What is clear is that those men who regularly pay cult to Macardit fall into a deprived category ; they are always the middle sons in a family who come out worst in the inheritance of their parents' property which is shared between the eldest and youngest (Lienhardt, 1961, p. 82).

These remarks on the Nuer and Dinka are not of course intended to be exhaustive. All I have tried to do is to suggest that further light may perhaps be shed on this material if we look at it in terms of the distinction between main and peripheral spirit cults and view it diachronically rather than synchronically.

MARGINAL CULTS IN THE HORN

Peripheral cults associated with women appear very clearly in the dominant Christian Amhara culture of Ethiopia. In this Christian orthodoxy spirit-possession has no major role, although the Church as a whole regards itself as inspired by God and leading figures in its hierarchy are believed to be variously endowed with divine grace.

In practice, however, it is, I think, only shamanistic in the sense that certain leading priests regularly exorcise evil spirits possessing afflicted persons in the name of God.[3] Such peripheral spirits or demons, whose benign analogues are guardian angels and other saintly spirits, are generally known as *agament*, or *saytans*, and are directly connected with the Devil (Levine, 1965, pp. 69ff.). As in the European Christian tradition, Amharas believe that individuals who desire to possess malign power achieve this by making pacts with these devils. These powers are thus connected with anti-social actions and seen as the motivating forces tempting people to commit sins or to yield to wayward impulses. Here it is important to remember that, while Ethiopian Christianity is essentially an eschatological religion promising heaven as the reward of the just and hellfire as the final punishment for sins, it is also strongly encapsulated in society in the sense that popular belief holds that the just should prosper and the unjust fail in this life. God, who is ideally just, may punish the wrong-doer in this life by ordering his guardian angels to neglect their protective duties, thus rendering the sinful particularly vulnerable to affliction and distress.

Closely associated with these demons are those similar spirits called *zar* which are regarded as the main carriers of physical and mental illness; typhus and smallpox, for example, are *zar* sicknesses. *Zar* appears to have been the name for the pre-Christian God of the Agau, one of the principal Cushitic peoples of Ethiopia subjugated and largely absorbed in the gradual expansion of Semitic Amhara rule. However, it appears that it is only in the nineteenth century that the use of this term to denote a category of disease-bearing spirits spread widely within Ethiopia and outside it into the Sudan and Egypt. This period for the rise of the *zar* cult appears very significant since it coincides with that of the final extension of Amhara rule and the emergence of modern Ethiopia. As well as being a time of extensive internal social change and culture contact, this was also when Ethiopian links with Western society began to be greatly increased.

As with peripheral spirit afflictions elsewhere, women loom large in the epidemiology of possession as do also men of low-caste occupational groups. It seems possible to distinguish three contexts of *zar*-possession activity.[4] There is first the standard situation where women in difficult circumstances use *zar*-possession as a means of putting pressure on their menfolk and of extorting gifts or favours from them. Second, there are well-defined *zar* spirit-possession clubs, led by a male or female controller (a master of spirits), in which the devotees fantasise their afflictions and deprivations in regularly held possession seances in which, as in group therapy, they act out their difficulties. The clientele of these groups is not exclusively women but includes also men, particularly those of subject, non-Amhara origin. Finally, a cadre of male *zar*-possessed diviners has arisen who fulfil an ancillary role within the main Christian religious system. Here, significantly, *zar* spirits play a directly positive role inspiring men to help those whose problems have not been satisfactorily dealt with by the orthodox religious establishment. Possession which in relation to women is truly peripheral and is accommodated to Christian orthodoxy through exorcism, seems here to have gained a more central role in the total apparatus of Amhara morality. To this extent, this aspect of the *zar* cult can no longer be regarded as entirely peripheral.

Amongst the Muslim Somali and in the Muslim Sudan the situation is rather similar. As with Christianity, the Muslim cosmology readily accommodates foreign peripheral spirits and offers them a comfortable ecological niche amongst the host of mischievous *jinns*. Thus the *zar* cult has spread to both these areas where it is again mainly associated with women and applied by them to further their interests in a world which still is heavily biased in favour of men. Its functional content here ranges from the mere relief of boredom (as for example in southern Somalia: see Luling, 1967) to the ventilation and alleviation of grievances in a mystical idiom when men will not permit these to be dealt with more directly in secular terms.

However, some of these spirits (though not *zar*) may also disturb men,[5] and not only those who are considered to be psychologically ill. To some extent these cults here enter the field of public morality, since it is believed (at least in the Sudan) that wrong-doing and situations of crisis alike expose individuals to the dangers of possession affliction (Trimingham, 1949, pp. 1 71 ff.). Moreover, despite the fact that neither the Muslim Sudan nor Somalia are in any complete sense shamanistic societies (as for example in Kafa or Macha), yet the charisma of some Muslim sheikhs and *walis* is linked to their employment of *jinn* servants and familiars (Trimingham, 1949, p.172). Thus for example of Sharif Yusuf Barkhadle, the twelfth-century saintly Muslim teacher in northern Somalia, it is related that God gave him control of *jinns* in such number that they filled 'the space between the earth and sky'. Similarly, the celebrated Somali Sheikh Mohammad 'Abdille Hassan, who led the latter-day *jihad* between 1900 and 1920 against the Christian colonisers of his country, is believed to have owed some of his miraculous-seeming power to the possession of *jinn* familiars (I.M. Lewis, 1965b, pp.63–91).

Such essentially peripheral spirits thus provide, potentially at least, a sort of reservoir of marginal power which may be tapped and fed into the central domain of male-dominated public morality. When this occurs it seems that those persons who are credited with utilising this source of power are usually themselves in some sense 'outsiders', coming from unusually deprived or remote social backgrounds. In any event, peripheral cults, as we have seen, are particularly susceptible to new influences, and frequently the means by which these acquire a foothold which may, with increasing syncretisation, carry them into the centre. It is difficult to say whether or not this is the process by which the Virgin Mary (*Mariam*) has today become assimilated among the Macha and other northern Galla to *Atete*, the female refraction of God (*waka*); or of the Prophet Mohammed to *Naba*, another refraction of this traditional Oromo God. But this does seem to have occurred in the case of the cult of Sheikh Husayn Baliale, the most important Muslim saint in southern Ethiopia, which has apparently developed with increasing Islamisation from the pre-Muslim traditional Galla cult of *kallu* high-priests. Today, by some strange irony of history, this cult which is now part of the central religious life of the Muslim Galla is spreading to southern Somalia as a peripheral spirit cult known locally as Borana (cf. Borana Galla), with a particular appeal for free-born *billis*, Somali women of the south. Indeed in this area south of Mogadishu, Sheikh Husayn is known particularly for his efficacy in finding lost property (Luling, 1967).

Many of the ambivalent and contradictory elements I have discussed are resolved in an arrestingly Lévi-Straussian fashion among the Semitic Gurage of Ethiopia with whom I close this survey (Shack, 1966). Here there are three distinct cults: one for men, one for women, and one which appears to be open to both sexes (I say 'appears' because the evidence is not entirely clear). The first cult is that bearing the main morality of the society and addressed to the male god (*waka*, cf. Galla *waka*). This spirit is the guardian of the moral world of men and receives annual sacrifices at his shrine which is the centre of Gurage political and religious life and where he is represented by a *female* priest consort. This ritual office is vested in a particular clan, but the office is here only potential. It becomes active by marriage to a ritual male consort who must again be drawn from a specified clan. However, it is this woman, human wife to the spirit, who, assisted by female members of the despised class of Fuga carpenters, leads the cult of men. Spirit-possession is not involved here. This, in contrast, is the dominant theme in the parallel women's cult addressed to the female deity Damwamwit, which is led by a male Gurage shaman assisted by male Fuga craftsmen. Through possession by this spirit Gurage women in general, and the despised Fuga men, are allowed special licence and a degree of status enhancement normally denied to them. This female spirit is credited with being capable of sending affliction to anyone who injures those thus under her protection: and women when in difficulties with their husbands, as can be imagined, are very ready to become possessed in this way.

Thus I see this cult (which, incidentally, is spreading to neighbouring Galla areas) as an essentially peripheral form of possession which has become institutionalised to the point where it is integrated in the total Gurage religious system in parallel to the male cult of the male spirit *waka*.[6] Here possession has not been allowed to intrude within the male-dominated main morality cult, but has been allowed to exist and persist among women under male leadership, apparently at the price of allowing female leadership in the former.

The third cult, which seemingly involves both men and women, is that of the thunder-spirit (*buza*) who is a male deity, represented by a male priest, and concerned particularly with the protection of persons and property against damage by lightning, fire and theft. Today, in the current situation of Christian and Muslim proselytisation, it so happens that the hereditary officiant of this cult has become converted to Islam and, having shed his traditional cult duties to a younger collateral, has become a leading figure in the spread of Islam in this region. What effect this will have on the assimilation of traditional Gurage cults within Islam cannot yet be determined. Elsewhere, and particularly among the Islamised Galla, it is the cult of *waka*, which, understandably, has become assimilated to that of Allah.

My primary aim in this chapter has been to argue that, appearances notwithstanding, in the Sudan as in Ethiopia and Somalia spirit-possession is an important cultural theme and one which will repay much fuller sociological and psychological attention than it so far seems to have received. What is required here, I suggest, is an approach which, while taking due account of psychological factors, also attempts to discover the social incidence of possession. The questions to be posed here are: is possession associated with some distinct social correlate such as sex, or occupational class; and what social functions does it serve? These latter, as we have seen, are likely to range widely. In what I have called peripheral cults, possession may simply function to relieve boredom amongst women who have little else to do with their time, in much the same way as spiritualist seances were once popular amongst certain classes of women in Europe and America. More seriously, possession may be used by women to take advantage of adversity, to press their claims for attention and regard in societies which are heavily biased in favour of men. And this strategy which involves an oblique line of attack, an exertion of pressure which does not seriously challenge the established order of society, may also be applied to advantage by men in low and despised status positions. On the other hand, where possession is institutionalised within a main morality cult, it clearly becomes an idiom in terms of which men compete for power and authority, a means of laying claim to and validating status.

In thus examining the sociological consequences of possession I am implying, of course, that it should be treated as a social institution, to some extent as a strategy either for ventilating grievances, such as might otherwise be achieved through witchcraft accusations, or as a device for gaining power. At first sight this is very different from the approach of the Western-trained psychiatrist who, except perhaps within the Catholic Church, does not himself believe in spirits (or for that matter in witchcraft) and regards possession usually as a form of hysteria or other mental illness, Yet again, this difference is more apparent than real since the functional approach in psychiatry today fully acknowledges the attention-gaining aspect of hysteria and of other neurotic symptoms, and relates these at least in part to the life situation and social circumstances of the patient (see e.g. Yap, 1960). And perhaps we should also remember that psychiatric diagnosis and treatment as well as the symptoms presented by patients are to a considerable degree culture-patterned (Shepherd, 1962): that, in short, psychiatry (and particularly psychoanalysis) is a cultural variant of shamanism.

There is thus every reason for advocating a joint sociological and psychological approach here. This is clearly what Nadel envisaged when, contrary to the traditional view that shamanism exists to shelter psychopaths, he argued that spirit-possession cults may serve to actually *reduce* the incidence of mental illness (Nadel, 1946, p.36). Here he was particularly interested in the stresses and strains which he took to be inherent in social change and cultural adaptation and which he saw possession cults as alleviating. Now, there is no doubt, as we have seen that possession cults are often a response to change. This may even be true of those peripheral cults involving women, where the ideal of at least temporary sexual equality seems to be involved and may represent the first hesitant stirrings of a local suffragette movement, or something approaching it.

But is possession always and necessarily a response to radical social change as Nadel (1947, p.446) seems to imply? To answer this question we need to know more of the history of institutionalised possession amongst such peoples as the Kafa. We also need to know more about the incidence of mental illness in static as well as changing circumstances. Traditional societies may deal with some tensions through the cathartic idiom of witchcraft accusation, or spirit-possession groups, but are such tensions any less deeply rooted, or disturbing, than those attendant on change? And if we thus discard the romantic view of an idyllic tension-free tribal existence, can we assume that traditional therapeutic techniques (such as those of exorcism and possession-groups) are in some instances as effective in dealing with psychiatric problems as modern methods?

These are questions which are of direct practical as well as theoretical interest and which are as yet far from being answered decisively, although a beginning has been made in the recent work of Field, Loudon, Leighton and others. As far as north-east Africa is concerned, one psychologist (Torrey, 1966) at least has argued that traditional *zar* therapy in Ethiopia fulfils a valuable function in the field of mental health, a view which he would presumably extend to the operation of the same cult in Egypt where current studies by Dr C. Nelson show that it continues to have a strong appeal for women in difficult circumstances. There seems scope for similar collaboration in the Sudan where the fruits of Professor al-Tijani al-Mahi's[7] intensive and superbly detailed research over three decades have yet to be fully published. The publication of this material will undoubtedly mark a new step forward in the comparative study of spirit-possession.

NOTES

1 Spirit-possession and witchcraft (or sorcery) are not necessarily (as some writers have claimed) mutually exclusive; on the contrary, as in the sixteenth- and seventeenth-century European tradition, they are often intimately inter-connected. See I.M. Lewis (1996, ch. 4).

2 As with misfortune generally, illness is otherwise regarded as caused by God in punishment of sins, but of course is not interpreted as divine possession.

3 One of the most renowned of these ecclesiastic exorcists is the priest Wolde Tinsanye Gezaw of Ghion in Shoa Province who claimed to have treated over a million patients, many of them successfully, in the late 1960s. See Giel, Gezahegn and van Luijk (1967).

4 Cf. Torrey (1966). Torrey seems to regard these as distinct 'types' of cult characteristic of different regions of Ethiopia.

5 In Somalia, men are particularly liable to possession by a class of learned spirits (the *jinn* counterparts of *faqs*) called *waddaaddo* which I translate as 'clerical sprites'. This epidemiological feature seems consistent with the fact that men rather than women play a more direct part in Islamic religious life. See I.M. Lewis (1969a).

6 Terrefe Woldetsadik (1967) reports a most interesting tradition to the effect

that the Damwamwit cult has developed from the degeneration of Christian practice at the Church of St Mary at Magarar in Muher. This would seem to imply that the veneration of the Virgin Mary had here become transformed into the cult of Damwamwit (cf. the assimilation of the Virgin Mary among the Galla to the traditional spirit Atete).

7 Unfortunately, the late Tijani al-Mahi's work still remains largely unpublished. The fullest ethnographic account of Sudanese *zar* to date is that of Janice Boddy (1989), based on research carried out in two northern Sudanese villages (in 1977 and 1984). In common with earlier work (e.g. Constantinides, 1985), this study emphasises the involvement of distressed housewives and their anxiety to produce children. Here, the engagement of husbands in meeting the costs of treatment for the spirit-inspired illnesses which disturb women's fertility, are seen as forcing men to accept some procreative responsibility. In addition to the psycho-social benefits conferred by possession and its treatment, explored in previous works on *zar*, Boddy adopts a 'cognitive' approach which views possession and trance episodes as 'texts'. Possession, she argues, enables women to confront and transcend the socio-cultural categories which constrain them. Through cognitive re-focusing or reframing, possessed women are, she claims, enabled to think and feel differently, being thus empowered to experience 'more felicitous outcomes in their encounters with others'.

This claim that, in effect, possession can change a woman's life in a deep, psychological sense beyond the advantages explored by previous researchers on the subject, is, unfortunately, undocumented and remains hypothetical. Space which might have been devoted to exploring how this bold hypothesis might be tested, is instead given up to a 'post-modernist' account in which the author's literary and other sensitivities are projected onto the Sudanese women concerned, without the adducing of any evidence that the latter share them. In this respect, Boddy's account can be seen as an elaboration of similar tendencies to ethnographic over-writing present in a more subtle and less intrusive form in Lienhardt's (1961) well-known study of Dinka religion.

For a more recent synthesis on possession in the region, see I.M. Lewis, Hurreiz and as-Safi (eds) (1991). G.P. Makris has carried out uniquely documented historical research on the *tumbara* possession cult in the Sudanese urban setting. See Makris (1996) and forthcoming.

CHAPTER 7

THE 'WISE MAN'S CHOICE'

CONVERSION THEORIES

Max Weber rightly characterised Islam as possessing a healthy respect for political power and wealth. In this chapter I want to explore aspects of the political economy of Islam in the context of Islamic identity in sub-Saharan Africa. While, as I shall argue, these features are highlighted when we examine the circumstances of the spread of Islam in Black Africa, they must not be allowed to overshadow the role of Islam as an international cultural identity and the diffuse significance in daily life of comforting Muslim remedies and panaceas. South of the Sahara generally, individual elements of Islamic cultural origin are widely diffused and have often been adopted by peoples who are not yet Muslim. The spread of Islamic cultural elements thus often outdistances the spread of Islam, although, of course, the situation is never static. Circumcision, geomancy, astrology and other divinatory techniques of Muslim origin regularly occur in cultures whose members do not yet profess Islam. In some places, bizarre cultural transformations have occurred. Amongst some West Africans on the Islamic fringe, the Muslim taboo on the pig has been turned upside down. This unclean creature is here transformed into a sacred fetish, uniquely linked with the Prophet Mohammed (Trimingham, 1959, p.67).

Where Islam has been formally adopted as a living religion, it has everywhere been accommodated to the local cultural and social context. Numerous dialogues have thus developed between the *universal* religion of Islam and *local* socio-cultural traditions, producing a wide spectrum of local styles of African Islam. More often than is usually acknowledged, this has led to the formation of unique new ethnic and cultural syntheses. The outstanding examples in west Africa are the Malinke-speaking Dyula trading community (Launay, 1983), and the part-Fulani Tukulor-Torodbe (literally, 'beg-hards'), peripatetic friars who played a crucial role in the local implanting and extension of

Islam. Similar processes of cultural synthesis, or 'ethnogenesis' led in east Africa to the formation of the distinctive Swahili culture (Arens, 1975) and, more recently, to the emergence as a local military élite in Uganda of the Muslim 'Nubis', epitomised by General Amin. Similarly, although the argument that historically the Somalis of north-east Africa are Islamised Oromo (Galla) is not entirely convincing, it is certainly the case that, where the two ethnic groups are today in contact, conversion to Islam implies a process of Somalisation (Baxter, 1966; Hjort, 1979). In the contemporary political context, the parallel anti-Ethiopian Somali Muslim and Oromo liberation movements have joined forces in a loose-knit alliance under the rubric of two branches of putative Somali identity: the Somali proper, called 'Somali *Warya*', and the so-called 'Somali Abo'. *Abo* is the corresponding term in Oromo for the Somali *'wariya'*, used to attract a stranger's attention. Similarly, today as in the past, the adoption of Islam in Nigeria is typically in the ethnic style of the Hausa (Salamone, 1975).

Where Islam has made its deepest impact it has been domesticated and acquired an authentic local patois. While the diffusion of Islam has automatically ensured the special prestige of the language of the Qoran, Arabic has usually only been adopted as a second, essentially religious medium. As with Latin in the Christian tradition, this has tended to enhance rather than diminish its status as holy writ. Only in the northern Sudan, with its history of extensive Arab immigration and settlement, has Arabic been accepted as the local, national language.

Africa's Black Muslims thus add fuel to the old issue of the ambiguous association between Islam and Arab identity. An ancient Islamic maxim affirms: 'The Muslim (convert) becomes a blood relative.' Islam certainly provides an important bridge between the Arab and African worlds, but it does not ensure that those Africans who embrace the faith will choose to identify themselves unequivocally as Arabs. Here, as elsewhere, today ethnicity remains fluid, opportunistic and problematic.

ISLAM AND AFRICAN RELIGIONS

Although Islam is many things, it is first and foremost a creed enjoining specific, externally observable ritual practices: the profession (or testimony) of the faith; the performance of the daily prayers; fasting; almsgiving; and, as an ideal goal, pilgrimage to Mecca. In its public ritualism, Islam is thus a very visible, even ostentatious, faith which readily impresses the observer. So, when they endeavour to discover whether or not someone is a co-religionist, the Hausa of west Africa ask simply: 'Do you pray?' 'Or do you drink beer?' (Last, 1979). In harmony with this antithesis, a huge motorway hoarding on the main highway north out of Lagos, juxtaposed with advertisements for Coca Cola and Scottish whisky, announces; 'Islam, the wise man's choice.'

Before examining how economic and political factors affect this 'choice' and its corresponding political and economic implications, we need to review the main similarities and differences in Islam's basic cosmological assumptions and those of its indigenous predecessors and rivals. Traditional African religions usually include a hierarchy of spiritual forces associated with different levels of social grouping. The cult of local deities, or lineage ancestors, ensures the well-being of the local community, while, at the national or tribal level, spiritual forces of a higher order are invoked. Whether they are seen as a series of manifestations or refractions of a single power or spirit, these mystical forces are charged with guarding the moral order of the community to which they relate. Undeserved afflictions and misfortunes are attributed to over-ambitious, self-seeking individuals who, as witches or sorcerors, seek to subvert the moral order by misapplying mystical power in pursuit of their own selfish ends.

It is easy to establish equivalences between these indigenous beliefs and those of the Islamic cosmology. The lofty omnipotence of Allah is readily assimilated to the distant and often otiose 'high god' of traditional African religion. Lesser spirits can be conveniently subsumed within the comprehensive categories of angels and spirits (both good and bad) sanctioned by the Qoran, and ancestors are readily converted into Muslim saints. Witchcraft and sorcery are likewise no strangers to the Islamic cosmology where they are identified as *sihir*. Similar parallels occur between traditional and Muslim divination, astrology and geomancy, although the Islamic lunar calendar may represent an innovation. The customary stress on the efficacy of ritual also accords well with Islamic practice and its emphasis on visible religious behaviour.

A more radical departure is the eschatological theme in Islam with its promise of an afterlife in which the devout are rewarded and sinners punished. This is generally contrary to the tenor of indigenous African religions which stress the immediacy of moral judgement – now, in this life, not in the hereafter. Where misfortunes dog the righteous, these are explained in terms of malicious witchcraft, rather than stoically endured in the confident expectation of compensatory rewards in the next world. As much as the interest in booty stressed by Weber, this dominant orientation towards the present colours the millenarian character of the great African *jihads*. Conversely, the pious duty to wage wars of conquest or rise against tyrannous rulers in the name of Islam adds new legitimacy to long-established patterns of conflict.

BEARERS OF ISLAM: MERCHANTS AND MIGRANTS

Coming now directly to political economy, in the history of Islam in sub-Saharan Africa it is not 'trade that follows the flag', as the old colonial slogan has it, but rather the flag (of Islam) that follows trade. Reflecting the facts of geography and the historical expansion of the Arabs from their homeland into north Africa, both the eastern Sudan and the Horn of Africa were by the seventh century already exposed to Muslim influence (Hasan, 1967; Cerulli, 1936). In east and west Africa, the foundations of Islamic penetration cannot be traced back securely beyond the tenth century (Trimingham, 1964; Trimingham, 1959). By this time, most of sub-Saharan Africa was included within an elaborate network of caravan routes, linking north and west Africa and the eastern Sudan with the Red Sea and Indian Ocean ports (Bovill, 1933). It says much for the positive appeal of Islam that, despite its early connexion with the slave trade and the discriminatory attitudes and practices of Arabs (B. Lewis, 1971), Muslim traders played such a prominent part in its dissemination. Only in the eastern Sudan was this trading factor significantly supplemented by the direct conquest and settlement of invading Arabs.

Although the conquest of pagan peoples in the western Sudan and of Christians in Ethiopia by local Islamised states helped to swell the numbers of those who professed Islam, elsewhere the trading factor was paramount. Those who played this crucial role in extending the boundaries of Islam were often not themselves Arabs. In the early period of the introduction of this mercantile creed in the western Sudan, pride of place must be assigned to the camel-owning Berbers whose great trade caravans plied back and forth along the Saharan routes. In the north-east, the nomadic Somali played a similar role, as caravan traders and through their western and southern migrations. There were also, of course, other similarly specialised trading peoples such as the west African Dyula and Hausa whose conversion to Islam made their widespread trading nexus a powerful proselytising instrument. These pioneering Muslim merchants had a pervasive impact on the traditional peoples whose lands they traversed and in which they often established their own self-contained quarters like the modern Hausa *sabo*.

While stressing economic factors favouring the expansion of Islam, we have also to recognise that here as elsewhere the relationship between religion and economics is complex. Thus, in a very interesting study, Murray Last has shown that amongst the predominantly Muslim Hausa of west Africa, non-Muslims are concentrated in pockets of low population density where extensive polygyny ensures that, as men say, 'our wives feed us'. Increasingly, involvement in the market economy, however, is associated with conversion to Islam and resettlement. As a trader's turnover grows, a point is reached where he must embrace Islam in order to maintain or increase his profits with consequent further involvement in the Hausa trading network (Last, 1979).

Although such merchants were usually not primarily themselves active missionaries, their very public if esoteric devotions attracted wide attention and prepared the ground for the itinerant holy men and mendicant teachers and scholars (known in west Africa as *mallams*; in east Africa as *mwalimus*) who either accompanied or followed them.

In the great traditional kingdoms in which these agents of Islam settled initially as minority enclaves, under the king's protection, they were soon found to possess useful qualities. Like the early colonial administrators who followed them, traditional kings and their courtiers quickly saw the advantages of these members of a far-flung trading network, linked with a great literate tradition. The tasks assigned them included accounting, tax-collecting, foreign diplomacy and diplomatic representation. Their lack of local attachments made such Muslim diaspora also uniquely attractive as recruits in palace bodyguards and special forces. It also became fashionable for a great pagan ruler to adorn his court with Muslim functionaries and to experiment with the new religion, seeking like Mansa Musa of Mali (1312–37) or the Askia Muhama (d.1528) of Songhay (Hunwick, 1966), so to enhance the ritual power of kingship – sometimes at the risk of alienating more conservative-minded followers. As a royal apanage, as Gouilly (1952, p. 42) so well put it, Islam provided, 'a doctrine, a flag and an arm' (and, he might have added a 'discipline'), and could thus promote and legitimise the conquest – for Islam – of surrounding pagan peoples.

But it was not only for the rulers of established traditional states in west Africa that Islam exercised this political attraction. In other times and places, the pattern of centralised government which Islam enshrines was not lost on ambitious leaders who, in traditionally uncentralised egalitarian societies, sought new justification for entrenching personal power. So, when radical socio-economic changes were in full spate amongst the republican Oromo pastoralists in eighteenth- and early nineteenth-century Ethiopia, petty chiefs and war-leaders turned to Islam (or sometimes Christianity) to legitimise the new personal dynasties they were establishing. With the negative as well as positive 'demonstration effect' of the centralised Christian Amhara Kingdom before them, a number of powerful figures thus established Muslim states along the Give river near the old Islamic province of Hadiya (H. Lewis, 1965).

Considerations of this sort, facilitating the extension of the faith, were, naturally, strengthened by Islam's minimal doctrinal stipulations and catholic tolerance of religious beliefs and practices which could be accommodated within the capacious Muslim cosmology without jeopardising the unique ascendancy of Allah. In the sphere of social relations, this assimilative process was assisted by the status accorded to local custom as a legitimate source of morality auxiliary and complementary to the *Shari'a*.

CURING AND CONVERSION

The majority of those who might, or might not, eventually become firm adherents assimilated elements of Muslim culture in piecemeal fashion. As *bricoleurs*, constantly seeking new mystical techniques to improve their mastery of their capriciously insecure circumstances, Africans were readily impressed by powerful-seeming Muslim rituals. These new remedies were all the more eagerly sought where new economic circumstances created novel possibilities for social advancement and hence encouraged uncertainty and conflict within society (e.g. Simmons, 1979). This is the other side of the coin in the picture we have already uncovered.

If, therefore, in the past as today there has always existed a steady demand for Qoranic amulets, therapeutic and prophylactic blessings, and divination, at times the path to conversion to Islam has taken more dramatic forms. So, for instance, when in the 1920s members of the Giriama tribe of Kenya began to follow the example of their Islamic neighbours, the Swahili, and changed from subsistence to cash-cropping,this new entrepreneurial class displayed a marked vulnerability to afflictions which were diagnosed as possession by Muslim spirits. This entrepreneurial illness could only be cured by adopting Islam (Parkin, 1972). Thus the sickness itself was in the nature of a spiritual crisis of the kind current throughout history and in all religions as heralding the adoption of new faiths where new recruits are summoned by this emphatic form of divine election (I.M. Lewis, 1971).

Such involuntarily selected 'therapeutic Muslims', as they are known locally, are in this manner protected from the malicious envy of their less successful tribesmen. The latter's traditional claims to participate in their success can be controlled by insisting on rigid Islamic dietary rules that isolate and insulate the new class from jealous neighbours. Thus, what are in traditional terms anti-social vices, ambition and personal aggrandisement, are here legitimised and protected by what amounts to a sort of spiritual embourgeoisement.

These striking examples of what is likely to have been a common pattern in the history of the adoption of Islam remind us that here, as elsewhere in the world, there are many different paths to the faith, and that no single model of conversion can do justice ot the rich variety of the facts. Note here the interesting contrast in the circumstances of Giriama and Hausa conversion. Giriama entrepreneurs are literally *forced* to yield to Islam: non-Muslim Hausa entrepreneurs appear to make a sober choice which has costs as well as benefits. Why should ecstatic conversion be involved in the Giriama and not the Hausa case? I do not know the answers to this intriguing question. I wonder, however, whether an explanation may be found in the fact that while most Hausa are Muslim, most Giriama are not and in their case Islamic conversion implies the adoption of a new, Swahili, ethnic identity. But this is a digression. If in sub-Saharan Africa, Islam (and later Christianity) were, as we have seen, often 'catalysts' associated with socio-economic changes promoting indigenous theistic conceptions which were thus already 'in the air', this does not entitle us to accept uncritically the 'intellectualist' (but also strongly Durkheimian) model of conversion proposed by Robin Horton (1971; 1975). Contrary to this mentalistic view, Islam is not simply or solely a way of explaining things intellectually at the conscious level. It is also a source of spiritual solace and pride and a set of rules for life. Whether selected deliberately and opportunistically, or forced upon protesting unbelievers according to the archetypical model of conversion, Islam above all provides an identity and a general orientation to the world, appropriate to particular spatial and historical contexts. As we have emphasised, it also introduces the radically different eschatological evaluation of moral wrongs and sins, which adds a new dimension to indigenous religion.

MILITANT AND POPULAR ISLAM

The spectre of idolatrous 'paganism' provides a powerful foil for the greater glory of Islam and fuels the perennial spirit of crusading *jihad*. In

Black Africa, the holy wars of the western Sudan, waged against pagans or Muslim renegades, only began at the end of the seventeenth century, sparking off the long chain of *jihads*, culminating in Usman dan Fodio's (1754–1817) famous conquests in Hausaland, and those of the 'Tukolor imperialist', Hajj 'Umar, in the Bambara states (1852).

In this period such millennial movements soon became caught up in the general reaction to Christian European colonialism which, of course, greatly extended their popularity. Thus, although Christian Ethiopia had constituted a target for Muslim *jihads* in the Horn of Africa since the fourteenth century, Usman dan Fodio provided an inspiration for the Sudanese Mahdi in his campaign against Anglo-Egyptian imperialism and the latter, in turn, was a shining example for the Somali *jihad* waged by Mohammad 'Abdille Hassan.

Each of these remarkable eruptions of militant political Islam has, naturally, to be understood in its unique historical and cultural setting. However, they share to a marked degree many common features. In the first place, the classical *jihad* formula, pioneered by the Prophet, was closely adhered to. In times of economic and social upheaval, the call to *jihad* was directed against 'polytheists' (*mushriqun*) and Muslim 'pagans' (*Kafirun*) by theocratic leaders who, though they rarely claimed or were given the exalted title *mahdi*, often called themselves or were called 'renewers' or 'pivots of the age'. It is scarcely surprising that the classical role of the *hijra*, often re-interpreted as withdrawal from Christian pollution, should have been so vigorously revived as the prelude to the fully fledged *jihad*.

Secondly, while different ethnic and class interests can be discerned in their leadership, it is difficult not to be struck by the prominence in their ranks of nomads like the Fulani and Somali and of merchants, traders and their associated itinerant friars. These are all, of course, mobile social categories with vested interests in the internationalist aspects of Islam and less firm commitment to particular, local states and chiefdoms. Settled farmers and rulers, in contrast, as Robin Horton (1975, p.389) puts it, 'sustained the more parochial aspects of the social order; merchants, pastoralists and holy men the more international aspects'. Where the interests of these disparate elements converged against a common threat, they constituted a formidable force.

Although these historic African *jihads* were often associated with particular religious orders (*tariqas*), through their frequent connexion with the cult of saints, the latter occupy a prominent place in what is often called 'popular Islam'. As elsewhere, pilgrimage to the major local shrines represents a kind of poor man's *hajj* and is often valued at an explicit fraction of the ideal pilgrimage to Mecca.

Supplementing the magical apparatus of Islam, these cults cater for those recurrent problems and vicissitudes in life which are not satisfactorily resolved by the lofty eschatological doctrines of the faith. There is an ambiguous overlap between the most frenzied of these cults and local spirit-possession cults such as those of the Hausa *bori* spirits, the *zar* spirits in Ethiopia, the Sudan, Somalia and elsewhere, and the *pepo* spirits of the Swahili coast. As the Hausa cult and that of traditional spirits amongst the Islamised Zaramo of Tanzania (Swantz, 1970) indicate, these are often traditional religions displaced by the adoption of Islam and reclaimed by those in subordinate positions – such as women generally in male-biased Muslim conditions, and other oppressed classes. In the case of women, possession by such spirits typically necessitates costly treatment and may lead to induction into a women's cult group whose members meet at regular intervals to perform rituals in honour of their spirits. Here the treatment is often more in the nature of accommodation or domestication of the intrusive spirit than a true exorcism.

Such mystery cults which regularly employ the same songs and Muslim rites as those of the Sufi orders provide an outlet for those who are acutely subject to otherwise unrelieved social stress. So, when other methods fail, the hard-pressed, segregated wife is liable to attacks of possession whose treatment enables her to exert pressure on her husband and other male members of her family (I.M. Lewis, 1971). Since these possession cults seem particularly attractive to the wives of bourgeois men concerned to maintain an image of Islamic respectability, they also offer the latter the privilege of vicarious participation in what they condemn as superstition and heresy. Thus if there is here a dual spiritual domestic economy, its two branches are interdependent and complementary.

CHAPTER 8

SHAMANS & SEX

A COMPARATIVE PERSPECTIVE

OBJECTIVES

Along with a number of colleagues in different countries, I have been arguing for some time that the sociological study of possession and shamanism illuminates both phenomena in a theoretically productive manner (cf. Siikala, 1978; de Sardan, 1996; I.M. Lewis, 1989; 1996). This approach to spirit-possession reveals the part possession regularly plays in shamanism itself – both in shamanic initiation, and in shamanising. This in turn enhances our understanding of the phased, career structure of possession-cult leaders who are, in effect, shamans. Taking as its point of departure the distinction made by de Heusch (1962; 1971) between cultivating spirit intrusions ('adorcism') and rejecting them, this sociological focus on social roles in possession and shamanism also highlights how shamanic exorcism may be applied to control the potential development of possession cults, or to constrain their proliferation. Where most of the possessed are women, this has major significance for the maintainance of male authority.

Following this path, this chapter seeks to explore further the social implications of different relationships between human beings and spirits.

SHAMANS AND SHAMANISM

The term 'shaman' (ecstatic healer and ritual expert) is, of course, in the first instance an ethnographically specific (i.e. Tungus) concept. Used comparatively, and cross-culturally, outside its native ethnographic context, it thus belongs to the category of such emic analytical terms as caste, compadrazgo, mana, potlatch and tabu, and so on, which, as I have pointed out elsewhere (I.M. Lewis, 1981; 1996), inevitably promote controversy and debate. For, as Roberte Hamayon (forthcoming) aptly puts it in relation to 'shaman', 'we must take into account that [this term] also designates a set of beliefs that is claimed by some traditional societies as their own'.

These problems are even more marked in the case of the concept 'shamanism' and the question of what is implied cosmologically by this term. Naturally, historians of religion and cultural anthropologists tend to assume that there is a distinctive shamanistic cosmology composed of various elements which may be present in various proportions in different societies. Thus, Ake Hultkrantz (1989, p.43) describes shamanism as a 'whole culture complex' in a tradition that includes Mircea Eliade (1951) and his classic emphasis on a supreme celestial being, and the shaman's 'mystical flight' along the axis of the 'cosmic tree' connecting this world and the upper and lower worlds which jointly constitute the universe.

As is well known, in common with various other writers on arctic shamanism, Eliade connected authentic celestial ascent with what he called 'pure shamanism', associated with prehistoric Siberian hunter-gatherer cultures and palaeolithic cave art. This seems also to be the view of some contemporary shaman specialists like Hultcrantz (1989) and is expressed even more strongly in Weston La Barre's (1970) grandiose assertion that shamanism is *the* origin of religion. According to him, shamanism is not merely a religion, but the original form of religion everywhere, with the shaman being the original prototype of god. With these associations and allusions, no wonder so many contemporary Western neo-shamanic cults seek to appropriate the label 'shamanism' as a source of revitalising exotic mysteries; and, in more populist fashion, in parts of eastern Europe those reacting against former totalitarian secularism reactivate 'traditional' religious beliefs and practices, including shamanism and Buddhism.

When all our data, in the past as well as the present, suggest such dynamic inter-cultural exchanges, it seems pointless to try to isolate a stable, unchanging cosmological setting for shamanism. This conclusion is entirely in harmony with Shirokogoroff's classic presentation of the shaman as a 'master of spirits', introduced into, or incarnated in his own body which serves, as he puts it, as a 'placing' or receptacle for his helping spirits which empower him to treat and control the actions of malign, pathogenic spirits. In the process of 'shamanising', to use Shirokogoroff's expression, the Tungus shaman negotiates with spirit – sometimes through what has become known as 'mystical flight', but, *pace* Eliade, on spiritual flights to the lower world, or in this world, as often as to the upper world.

THE PLACE OF ECSTASY

Shamanism, I am arguing, is simply the practice, in whatever cosmological or religious trappings, of the shaman's role. Just as a wit defined social anthropology as 'what social anthropologists do', so we can conveniently define shamanism as the work of shamans. As the Siberian specialist, E. Lot-Falck (1973) put it, over twenty years ago: 'To be a shaman does not signify professing particular beliefs, but rather refers to a certain mode of communication with the supernatural'. If this is correct, what is to be said about the shamanic 'ecstasy' on which Eliade and others have placed such emphasis?

In terms of Shirokogoroff's classic account, this emphasis actually seems fully justified. 'No one', he reports ,'can be accepted as a shaman unless he can demonstrably experience ecstasy – a half delirious hysterical condition "abnormal" in European terms.' (Shirokogoroff, 1935, p.274). Shirokogoroff also gives detailed descriptions of the highly charged psychological atmosphere of the shamanic seance, and of the emotionally intense interaction between the shaman and his audience, as he works himself up to a pitch of what is described as 'ecstasy'. To quote our classical source again:

> When the shaman feels that the audience is with him and follows him, he becomes still more active and this effect is transmitted to his audience. After shamanising, the audience recollects various moments of the performance, their great psychophysical emotion and the hallucinations of sight and hearing which they have experienced – because in shamanising the audience at the same time acts and participates (Shirokogoroff, 1935, p.331).

Moreover, Shirokogoroff, who was a medical doctor, specifically noted physiological changes in the shaman's comportment during and after 'ecstasy'. The shaman's dramatic role in the seance, he observed, required the expenditure of enormous energy, leaving the shaman afterwards unable to move, covered with perspiration, his pulse weak and slow, his breathing shallow'.

In the classic Tungus case, it is thus evident that ecstatic behaviour was a crucial feature in shamanising and central to the shaman's performance. Naturally, the exaggerated gestures and theatrical role playing were conventionalised, and even to some degree standardised. Hence, although as Shirokogoroff insisted, at the peak of his seance performance the shaman was in a state that literally involved some degree of altered consciousness, this does not allow us to conclude that in every case he was actually in the same heightened psychological state. To a certain extent, this parallels the pattern with spirit-possession which, where it is culturally developed in a society, does not in all circumstances imply a state of 'trance' – understood as involving some degree of altered consciousness. In many contexts, people are considered by other members of their community to be possessed by spirits when they are still manifestly fully conscious, in the normal everyday sense. Trance generally enters the picture, corresponding literally with possession, in the heightened atmosphere of possession rituals which are indeed seances (cf. I.M. Lewis, 1989, pp.32–58).

THE SHAMAN AND THE SPIRITS

In her exciting recent works on the shamanism of Tungus and Buryat hunters and herders, Hamayon (1990; forthcoming), in effect resurrects the image of hunting shamanic cultures. She does so, however, with as far as I know, much greater sophistication and depth of cultural and sociological analysis than most of her predecessors. In the context of prolonged and sensitive fieldwork, she examines the multi-layered complexity of the shaman's relations with the spirits which control the supply of game, a crucial aspect of the wider interdependence between humans and spirits. Essentially, local beliefs hold that spirits allow game (which also have souls) to be killed as food for humans, with the latter in turn eventually becoming the quarry of animal spirits. This complex exchange is managed by the shamans through their marriages with female animal-spirits, or the spirit daughters or sisters of game-giving spirits. Thus marriage, with the shaman in the role of husband, and the game spirit in the role of wife sets the terms to the game-supply contract between humans and animals.

That the shaman is cast in the role of husband, rather than wife, in these patriarchal cultures, Hamayon argues, expresses the dominant position of men over game – although in the end, 'once his grand-children are old enough to hunt, a hunter should disappear once for all in the forest, as if he were returning his own flesh to the spirits of game animals' (Hamayon, forthcoming, lecture 2). The centrality of the marriage alliance between shamans and spirits, as Hamayon con-vincingly demonstrates, illuminates the sexual imagery which abounds in shamanic discourse (cf. Sternberg, 1925; Zolla, 1986), especially in the rituals performed by the Siberian shaman. The shaman's theatrical 'play acting', in his animal costume, mimes the act of rutting or coupling with his animal partner. The terminology here, which has been explored by a number of linguistic specialists, clearly establishes the sexuality of these actions and gestures which collectively constitute sexual 'play'. According to Hamayon, consistently with this strong emphasis on the seance as a sexual encounter, even the shaman's drum and the stick used to beat it, while he leaps and jumps ritually, are representative of sexual intercourse. All this accords with the etymology of the word *shaman* itself as expounded by Siberian specialists who emphasise that the root *sam* signifies the idea of violent movement and of dancing exuberantly, of leaping and bounding, and of violent agitation (Lot-Falck, 1977). Such is the importance of the shaman's spiritual union, of which these are the physical signs, that the idea of the shaman's voyage to the realm of the spirits is only a 'secondary process'.

Amongst those related Siberian pastoralists who no longer practise hunting, the locus of the shaman's celestial union shifts. The shaman's vocation, involving the spiritual aid of lineal ancestors, becomes hereditary but – according to Hamayon – also implies union with an animal spirit wife, typically a spirit wife inherited from the ancestors. (At this point it should be noted, she parts company with Shirokogoroff (1935, p.369) who specifically rejected the idea of sexual differentiation between shaman and spirits, accusing Sternberg of being factually wrong.) Presumably because of this amalgam of pastoralist and hunting shamanic ideology, Hamayon (forthcoming, lecture 3) argues that a 'hunting attitude can be maintained even though hunting is no longer practised'.

With this emphasis on eroticism, it seems somewhat paradoxical of Hamayon to question the status of shamanic ecstasy, which, after all, is often explicitly identified with orgasm. So, for instance, orgasmic seizures are reported in Nepalese shamanism by Mastromattei (1988). Even more flamboyantly, this features in Christian Sri Lankan exorcism (Stirrat, 1977; cf. also Gombrich and Obeysekere, 1988) where, at the climax of exorcism at a Christian shrine, female pilgrims achieve orgasm and are penetrated, as they believe, by Christ himself.

For that matter, human orgasm is not immune from conventionalisation – there are after all instruction manuals on the subject, not to mention advice in glossy popular magazines. Indeed, orgasm is sometimes reported to be simulated, especially by women. Ironically, for Hamayon, the fact that shamanic ecstasy is subject to similar constraints and conventional pressures, casts doubt on its authenticity – indeed, invalidates the concept. In this context, it is interesting to note that medical research in Canada has been reported to be under way, comparing orgasm and ecstasy – but I do not know the outcome.

Perhaps we should raise the wider question: why is sexual imagery and symbolism so widely employed to express religious experience? Here the American anthropologist, Manning Nash, suggests a plausible answer which fits this discussion of shamanic sexual play rather well. In his opinion: 'Erotic love is frequently a template for religious meaning since this form of strenuous play provides a readily available expression of self-transcendence.' If the peak of ecstasy thus mirrors (or re-enacts) the experience of orgasm, this, of course, applies to male as well as female ecstatics in shamanism and possession. Hence, although spirit-possession dramatises an ideology of immanence and incarnation, this cannot be exclusively linked to women's experience of genital penetration in sexual intercourse (as Sered, 1994, p.191, argues).

MYSTICAL MARRIAGE

Actually, marital unions with empowering spirits are a very common method of shamanic legitimation in other arctic societies and in other parts of the world. Thus, in Malaysia where in 1988 I carried out a small-scale field study of local Malay shamans, known as *bomohs*, I found that the majority claimed to have spirit spouses as their main helping spirits (*hantu*) which regularly included ancestors, tiger spirits and Muslim saints (cf. Laderman, 1991). One *bomoh* who claimed to treat AIDS successfully as well as drug-addiction, casually told me how at the outset of his career he had lived as a hermit for over two months on a mountain in Johore. In the course of this, he experienced an apparition of a female spirit who was desperately pleading to marry him. The young shaman married this spirit in traditional fashion, and fasted for 68 days. On the 80th day, he said, he descended the mountain with a sack full of medicinal herbs and, of course, his spirit wife. When he arrived home, talking to this invisible companion, people thought he was mad. This caused some marital stress. After thirteen years of marriage and the birth of two spirit children, a boy and a girl, they separated – but his spirit wife remained as his spiritual guide and medical adviser.

The Malay *bomohs* (males and females), whose practice I observed in the course of my brief study, invoked their helping spirits to treat what they diagnosed as spirit possession in their patients, usually in a form of exorcism (cf. I.M. Lewis, 1996, pp.132–6). In their most elaborate version, these exorcist rituals are a dramatic enactment of traditional cosmology, with the patient representing a disordered realm to which the shaman restores order (Kessler, 1977).

Similarly, to cite another excellent illustration, amongst the Saora tribesmen of Orissa, Verrier Elwin (1955) recounts how novice or trainee shamans frequently suffer from a kind of sexual harassment by female spirits who goad them into marriage. Unlike their partners, these spirit wives are Hindus. When their shaman spouse dies, he is carried off to the underworld where he in turn becomes a Hindu spirit. In other cultures, the male shaman's spiritual partner is sometimes, as among the Akawaio Indians of Guiana, an animal spirit (Butt, Wavell and Epton, 1967). When we widen our gender spectrum to include the female shamans who regularly lead women's possession-cult groups around the world, the uxorial symbolism becomes even more striking. Here, however, we are concerned with women, considered to be brides to the spirits. These spirit spouses are treated as the males in this matrimonial relationship, even though they may include female spirits. This raises issues of the relationship between shamanism and possession to which I shall return shortly.

For the moment I simply want to stress that outside the classical Tungus context described by Hamayon, shaman's marriages are not necessarily only with animal spirits which regulate the supply of wild game. Nor, I think, are these unions necessarily concerned generally with ecological control. To the extent that this is the case in the Tungus socio-cultural setting, it is evidently closely associated with the ambient 'shamanic' cosmology. More generally, however, it seems more pertinent to regard the shaman's celestial marriage as a unique validation and guarantee of his spiritual power, rather than as essentially a cosmic instrument to control the game supply.

SPIRIT-POSSESSION AND SHAMANISM: DIFFERENT PARTNERS?

This, finally, brings us to the topic of spirit-possession itself and its place in shamanism. As Shirokogoroff long ago demonstrated, and as Hamayon has recently re-emphasised, since the shaman is defined as a master of spirits, it is hardly surprising that his interaction with spirits includes being possessed by them himself. Indeed, in the arctic hunting societies discussed by Hamayon and other Siberian specialists, as we have seen, the shaman is literally empowered by his marriage to a female nature spirit and his erotic, shamanic ecstasy dramatises this relationship. In women's possession cults elsewhere, as we have noted, devotees are regularly considered to be 'brides' of the spirit – with whom, in their turn, they make love.

Hamayon has made the bold suggestion that this uxorial contrast might provide a clear point of distinction between possession and shamanism, with the former essentially a 'wife to husband' relation in contrast to the shaman's 'husband to wife' relation with spirits. The idea here is that the shaman's masterful behaviour, and control over spirits, is validated by his gender and the authority he exercises over a female spirit.

Sociologically, this is an exciting hypothesis. However, I am afraid that the facts are perhaps too complex to conform to this formula. Thus, for example, the leaders of female possession cults who 'master' spirits may often be older women past child-bearing and so considered to have masculine characteristics. But, such reading as I have so far done of the comparative literature does not confirm the idea that they should then also be 'husbands' to spirits, while the bulk of their followers are simply spirit 'brides'. Since, moreover, such shamanic leaders graduate from the ranks of spirit-possessed women, who are 'brides' of the spirits, this would entail a sex-change in spiritual relations for which there does not seem to be any evidence.

At the same time, in Dahomey and Haitian vodu, where shamans may be of either sex, irrespective of their gender they are classified as 'wives' of the spirits. This differentiation, we are told, expresses human subordination (cf. Verger, 1969, p.50). This, presumably, must also ultimately be the case with Siberian shamans who are nevertheless 'husbands' to spirit 'wives'. Of course, as Hamayon emphasises, there are also female shamans, whose spirit partners are souls, but which nevertheless are apparently apt to become confused with animal spirits. In any case, whatever the gender of the shaman, and for all its fiery eroticism, the Siberian shaman–spirit relationship is inherently ambivalent. Mastery, by male or female human partner, is not a secure property, and can slip from the shaman's grasp.

It could be argued, perhaps, that differences in the relative power of shamans, possessed persons, and gods and spirits, and variations in gender definition, may enter the picture here. If this is so, we may have to take account of non-sociological, cultural factors (cosmology).

While I thus think that it would be premature to draw conclusions here at the moment, something further of a sociological nature can be said about spirit marriages. Where it is deemed possible for humans to marry spirits, we have a spirit cult (and shamanism); whereas, if the only possible treatment for possession is exorcism, we will not find marriage with spirits – or, at least, not with those spirits. (Others, conceivably, might authorise the power of exorcists through spiritual unions.) But this is almost a tautology!

CHAPTER 9

ETHNOGRAPHY & THEORY IN ANTHROPOLOGY

Our historiographical opening chapter demonstrated how, even in its heyday, functionalism did not succeed in exorcising history in British social anthropology. Although, at various times and in the works of various authors, functionalism assumed a privileged status in explaining social facts, in principle, and in practice also as we have seen, it never actually necessarily excluded a concern with historical causes. History might have been muted, but it was still waiting in the wings ready to be summoned on stage. It is thus perhaps a kind of poetic justice that, in the social anthropology of the 1980s and 1990s despite the conspicuous prominence of historical trends, arguments about the relationships between ideology and institutions (and between cultural and social formations) should still have remained basically functional in character. This, of course, is frequently not what the authors concerned supposed they were doing. Hence, we enter a period dominated by what we may call 'unconscious functionalism' where, whatever the official prominence of other theoretical para- digms, functionalism lurked uneasily in the background ready to play an anonymous role in clinching the arguments of the principal characters.

   This concluding chapter, in a book dedicated to the enduring value of a substantive anthropology based on the comparative method in the analysis of ethnography, again employs a historical framework within which it endeavours to elicit a number of significant (functional) relationships. It proposes a multi-factorial interpretation of how the contrasting classical emphases in British social and American cultural anthropology appear to reflect and embody the circumstances of their formation.

THE FIELDWORK MODE OF PRODUCTION

Traditionally, British social anthropology analyses social institutions from the perspective of an ethnographically based comparative sociology. This contrasts sharply with the culturological focus of American anthropology, particularly in its formative stages. Although as I argue here, these surface differences can be traced to a significant extent to their contrasting origins, they are not, actually, as all-pervasive as at first appears. In fact, as I hope to demonstrate, even at its most resolutely sociological, social anthropology rarely manages to escape a significant degree of cultural contamination. Its theoretical propositions are actually insidiously subject to acculturation in a manner which, unlike the classic anthropologist's own personal Eurocentric bias about which so much has been written, often passes unnoticed and unexamined.

In social anthropology, there is always an intrinsic tension between the particularistic description and celebration of a given community's culture ('thick description') and the cross-cultural analysis of social institutions which seeks patterns and interdependencies transcending a given cultural logic. In exploring this creative dynamic, I hope to show how, despite the quest for culture-free generalisations, unrecognised culture-bound assumptions are nevertheless apt to find their way into our debates. Hence, they influence the development of empirically based anthropological theory.

Historically, while they obviously treated their findings very differently, cultural and social anthropology shared the same general aims. These were, as I assume they still are (notwithstanding the liberties taken by post-modernism), to record and analyse as completely and as accurately as possible the social and cultural systems under scrutiny. Traditionally, moreover, both styles of anthropology concentrated on the more or less 'subaltern' cultures and communities of the Third World, those which in colonial days lived outside, or on the margins of the Western and Oriental worlds and were not included in the purview of oriental studies. (This, ironically, did not deter politically correct American anthropologists in the 1980s, under the influence of Edward Said, from accusing their predecessors of 'orientalising' and 'othering' the people they studied.)

With this regional (and political) focus, each anthropologist aspires to understand what his or her subjects, or interlocutors, say and think, how they express their ideas, and what they do in practice. Anthropologists thus inevitably share with other social scientists all those methodological (and ethical) problems that derive from studying self-conscious, articulate people, rather than things. Sociologists and economists may routinely find refuge from the exigent pressures of their ultimate subject-matter in statistics. Psychologists contrive elaborately artificial experiments that treat people like rats. In history, the ghosts with whom historians wrestle can be easily exorcised and laid to rest. But anthropology is very different. There the people studied are irrepressibly present and may become exceedingly obtrusive, clamorously imposing a particular version of events, or narrative, on the observer: their 'fictions' are then apt to become our 'facts'.

The anthropologist's corresponding defensive 'distancing' is built into the conventional fieldwork situation. There, according to the classic formula, the European anthropologist heroically confronts exotic alien communities, whose unfamiliar languages and cultures are at once a barrier and a challenge to mutual communication and understanding. The solitary anthropologist (or, more sociably, the American, French, German or Italian team[1]) thus sallies forth to penetrate remote jungles in pursuit of the elusive quarry, an exotic, hitherto unchronicled (or unrecorded) people. Here the foreign observer lives for perhaps a year (and, if British, sometimes longer), immersing himself (or herself) in the lives of his hosts while seeking to learn and internalise their culture and institutions. The 'translation of culture', which this method of research aspires to achieve, makes linguistic competence an important, though insufficiently addressed, issue.

Command of the language of the people he (or she) is studying, not only enables the foreign fieldworker to follow what is going on around him, but, above all, enables him to interact with them in terms of *their concepts*, and in their own linguistic idiom. Linguistic fluency, even if it is at a rather basic level, enables the anthropologist to internalise, in some measure, and so directly to savour, local culture and values in their own terms. The ability to formulate the ideas of one's interlocutors, in their terms, and to directly register their response is a powerful methodological research tool. As I well know from my own experience, however indispensible initially, interpreters inevitably eventually become a barrier to this kind of 'living one's way' into another culture.

American anthropologists usually possess a more sophisticated training in linguistics, yet paradoxically often seem less fluent in the relevant vernacular than their British colleagues. But, in any case, whatever his command of the local language (the ultimate key to 'local knowledge'), the foreign field anthropologist tends to rely much more heavily than he cares to admit on those whom, in unguarded moments, he is apt to describe as 'reliable' informants.

As a kind of micro-sociology, based upon the intensive study of a manageably compact and homogeneous community, the research technique characteristic of anthropology is, of course, that known loosely (and often rather optimistically) as 'participant observation', where the observer behaves like a highly permeable cultural sponge. Here, as Descola (1996) succinctly puts it, 'the workshop of the ethnologist is himself and his relationship with a given population'. As his (or her) own chief research instrument, and through the contacts and relationships he establishes, the foreign fieldworker thus strives to construct a comprehensive picture of what it is like to be a member of the host community. At its most successful, this research technique (including linguistic fluency) engenders a kind of intimacy between the traditionally alien observer and his subjects at the community level, which, as has often been noticed, has analogies with that at the individual level in psychoanalysis.

It is thus not difficult to appreciate how such cross-cultural anthropological research, particularly where there is strong empathy, regularly administers a massive dose of 'culture-shock' as the trainee anthropologist's own ethnocentric verities risk dissolving into incoherence and arbitrariness (cf I.M. Lewis, 1996, pp.1–26).[2]

It can equally readily be appreciated how, in this Malinowskian tradition, fieldwork in an alien setting should have become the *sine qua non* for professional recognition as a *bone fide* anthropologist. As a routine initiation ritual, as has often been noted, fieldwork thus plays a similar sociological role (as well as sharing something of its character) to the psychoanalyst's training analysis in which the neophyte has in effect to assume the sick role in order to become a qualified healer.

If, however, the newly qualified analyst owes his (or her) specially sensitised insight to his teacher, the anthropologist owes a wider and more comprehensive debt to the people he has studied. It is not simply that, through having studied one foreign community, he is now properly licensed to study others (including his own society). In addition to this, his professional working capital consists of the mass of information he has culled in the course of his fieldwork, the publication of which may well take most of his working career. This capital – ethnography – is the greatest and most obvious debt we owe to those from whom we learn our trade. No wonder, therefore, that anthropologists of every denomination unite in paying homage to ethnography, that most precious 'Golden Fleece' (Forge, 1972) without which the anthropological voyager would return home empty-handed, possessing neither raw data, nor (as I shall argue) theory.

THE THEORY OF THEORY

Where fieldwork of this type has such profound personal significance, it is not surprising that it should endow the ethnographic treasures the anthropologist brings back with magical powers akin to those of an Aladdin's lamp (cf. I.M. Lewis, 1996, pp.1–22). It is equally obvious that the anthropologist's personal equation must bulk large in his or her fieldwork (an issue elaborated *ad absurdem* by post-modernists). The ideal picture of successfully intensive fieldwork, outlined above, may be very different in practice. This prompts a string of supplementary questions. Were one's colleagues as warmly welcomed as they make out? How did they really conduct their fieldwork, and how thoroughly did they immerse themselves in the language and culture of their hosts? In these terms, did the community studied get the anthropologist it deserved?[3]

Whatever the true answers here, subjectivity and personal involvement are deeply engrained in our most cherished and characteristic mode of research. It is perhaps an acute consciousness of this subjective overlay which helps to sustain the received view of the relationship between our data and our theories. This asserts that theory is primarily the brain-child of the anthropologist, something which he imposes on the evidence he collects.

Clifford Geertz (1967, pp.25–32) provides an eloquent, if somewhat circular, exposition of this view. The anthropologist's 'personal relationship to his subject of study is', Geertz says,

> perhaps more than any other scientist, inevitably problematic. Know what he thinks a savage is and you have the key to his work. You know what he thinks he himself is and, knowing what he thinks he himself is, you know in general what sort of thing he is going to say about whatever tribe he happens to be studying. All ethnography is part philosophy, and a good deal of the rest is confession.

(This might be taken to be post-modernist anthropology's credo – so much of which, in any case, is repetitiously derivative of Geertz.) From this perspective, the biography of culture turns out to be significantly autobiography – a state of affairs for which *Father and Son* (1907), the literary classic by the celebrated Victorian man of letters, Edmund Gosse, might have provided a productive paradigm (although I have not seen it cited in this context).

In this vein, and without the benefit of Geertz, Evans-Pritchard used to counsel an earlier generation of students (of which I am one) to make it their business to meet personally the various anthropologists whose texts they were studying. Thus, we were told, we could see plainly for ourselves the authors' temperaments, discover their biases and quirks at first hand, and so know how to assess their works. For past heroes no longer directly accessible to such personal scrutiny, as for instance Malinowski, Evans-Pritchard was always ready to supply his own colourful assessment. It is perhaps poetic justice that Evans-Pritchard's own commentators should draw attention to the striking difference between his famous study of Zande witchcraft (Evans-Pritchard, 1937) and his later book on Nuer religion (Evans-Pritchard, 1956). The first was written before its author embraced Catholicism and makes little reference to God. The second study, written after its author's conversion, dwells at length on Nuer theism, and scarcely refers to scepticism or disbelief – themes which receive considerable attention in the earlier book. Leach (1984), rather late in the day, added his voice to this view of the ethnographer's dialogue, declaring forcefully, 'every anthropological observer . . . will see something that no other such observer can recognise, namely a kind of harmonic projection of the observer's own personality.' (How precisely this accorded with Leach's eventual espousal of structuralism remained unclear.)

Personal information of this sort is often held to be all the more necessary, since in many cases a given culture may still today only be known to us through the research and publications of a single anthropologist. The discrepant reports which we thus tend to expect when two or more anthropologists study the same people seem to confirm this doctrine of the subjectivity of anthropological testimony. The stock example, traditionally cited here, concerns the conflicting accounts of the Mexican village of Tepoztlan provided by Robert Redfield in 1930 and by Oscar Lewis some twenty years later. As every American anthropologist knows (or used to know), where Redfield found a pleasing sense of harmony and dignity in the 'Little Tradition', Lewis found rancorous misery – the basic traits which he later thrust into general currency under the impressive title of the 'Culture of Poverty'.

It is not difficult to find other examples of such conflicting eth-nographic evidence, suggesting anthropological subjectivity. One of the most clamorous in academic anthropology must surely be Derek Freeman's (1983) categorical denunciation of Margaret Mead's (1928) idyllic picture of teenage Samoan culture. The graceful and innocently uninhibited adolescent sex which Mead found so charming and attrac-tive (and contrasted with her own American experience) is, according to Freeman, a complete myth. The real Samoan culture, he claims, is rigidly hierarchical, punitive and generally violent. The discordant images produced by these two anthropologists are presented in equally contrasting theoretical frameworks (Mead stresses cultural, Freeman biological imperatives) which might also, of course, be argued to reflect differences in temperament.

Similar contrasting judgements, with more serious political implications, occur in the contemporary Belgian anthropological literature on Rwanda. Here in his well-known and influential political analysis, Maquet (1960) presented a benign, consensual view of Tutsi hegemony and Hutu acquiescence. D'Hertefelt (1965), in contrast, stressed the inequalities in power between the Tutsi ruling caste and the Hutu peasantry, and the obvious potential for revolutionary conflict (cf. Newbury, 1988). It is this, notoriously, which has turned this region of central Africa into a vicious, perennial blood-bath, and (more hopefully) contributed in 1997 to the collapse of Mobutu's tyrannical and corrupt regime in Zaire (cf. Prunier, 1996).

Such apparently subjectively coloured reports are, moreover, our sources not only for descriptive accounts of individual peoples, but also for high-flown interpretative analyses which we can only check against the author's own data, selected in the light of his or her theoretical preoccupations. (In this connexion, I recall Evans-Pritchard shocking his young acolytes at Oxford by criticising a monograph by one of his peers, on the grounds that it was written so loosely that it contained evidence that contradicted the argument. It was remiss of the author to be so careless!)

Every anthropologist conventionally answers hostile critics by saying in effect: 'I was there and know what happens: you were not!' As Evans-Pritchard loftily observed in his influential Marett Lecture in 1950: 'The social anthropologist discovers in a native society what no native can explain to him, and what no layman, however conversant with the culture, can perceive – its basic structure'.[4] This elusive structure, he intriguingly remarks, 'cannot be seen. It is a set of abstractions, each of which though derived it is true from analysis of observed behaviour is fundamentally an imaginative construct of the anthropologist himself.' The difference between native knowledge (the 'emic' level) and the anthropologist's analysis (the 'etic' level) is, Evans-Pritchard explains, like the difference between a native speaker's knowledge of his language and a grammarian's analysis.

If such a brilliant and widely experienced fieldworker can so strongly proclaim the subjective creativity of the anthropologist's analyses of the ethnographic data he personally collects, we can readily appreciate how such subjectivity is further compounded by armchair anthropologists who rely heavily on other anthropologists' field data. The gap between the analyst's 'structures' and the 'raw ethnographic data' must increase correspondingly. This is largely the situation with Lévi-Strauss's version of structuralism which is so extensively based on secondary sources.

Lévi-Strauss's structuralist apparatus rests on even more abstract principles, the master adding the grave warning that when analysing his material, while paying some attention to what his informants say, the anthropologist should not believe everything he is told. As the French *savant* states in a much-quoted passage: 'conscious models, which are usually known as "norms", are by definition very poor ones since they are not intended to explain [the] phenomena, but to perpetuate them' (Lévi-Strauss, 1963, p.281). Here Lévi-Strauss invokes the weighty authority of Franz Boas, whose voluminous collections of American Indian myths provide so much of the raw ingredients for the rich French structuralist cuisine. Boas, he recalls, demonstrated that 'facts can more easily yield to structural analysis when the social group . . . has not elaborated a conscious model to interpret or justify them' – where, in a word, there is action without explicit rationalisation.

In this spirit, Lévi-Strauss's formidable corpus of myth exegesis, like so many of its predecessors, is based mainly on second-hand data collected by other ethnographers and interpreted out of context. This detachment from their original living setting enhances their character as inert data to be fed into Lévi-Strauss's miraculous thought-machine. This is consistent with Lévi-Strauss's treatment of myths as politically and socially neutral, and hence immune from those distracting politico-economic forces which colour, and from his point of view distort other social phenomena. No wonder also that Lévi-Strauss should seek to confine the field of operation of structuralism to those truly 'primitive' societies which, significantly, he distinguished as 'cold' in opposition to the 'hot' changing societies of the modern world. To borrow his own terminology, Lévi-Strauss has apparently performed the notable feat of transforming cultural into natural data. This naturalisation effectively deprives socio-cultural data of their unique human status, making them part of the inarticulate world of nature. The final paradox here is that despite being thus rendered speechless, Lévi-Strauss's myths nevertheless engage their analyst in lively dialogues.

Lévi-Strauss's case is an extreme one.[5] But besides having become a household name (for the intelligentsia), he does illustrate a general tendency which I seek to identify and explore. Rather surprisingly – for he had no truck with French structuralism – we can indeed find the same sort of sleight-of-hand between Culture and Nature in Evans-Pritchard's methodological directives. In reaction to Radcliffe-Brown, and proposing a new influx of anti-positivist illumination from the humanities to counter the baneful influence of what he considered spurious scientism in social anthropology, Evans-Pritchard forcefully urged an alliance with history (his own undergraduate discipline). This was also designed, I believe, to encourage higher standards of scholarship in social anthropology.[6] The unintended effect, if taken to its logical extreme, would be to assimilate the over-articulate subject-matter of anthropology to the drier, more remote material of the historian – (a paradoxical dehumanisation in which social anthropology could be reduced to a kind of spatial archaeology).

On these views of the generation of anthropological theory (which, following Kuhn, should presumably qualify as 'normal anthropology'), doing fieldwork, especially after the initial initiatory ritual, is almost like being on vacation in a think-tank. After a spell away from his (or her) humdrum routine teaching responsibilities, the anthropologist returns to his colleagues refreshed and charged with brilliant new ideas which he has dreamed up during his field-trip. Of course, as he may generously acknowledge, he may well have enjoyed stimulating intellectual company amongst his genial 'tribal' hosts who, also, obligingly, provide the raw material – the ethnography – from which he confections anthropological theory. If this really was all that happened, it would reduce our subject to what it has always teetered on the brink of becoming: a fashionable literary pursuit, a dilettante traveller's *belles lettres*. (This was virtually the point of departure for the post-modernist tendency in 1980s anthropology, with a spate of publications on the 'poetics' of different aspects of culture by authors whose literary talents sometimes seemed rather questionable.)

With this highly Eurocentric model of anthropological fieldwork and theorising, it would also follow that the differences and similarities between the two traditions of anthropology which mainly concern us here, the British and the American, could be explained mainly in terms of such chance factors as diverging or coinciding *zeitgeist*s, and the personal eccentricities of their leading exponents.

This is patently an exaggeration. After all, even in history there is a discernible relation between data and interpretative theory which, moreover, spills over into historiography. There is, for instance, a world of difference between the general picture of history and of the historian's task proposed by E.H. Carr (1964) and by G.R. Elton (1967).[7] This contrast is not merely a reflection of the parochial differences between the Oxford and Cambridge history schools: it also surely relates to the different periods in which these two famous historians specialise. As a modern historian, Carr is faced with a surfeit of information and so stresses the problem of selection in history. As a Tudor historian, Elton's situation is very different. He has less confusing and contradictory material to contend with, and correspondingly finds in history a more confident and purposive sense of direction.[8] In this sense, ghost-writing in history is perhaps more common than is generally supposed by those who assign such importance to the political loyalties of individual historians, irrespective of what they write about.

CONTEXTS AND CHARACTER: AMERICAN ANTHROPOLOGY

If in history the dead subjects of study can posthumously exercise such palpable influence, surely the impact of the living must be even more marked in anthropology? With this in mind, I now turn to consider whether, and in what way, the setting and character of ethnographic data seem to impact upon the theoretical preoccupations of anthropologists (cf. Fardon, 1990). First, American cultural anthropology. From its inception virtually to the present, and apparently in all subsidiary traditions and schools, what is striking here (especially to a British social anthropologist) is the consistent and emphatic stress upon culture as the driving force, distinguishing and explaining different human communities. As Ward Goodenough (1970) put it in his Henry Morgan Lectures, culture is above all 'authoritative', and indeed possesses such magisterial power that social structure is to be regarded as a subordinate 'artefact'. But perhaps the essence of the American view here is still best summed up in Kroeber's famous conception of culture as 'superorganic'. Thus, whatever may be the case amongst those they study, in American anthropology, at least, Custom is king and reigns supreme – no wonder some latter-day American anthropologists fastened so enthusiastically on Bourdieu's opaque slogan 'habitus'.

This emphasis upon *culture patterns*, rather than upon *social relations*, as the fundamental determinant and boundary marker in social life seems consistent with American anthropology's formative historical circumstances as, virtually, a backyard industry set in a plural society, characterised by a pervasive sense of ethnic difference. The same all-pervading sensitivity to ethnic distinctions also colours American sociology, especially that of the Chicago School, giving it much of its vitality and interest – in the eyes of a British social anthropologist. However great the cultural distance, the founding fathers of American anthropology did not have to travel far geographically to study exotic communities which, in a subordinate capacity, formed part of their own native political system. The American Indians, or what was left of them, constituted a convenient ethnographic resource for anthropological research, a living ethnographic museum of dying Indian cultures. Boas and his colleagues and students sought to record for posterity what remained of this precious heritage, from the lips of the oldest and most knowledgeable Indian informants they could find.

In the beginning, American anthropology was thus a rescue-operation, directed towards salvaging as much as possible from an archaic world smashed to pieces in the process of colonisation. Here the gentle Yahi Indian, Ishi, the last survivor of his tribe, who in 1911 found sanctuary in the Hearst family ethnographic museum of the University of California, epitomises a whole anthropological tradition (see T. Kroeber, 1961). In the 1960s his spirit rose phoenix-like from his mortal ashes to achieve a modern incarnation (at one remove) in the Yaqui Indian *guru*, Don Juan, whose fame spread throughout the world through the popular works of his UCLA-trained anthropological spokesman, Carlos Castaneda. Like Castaneda, although applying different methods, the early American ethnographers were forced to try to collect and piece together the assorted remnants of information gleaned from a few venerable Indian elders. As Robert Murphy (1972, p.24) has pithily commented, this led the founders of American anthropology to concentrate on the 'cultural residues of the mind', as they sought to retrieve the last particles of remembered custom, and produced a series of monographs that read like those impressively detailed laundry lists formerly found in the most exclusive hotels.

The risks attached to this particular American version of anthropology's perennial romantic quest for pristine savage cultures are illustrated in a poignant case involving the Cushitic-speaking peoples of north-east Africa. While researching in Kenya, a young American anthropologist had the good fortune to meet two venerable elders who introduced themselves as the 'last survivors' of their tribe. They spoke what sounded like an unknown form of Cushitic, a language that had, apparently, not previously been recorded by Western scholars. Here surely was a true example of anthropological serendipity. So the young research worker engaged the services of these two obliging sages to work with him on a regular daily basis, and spent months systematically recording their language and their accounts of their culture. He then rushed to Europe, with his valuable tapes, to present his discovery to the leading Cushitic experts there. After hearing his recordings, these experts had the delicate task of informing their enthusiastic young colleague that the two old gentlemen were in fact speaking a form of well-known standard Somali. They had apparently also added insult to injury by engaging in obscene exchanges while ostensibly responding to the questions the researcher had read out from his questionnaire. How ironic that the eager young scholar was studying language-switching!

This cautionary tale is not intended to cast doubt on the veracity of honest Indians such as Ishi (Don Juan might be another matter). It simply illustrates the formidable problems of assessing source material which inevitably confronted the pioneering scholars who established Amerindian Studies and American cultural anthropology. In a part of the world containing the miscellaneous debris of so many shattered indigenous cultures, and within a wider political system dominated by the White Anglo-Saxon Protestant (WASP) 'Great Tradition', which the subordinate Black tradition further underscored, the stress on cultural elements and the quest for meaningful patterns, and combinations or complexes of these 'shreds and patches' (in Lowie's famous phrase), seems a natural, even almost inevitable outcome. For 'shreds' read 'sherds' and you get the same common origin which, surely, explains the early, and enduringly close association between anthropology and archaeology in America.

But we cannot pursue that linkage further here, and must restrict our attention to the American cultural anthropology tradition. Within this, it is possible to trace a virtually unbroken line connecting the early diffusionist treatment of this ethnographic material by Boas and his contemporaries and its modern analysis in and outside America, in terms of French structuralism and cognitive anthropology. As George Stocking (1978, p.26) has observed, the focus of Boas's student and colleague, Edward Sapir, on 'archaic residues' – those 'fundamental features of structure, hidden away in the very core of the linguistic complex' . . . 'implied a "structuralist" view of language, and by extension of culture itself'. (The focus on language and 'narratives' of the 'other' can also, perhaps, be seen as preparing the ground for the post-modernist craze of 1980s American anthropology.)

An area strewn with so many marinaded culture elements, and appealing as much to archaeology as to ethnography, prompted earlier generations of anthropologists to explain the similarities they found between one culture-complex and another in terms of diffusion from a common source. Culture traits were thus, as it were, the visiting cards or trade-marks of different peoples. Although they draw different conclusions, both diffusionists and structuralists treat cultures and culture-complexes as composite assemblages of elements which can be permutated in a kaleidoscopic assortment of patterns. Indeed, when one examines Lévi-Strauss's publications chronologically, the transition from the earlier diffusionist search for cultural continuities and identifiable patterns to modern structuralism is in places quite explicit. Furthermore, in the work of the earlier American anthropologists, which in some cases he disavows and in others assimilates, it is not difficult to discover, under a different name, the starting point for his entire enterprise. Thus, in a prescient phrase which Lévi-Strauss himself might have written, Ruth Benedict (1923) concluded her Ph.D. thesis with the judgement: 'It is, so far as we can see, an ultimate fact of human nature that man builds up his culture out of disparate elements, combining and recombining them'.[9]

THE FRENCH CONNEXION

This, surely, is as succinct a statement as one could hope to find of Lévi-Strauss's basic assumptions and methodology which, of course, he shares (to varying degrees) with those brands of American anthropology practised under such names as new ethnography, cognitive anthropology, and so on. Lévi-Strauss (1963, p.206) himself traces his own intellectual pedigree within the same tradition to Franz Boas whom he approvingly quotes as follows: 'It would seem that mythological worlds have been built up, only to be shattered again, and that new worlds were built from the fragments.' (Boas, 1898, pp.18).

This insight, shared within Amerindian ethnographic tradition by Boas and Benedict, is surely the lineal ancestor, or one such, of Lévi-Strauss's conception of those whose cultures he studies as *bricoleurs*: cerebral do-it-yourself men who, as wayward beachcombers, pick up and ingeniously recombine the richly assorted remnants deposited on the sands of time by successive tides in the perennial movements of cultures and civilisations. It would be easy, I believe, to go further to demonstrate how the well-worn schema of binary oppositions between Culture and Nature, male and female, right and left, and so on (which Lévi-Strauss shares with some cognitive anthropologists), is also in fact part of the *surface structure* of the cultures of those South American Indians whom he has actually encountered in the flesh in the course of his own limited fieldwork. (Lévi-Strauss's student Descola (1996), in an otherwise enlightening account of his structuralist fieldwork among the Jivaro of Ecuador, does not appear to consider this issue.)

It would take us far outside our present concerns to further pursue Lévi-Strauss's much misrepresented intellectual antecedents. I mention him again here simply to illustrate how, as much as any of his American predecessors and contemporaries, his work bears the stamp of the ethnographic specifics with which it is fashioned. Thus, it seems to me justified to go further in this direction than his critic Ricoeur (1963, pp.596–627) does, when he delicately suggests that Lévi-Strauss's theory of totemism draws its inspiration from, and so may only apply to, 'totemic societies'. I would also naturally concede that other ethnographic regions, such as Indonesia, would, as Lévi-Strauss (1963, p.133) himself acknowledges, provide equally apt material for his structuralist mill.

It may, of course, be reasonably objected that, if Lévi-Strauss is unquestionably an Americanist, he is only honorarily an American, and that this argument might be more persuasive if it stuck to native American examples. Let us therefore now consider specific trends and tendencies within the American tradition of cultural anthropology which reflect the pervasive force of the local ethnographic situation. The abiding emphasis on *culture* here is equally evident in the treatment of social change in terms of *culture change* or of *acculturation* (cf. Bastide, 1968, p.1031) in child development studies couched in the idiom of *enculturation*, in the related culture and personality studies, and even in American Marxist anthropology where it infects the terminology and leading concepts of both the evolutionists and environmental determinists. If the former attempted to chart the evolutionary thrust, of successively more complex *cultural* formations, the latter significantly adopted the title of '*cultural* ecology' to describe their modern version of Malthus's demographic determinism.[10]

Leslie White, himself one of the high priests of 'culturology', defined culture as

> a mechanism for providing man with subsistence, protection, offense and defense, social regulation, cosmic adjustment, and recreation . . . to serve those needs of man energy is required. It becomes the primary function of culture, therefore, to harness and control energy so that it may be put to work in man's service.' (White, 1949 p.367).

Here, and indeed I think one can virtually say that throughout American anthropology, as in biochemistry, there has been a marked tendency to treat culture (as to some extent with Boas) as an adaptive medium, enabling a human community to adjust to its environment. So, for instance, to quote a well-known and pioneering study of the Cultural

Ecology School, Robert Murphy and Julian Steward (1956) argue – rather unconvincingly – that the relationship between ecology and society among hunters is so close that those who share this mode of production end up possessing the same *culture*.

If those who employ Marxist assumptions cannot escape from the culturological tradition in American anthropology, we can scarcely expect anthropologists of other persuasions to be more successful. Finally and self-evidently, Black Studies and Amerindian studies, indeed ethnic studies generally, as well as cultural studies (and, for better or worse, post-modernist anthropology), are further testimony to the all-consuming power of the cultural paradigm in American anthropology.[11]

BRITISH SOCIAL ANTHROPOLOGY

From this outline of trends in American cultural anthropology, we pass now to its British counterpart, social anthropology. Here, under the inspiration of Radcliffe-Brown's domestication of Durkheim (and *pace* Malinowski), the persistent, explicit emphasis is not on *culture* but on *society*. Culture is seen essentially as a mode of expression, like language, a way of communicating in the conduct of social relations. (This view, interestingly, is clearly illustrated in the title of Leach's (1976) popular exposition of his British, sociological, version of French structuralism, *Culture and communication*.) Culture thus becomes a means rather than an end, at best an important secondary phenomenon. For American anthropologists this amounts to a heresy against which Alfred Kroeber had sternly warned many years ago (Kroeber, 1948). In this contrasting British tradition, social relations rather than community of culture define significant boundaries (although social divisions may generate cultural distinctions). Society and culture need not even coincide. As Edmund Leach (1954, p.17) himself long ago expressed it, perhaps unconsciously reflecting the discordance of cultural and political frontiers characteristic of Britain's former colonies (as we have seen in Chapter 4): 'there is no intrinsic reason why the significant frontiers of social systems should always coincide with cultural frontiers'.

More generally, I think that to a significant extent the British preoccupation with *social* rather than *cultural* differentials is consistent with the classical fieldwork political context. In the colonial era under the 'White Peace', British anthropologists carried out research on societies within their overseas dependencies which, in the main, were administered by expatriate rather than settler officials. Unlike the American Indians, these were usually vigorously alive communities. Indeed, their vitality and the effectiveness of their political institutions prompted the development of Lord Lugard's famous system of colonial administration, known as 'indirect rule', under which indigenous local units enjoyed a high degree of autonomy. The situation here (like that in group psychotherapy) was also that, since there were not sufficient expatriate officials to control large areas and populations, it was more economic to co-opt local leaders and authorise them to rule themselves within the overarching colonial system. Naturally in this process (literally a matter of political economy), it was not always a straightforward issue to identify 'authentic' local leaders, and in some cases entirely novel administrative units were established which gradually acquired their own distinctive political culture and ethnic identity. So, 'tribes' were sometimes actually created (see above, Chapter 4), as well as simply recognised and reinforced.

In this 'tele-anthropology' we British social anthropologists discovered and investigated our subject-matter as it existed *in situ*, and at a safe distance from home (cf. Goody, 1995). Typically and prior to the processes of mass immigration and globalisation, those we studied lived in territories which were only tenuously, and ultimately transiently, linked to our metropolitan world. It was in their indigenous setting, not in our metropolitan haven, that our subjects then seemed destined to achieve local independence and autonomy in their own fashion. As was later discovered, British passports related primarily to that situation, rather than conferring full metropolitan citizenship.

In this colonial dialogue, the anthropologist's home culture thus remained unthreatened by exotic ethnic forces. Ethnicity, at this time, was consequently usually only an issue in the life of the expatriate anthropologist in remote and fleeting contexts overseas. The question of cultural assimilation only arose significantly in relation to education and development for local self-government. Culture, thus, was not such a controversial and sensitive personal issue for the transient British fieldworker. Nor, in contrast to the 'vanishing American Indian' context, was culture an elusive quarry that could be discovered only after the most energetic and persistent detective work. On the contrary, it was immediately salient, and the first challenging barrier to overcome as the anthropologist's command of the local language gradually increased.

Even in South Africa where issues of ethnicity and cultural assimilation obviously did confront the anthropological fieldworker, both in urban and rural contexts, it was primarily the most committed

Afrikaans-speaking settlers, rather than the essentially more cosmopolitan Anglophone anthropologists, who elaborated cultural distinctions into the political ideology of *apartheid* (see e.g. Schmidt, 1996; A. Kuper, 1998; and above, pp. 6–7). This culturological approach was largely rejected by the Anglo-Saxon School of Social Anthropology (implanted by Radcliffe-Brown and developed by Isaac Schapera and his colleagues) which was adapting the British social structural approach to the particular circumstances of southern Africa as a vast plural society in the throes of complex change and development.

The colonial setting in which they generally conducted their fieldwork, it seems to me, thus tended to encourage British social anthropologists to take culture for granted, devaluing its diacritical significance, and promoted an approach which focused primarily on different types of social system. The fact that we were also usually studying living social communities (rather than attempting to resurrect dead or decaying cultures) may well have contributed, as some have suggested, to the strongly functionalist orientation of British social anthropology where the primary concern was to understand how particular social institutions (and at a more abstract level) social systems actually worked. Here I have in mind especially the 'desert island' setting of the formative classic British studies in the tradition of Malinowski and Firth and their disciples.

In contrast to our American colleagues, this established a tradition where culture tended to be treated as an arbitrary appendage. This disposed us to view history, and developments over time, in terms of *social* rather than *cultural* change, and to endeavour to explore correlations between *social* relations independently of their *cultural* trappings. The ambition here, is of course, to produce culture-free theory. So, if in American anthropology *culture* is the key determinant, for us it is often regarded as little more than a constraint (see e.g. Loizos, 1975) . Hence, it may ultimately be seen by British anthropologists as a product of social interaction, a device, even an embellishment, to give substance and mystery to shared political and economic interests as with nineteenth-century European nationalism, or the synthetic ethnicity sometimes encouraged in Africa by the colonial (and post-colonial) experience. This is particularly the position taken by those who work at the 'transactionalist' end of the spectrum in British social anthropology (e.g. F. Bailey, and A. Cohen). Here, naturally, convergence and interpenetration occurs with the work of 'symbolic interactionist' American sociologists.

In the tradition of their master (in this context at least) Durkheim, over fifty years ago Fortes and Evans-Pritchard (1940, p. 3) uncompromisingly proclaimed social anthropology's basic creed: 'comparative study . . . (has) . . . to be on an abstract plane where social processes are stripped of their cultural idiom and are reduced to functional terms.' In the inaugural Malinowski Memorial Lecture, twenty years later, apparently under the impression that he was suggesting something new, Edmund Leach (1961) proposed the same objective in slightly different terms.

It will be evident by now, I think, that many mainstream British social anthropologists (at least until the rise of the post-modernist fashion) generally accepted without serious demur the charge that they 'ignored culture', advanced in a friendly critique by G.P. Murdock as early as 1951. (They would, of course, have tended to retort that they did not 'ignore' culture but just treated it appropriately, as a secondary phenomenon.) They would naturally, however, hardly have shared his conclusion that they thereby became 'sociologists of a rather old-fashioned sort' (Murdock, 1951 pp.46–7). Durkheim was not so easily displaced, even when efforts were made to replace him (or reconstitute him as Marx). More generally, British social anthropologists might claim that they studied the *content* of social relations, independently of their cultural form. This, needless to say, would entail repudiating the artist's contention that content *is* form.

ETHNOGRAPHIC BIAS IN ANTHROPOLOGICAL THEORY

So far, I have sought to argue that the surface differences between American *cultural* and British *social* anthropology reflect, to a signifi-cant degree, the contrasting fieldwork settings in which each tradition developed its distinctive features. These were elaborated with the crucial influence of Durkheim on British anthropology and his relative neglect across the Atlantic. My thesis, which I have naturally overstated, assigns greater weight to the raw data and complex character of the ethnographic experience – including the circumstances (political and other) in which such information is collected, than is usually recognised by anthropologists when they write about theory. Further support for this interpretation can, perhaps, be found in the fact that many of the American anthropologists who, in the period between the two world wars became closely associated with British social anthropology and produced similar works to their British colleagues, also did their fieldwork in Africa. (This convergence, naturally, was further encouraged by those British anthropologists who, in the 60s and 70s, assumed teaching posts at United States universities.)

Confirmation for this heretical view can, perhaps, be found in the French anthropological tradition which, despite language differences, may be seen as mediating between the two Anglophone schools. Like the British, the French practised their anthropological fieldwork mainly overseas, but usually in territories governed (officially, at least) by *direct rule*, where traditional political systems had often been destroyed rather than renovated and adapted, and under the guiding ideology of cultural assimilation to the metropolitan French norm. Thus, if in its formative empirical period the French anthropological encounter took place abroad, it was nevertheless within a more tightly integrated *plural political system* which, like its American counterpart, was dominated by the White ruling élite. Cultural assimilation (which was also part of colonial ideology in the 'civilising mission'), was thus again a critical issue.

These latter factors seem to me to have played a part in shaping the mainly *cultural* emphasis which, despite the sociological legacy of Durkheim (so prominent in British anthropology), was until recently generally such a marked feature in ethnographic monographs by French anthropologists. (It has to be added, however, that this did not prevent the development of a comparative sociological tradition associated in its colonial fieldwork context with names such as Balandier.) As we have already seen, culture is peculiarly prominent in the work of the leading French theoretician, Lévi-Strauss, and coupled with the fact that he makes such extensive use of American data, this helps to explain his appeal to American anthropologists (particularly those engaged in symbolic anthropology). Here there is a striking cultural convergence.

This cursory reference to the history of French anthropology cannot be pursued further here (for broader treatment see Leclerc, 1972; Balandier, 1974; Panoff, 1977; Auge, 1982). My oversimplified generalisations would, obviously, have to be considerably modified in relation to parts of French north Africa (and, perhaps, elsewhere).

We must now return to concentrate on my central thesis. The distinction I have been urging between the two great Anglophone traditions, which is not simply one of style, paradoxically breaks down as soon as we consider the finer structure of the relationship between data and theory.

Indeed, the more closely we examine it, the more self-evident becomes the *cultural* character of so-called *social* anthropology. (Cultural anthropology is not however correspondingly really sociological.) For a start, some of the standard analytical categories we social anthropologists utilise in comparative analysis are direct borrowings from specific cultures. Typical commonplace examples are: shaman, totem, taboo, mana, cargo-cult and caste. The intrinsic ambiguity of such terms as on the one hand, culturally specific and on the other, cross-culturally useful, is well illustrated in the case of the word 'caste', whose applicability outside the Hindu caste system has long been a matter of protracted controversy.[12]

In the same plagiarist style, English translations of cultural concepts, shared by an entire ethnographic area and taken to be characteristic *leitmotifs*, are regularly thrust into general circulation. This leads again to vigorous debate over the limits of their applicability and analytical utility. So, 'honour and shame' has become one of the key 'theoretical' concepts in the comparative anthropology of the Mediterranean peoples, and ecumenically embraces Christian and Muslim cultures. There are two principal competing versions of 'honour and shame' theory. One treats honour as the prize of worldly success: the other presents honour as the consolation which dignifies failure (both views are obviously justified, given the ambiguity of the concept). More recently, the great expansion of anthropological research in New Guinea has resurrected and given new prominence to the role in small-scale, politically uncentralised communities, of charismatic entrepreneurial leaders known familiarly as 'big-men'. This New Guinea paradigm, associated with the culture of competitive exchange (and what in Asian ethnography are usually known as 'feasts of merit'), as Mauss long ago appreciated, provides theoretical links with the familiar North American Indian potlatch.

Theory in comparative social anthropology is thus riddled with examples of singular (i.e. emic) cultural (and ideological) forms and complexes, elevated to the status of general archetypes or paradigms claiming 'etic' identity. So, for instance, the distinction that Evans-Pritchard found in the religious beliefs of the Zande people of the Congo between what he chose to translate into English as 'witchcraft' on the one hand, and what he called 'sorcery' on the other, has become part of the general currency of theoretical social anthropology. It has also even diffused into the theories of the American Culture and Personality School! As those who have read Evans-Pritchard's text carefully know, this contrast rests on 'witchcraft' conceived of as a psychic capacity to cause harm, and 'sorcery' viewed as malevolent magic, essentially an observable technique involving spells, potions and other tangible substances.

Despite the readiness of anthropologists to fit their data from other societies into this Zande strait-jacket, and to weave highly implausible theories on the basis of this distinction,[13] witchcraft and sorcery are in fact rarely distinguished elsewhere so sharply and, indeed, more characteristically blend into a hybrid malevolent power. Thus it is not surprising that in African societies in the era of modernism and nationalism, and reflecting Western secular influence, there was a tendency for witchcraft to become sorcery and assimilated to 'poisoning'. The currency acquired by Evans-Pritchard's distinction evidently represents a case of ethnographic imperialism, based on a particular (i.e. Zande) cultural source. A more interesting example, perhaps, and one at least enjoying considerable cross-cultural validity, is that of the so-called 'anthropological' social tension theory of witchcraft and sorcery. This, of course, explains who accuses whom of witchcraft (or sorcery) in psychodynamic terms, invoking interpersonal conflict and rivalry, and is lifted straight from the practice and precepts of those to whom it refers. It is a good theory, but hardly one for which anthropologists themselves can claim much originality – other than that of serendipity (cf. I.M. Lewis, 1994, pp.12).

Again, the ethnography of the Nuer people of the southern Sudan, relayed by their forceful spokesman, Evans-Pritchard, has spawned a whole theoretical system of 'segmentary lineage organisation' which, until it was challenged by the competing 'alliance theory', based initially on south-east Asian and South American ethnography, reigned virtually supreme in anthropological analysis of uncentralised, kinship-based political systems. As with other arguably culturally specific, and hence questionable, analytic constructs, protracted disputes ensued as to whether or not other societies possessed Nuer-style kinship organisation (cf. above, Ch. 2). Eventually, this provoked Marshall Sahlins (1961) into proclaiming that this structure was specific to a particular evolutionary stage, and to particular ecological conditions. This had a dramatic effect on Evans-Pritchard's prototype since, according to Sahlins, apart from the Nuer there was only one other example (the Tiv) to be found in the whole anthropological kingdom. The concept had thus become somewhat rarefied. Taking this assessment a stage further, from a rather thin selection of ethnographic data, Adam Kuper (1986) has claimed dramatically, if unconvincingly, that lineage ideology (never mind lineage organisation) did not even exist (see above, Ch. 2).

The tendency illustrated here of seeing the world through the spectacles of the culture the anthropologist has studied intensively, is actually an occupational hazard which exerts a pervasive effect on theory-building in social anthropology. As we have seen, this form of anthropological acculturation, aptly termed 'secondary ethnocentricity' by the American cultural anthropologist, Herskovits, operates simultaneously at several different levels, and often only becomes apparent in debates involving ethnographic data from different regions – which, naturally, is a powerful argument for the comparative method advocated in this book. This professional ethnocentricity achieves its extreme form in those hypothetical declarations which anthropologists grandly issue on behalf of those they study, to the effect that, although they do not happen to have actually recorded it during their fieldwork, 'their people' would nevertheless never indulge in some belief or practice described elsewhere, and would, moreover, be scandalised at the suggestion. Here we confront very clearly an unthinking reification, virtually an ossification of the anthropologist's cultural experience, divorced from actual social contexts and generalised virtually *sub specia aeternitatis* – all the more remarkable in being entertained by anthropologists who would blench at the mention of the idea of national character. (I always think of the Tallensistic pronouncements of Meyer Fortes in this connexion.) All this, clearly, is a far cry from the methodological directive of Evans-Pritchard and Fortes, issued to their colleagues in 1940, outlawing cultural specifics in comparative analysis (cf. above. p.131).

This largely ignored variety of anthropological subjectivity – brainwashing by those studied – is, arguably at least as prevalent and important as the other aspect of the personal equation which has received so much attention in the official theory of fieldwork and theory-building. If, as I believe, this diagnosis is correct, a great deal of high-sounding theoretical debate in social anthropology is in large part a dialogue, conducted through unconscious anthropological agents, between the various cultures we study (and absorb). The most promising pieces of empirically based theory, really minor hypotheses, postulate correlations between two or more institutions, and follow the discovery of their concurrence or co-variation in one or more societies. Here I might instance my own hypothesis relating ecstatic forms of religiosity and spirit-possession to the experience of stress and constraint (I.M. Lewis, 1971; 1989; I.M. Lewis *et al.*, 1991; see also above, Ch. 6), and hence suggesting links with the setting typical of millennial movements. This 'theory' derives directly from observing the behaviour of spirit-possessed Somali women, and listening to their own and their husbands' mutually contradictory explanations of its causes and meaning. My 'hypothesis' is a generous bequest from the northern Somali people with whom I was working in the late 1950s. This particular 'discovery' prompted me to search the literature for other ethnographic parallels which, fortunately, I found in some profusion.

Max Gluckman's once famous hypothesis, postulating a correlation between an emphasis on kinship traced in the male line, patriarchal power, the size of marriage settlements and the stability of marriage itself, derives from the data he collected on the kinship systems of two contrasting southern Bantu peoples. Gluckman's theory (Gluckman, 1950) has thus a dual cultural origin, and as he demonstrates, fits a considerable range of other ethnography quite satisfactorily. This encouraged him to generalise about the nature of patriarchy and patrilineal descent in ways that others have subsequently shown (e.g. Fallers, 1957; Leach, 1957; I.M. Lewis, 1962b; see also above, Chapter 3; Jacobson, 1967; Comaroff, 1980; Solivetti, 1994) turn out to apply only to certain specific cultural forms and social conditions. To his credit, Gluckman later admitted (albeit in another context) that he had been misled by the 'ethnocentrism derived from studying Zulu and Barotse'.

To cite further examples of such cultural imperialism would serve little purpose here. Those discussed above show how the genesis of empirically based theory in the works of social anthropologists can usually be traced to the cultures they study and plagiarise in the name of social structure. These provide healthy empirical roots which, for those committed to a genuinely substantive anthropology, give our subject worthwhile intellectual rigour and vitality, and make it more scientific and less personally subjective than the various declarations I cited earlier would suggest. Although American cultural anthropologists (e.g. Sahlins, 1989; Mintz, 1996) have also made significant contributions to comparative theory (G.P. Murdock's monumental labours notwithstanding (Murdock, 1949; 1972), this emphasis is generally less pronounced than in British social anthropology (for recent examples here see Fuller, 1992; Gell, 1998; I.M. Lewis, 1996). Part of the reason for the latter, I suspect, is that, naively confident that they were transcending the cultural particularities they confronted, British social anthropologists had less inhibitions in drawing conclusions and elaborating hypotheses about relationships they then took to be culture-free and of general validity. I refer, of course, to the empiricist tradition in social anthropology where those in the classical fieldwork situation were generally not part of a political structure based on the melting-pot ideology, which, paradoxically, must first accentuate ethnic differences in order to homogenise them.

In these circumstances, the most impressive evidence of the seminal power of ethnographic data in theory-building is, thus, that contrary to appearances, whether we choose to call it *social* or *cultural*, empirically based anthropology persistently bears the stamp of the cultures in which it has been forged. Through its ultimate reliance on ethnographic data (which are partly cultural and partly sociological), and with its tendency to unconsciously absorb and re-cycle such emic insights, theory thus often transcends those other powerful influences that have led to the initially impressive differences in orientation of the two Anglophone anthropological traditions. These, of course, were always only differences of emphasis, since it is in reality extremely difficult to eliminate all traces of cultural loading in the comparative analysis of social institutions. In a sense, although cultural anthropology can be virtually emptied of sociological content, social anthropology has never been free from cultural contamination – however implicit.

Thus, whether labelled 'cultural' or 'social' anthropology, it seems clear that the minimum paradigm for understanding the flow of anthropological ideas includes, at its simplest, at least three broad headings (cf. Ch. 1, above). These are: the subjective anthropologist; his understanding and mobilisation of current anthropological theory; and the multi-layered socio-cultural 'ethnography' of the people(s) studied. As I have argued, the relationship between ethnography and such empirically based theory is complex and is strongly affected by the ambient political circumstances in which data is collected and analysed. Ethnography itself always includes both social and cultural data as the people we study act in terms of, but not necessarily always in obedience to, their own (culturally specific) beliefs and theories, and within a particular political setting, colonial or post-colonial. Indeed as Chapter 1 explored more fully from a historical perspective, the situation is actually more complicated than this. Unlike molecules that do not confidingly whisper their secrets to those who study them, our subjects thrust their ideas and ideologies upon us with gay abandon. At the same time, 'meta-theoreticians' in the shape of irregular amateur local anthropologists – true Man Fridays – suggest unorthodox but highly insightful interpretations which, clandestinely, filter into our ethnographically distilled theory (cf. I.M. Lewis, 1996, pp.14ff). Here, again, what anthropologists often glibly call 'ethnography' is the product of many different voices and sometimes more in the nature of an argument than a simple dialogue.

This latter point leads to the issue of what might be called 'endo- or auto-anthropology', where professionally trained social anthropologists study their own cultures and societies. Such anthropologists, engaged in what is effectively Black Studies, have obviously much to contribute in terms of superior command of a local language and culture – as I know from my own experience with Somali colleagues. Whether these obvious advantages completely outweigh the culturally innocent insights of the conventional anthropological outsider is obviously a matter of opinion (see e.g. Nakane, 1970; Cutileiro, 1971; Jackson, 1986; Ohnuki-Tierney, 1987; Srinivas, 1997). But, I wonder if we should not learn even more from research by Third World anthropologists on the industrial cultures and societies from which anthropologists are conventionally drawn. Such a reversal of roles would certainly be in the authentic spirit of our discipline and bring a new infusion of blood far more potent than any yet proposed to keep our subject alive and 'relevant' to the globalised world in which we all now live.[14] In the late 1990s these were still largely aspirations for the future.

We must now return to our consideration of the converging parallelism between British and American anthropology. With the post-Marxist decline in the empirical vigour of the European sociological tradition, 'culture' had come home. Some British anthropologists soon started to produce explicitly cultural analyses, sometimes invoking 'cultural logic' as a way of explaining particular socio-cultural phenomena. So, in the wake of the French Indianist, Louis Dumont (1972), British specialists on Indian caste sometimes employed 'hierarchy' as a general explanatory principle in Hindu culture and society (see, e.g. Parry, 1994).

One of the more extreme examples of this tendency to utilise culturological determinism occurs in Kapferer (1983)'s analysis of Buddhist exorcism in Sri Lanka. He evidently believes that culture explains itself, interpreting the prevalence of largely working-class and peasant female victims of spirit attack as a 'function' of the 'cultural typification' which places women in 'a special and significant relation to the demonic'. (Note the reliance on functionalist concepts in this 'post-functionalist', 'post-modernist' study.) That women and demons are so conceived is not in question – so they are in many societies – but these are cultural stereotypes which are themselves part of the surface structure of the culture Kapferer is describing and they invite analysis at a deeper sociological level. They constitute the beginning, not the end of analysis. Culture (however it may be designated) in such anthropological treatment is obviously no longer a mere *constraint* (cf. above, p.131): it has become a major determinant.

The circumstances in which British anthropologists regularly worked, and particularly those governing field research in the Third World, had now, of course, also changed dramatically. In the insecure post-colonial world, European researchers no longer enjoyed privileged, safe access to field sites of the kind which had played such a formative role in distinguishing their anthropology from that of their American counterparts, and cultural pluralism was rampant everywhere.

No wonder therefore, that cultural studies and American-inspired post-modernist 'reflexive' anthropology (the new 'armchair anthropology'), should have received such a warm, if often rather uncritical welcome on this side of the Atlantic (cf. A. Kuper, 1994). Somewhat portentously, Marcus and Cushman (1982, p.25; cf. Clifford and Marcus, 1986) had introduced the new programme for 'experimental ethnographies' which 'integrate, in their interpretations, an explicit epistemological concern for how they have constructed such interpretations and how they are representing them textually as objective discourse about subjects among whom research was conducted'.

The danger here, of course, is that the writer of the ethnographic text becomes so self-consciously and so self-indulgently intrusive (projecting her own sensibilities) that the culture which she (or he) seeks to depict in all its rich authenticity recedes into the background and becomes a rather colourless setting, or foil, for the anthropologist's exercises in introspection. This is a profoundly ethnocentric (and even egocentric) process in which the original vernacular ideas and values so elaborately elucidated become so heavily encrusted with thick deposits of foreign interpretive over-writing that they are likely to disappear from view, like a picture on an old canvas that has been repeatedly over-painted by lesser hands (cf. de Sardan, 1996). In my opinion, this constitutes a kind of 'thick description' that can, paradoxically, easily amount to virtual ethnocide (see e.g. Stoller, 1995;[15] Rasmuseen, 1995[16]). Even at its best, and in more skilful hands, the genre is apt to produce highly problematic results (see e.g. Reisman, 1977; Favret-Saada, 1980;[17] Parkin, 1991;[18] for a discussion of Lienhardt and Boddy see above, Ch. 6).

If our subject is to avoid this drift towards narcissistic 'meta-twaddle' (Gellner, 1995; cf. Polier and Roseberry, 1989; Reyna, 1994), and is not to degenerate into the whimsical 'Anything Goes School of Cultural Studies', it is essential to reassert the overriding sociological importance of a robust, cross-cultural, comparative anthropology. This should embrace historical and regional processes and, notwithstanding implicit cultural influence on theory, rigorously pursue the quest for significant cross-cultural correlations between social institutions. This is a far cry from the subjective anthropology criticised above, which can also be viewed as an extreme development of omniscient conceptions of the anthropologist's creative role in the construction of theory. In reality, as

I have sought to demonstrate here and in other chapters, theory-building is a complex, multi-stranded process and more dependent than is usually recognised, or admitted, on the inspiration of the peoples anthropologists study. This, surely, is further justification for the kind of empirically based comparative social anthropology advocated in this collection of essays.

As I have argued, in this endeavour there is always an inherent tension between cultural particularity and cross-cultural generalisation. But if we abandon the latter sociological goal, we risk, at best, simply producing miniaturistic celebrations of cultural particularities, and so contributing to the international portrait gallery of diverse cultures. This, of course, has its own value. But as the previous chapters have endeavoured to illustrate, that is only the first step towards a serious, comparative social anthropology that explores significant affinities between social institutions.

It is of critical importance, also, to stress the value of comparative study as a cumulative process in which new studies set their findings in the context of established knowledge. Without such scholarship, those who are ignorant of relevant comparative work may inadvertently replicate it less competently. This can have curious effects when anthropologists naively borrow from other disciplines theoretical ideas which are already firmly embedded in their own tradition. A typical case in the 1980s and 1990s involved the so-called 'invention of tradition', an idea usually attributed by its anthropological enthusiasts to the Africanist historian T. Ranger (e.g. Hobsbawn and Ranger, 1983). The central idea here is that not all that presents itself (in ritual, in tribal organisation etc.) as 'tradition' is necessarily as venerable as it may appear. In the colonial era, moreover, according to this formulation, most tribal formations are claimed to be untraditional reactions to colonial domination (which, as we have seen in chapter 4, is far from being generally true). The imputation that pre-colonial Africans (and others elsewhere) could not invent institutions for themselves until they were inspired by the colonial experience seems to me patronising and eurocentric. Oblivious to these derogatory implications, and beguiled by the anti-imperialist packaging, anthropologists who were apparently ignorant of their own intellectual 'traditions' proceeded to reinvent them. What they heralded as a novel analytical paradigm was already firmly ensconced in the anthropological analysis of political legitimation and identity formation in a tradition running as far back as Malinowski (1926), with more proximate elaboration in Laura Bohannon's (1952) work on lineages and genealogical manipulation.[19]

My aim here is not to attempt to establish a patent in the concept of the 'invention of tradition', or to claim unique anthropological inspiration for it. After all, it is surely self-evident that tradition is at some point inevitably invented (cf. Bernardi, 1993, p.16). My purpose is merely to point out that in the 1980s and 1990s it was hardly necessary to go outside the discipline in order to discover (and recycle) an idea which was already firmly embedded in mainline social anthropology.

This borrowing is, I think, far from being an isolated example of what can most charitably be attributed to lack of anthropological knowledge, and may also be a sign of intellectual insecurity and, more significantly, of the desire to display political correctness.

It is thus essential for those who wish to be considered serious anthropologists (social or cultural) to maintain an informed knowledge of the work of their predecessors as well as of their contemporaries. Unless it retains its character as a cumulative scholarly discipline, based on well-informed theories, rigorously tested against empirical data, social anthropology risks losing its substantive anchorage and its claim to make a distinctive contribution to the social sciences.[20]

NOTES

1 For a robust examination of the methodological benefits of teamwork, see de Sardan (1996).
2 Amongst the many telling accounts of this experience, Laura Bohannon's (colonial Africa) and Read's (New Guinea) remain outstanding evocations, while Gardner (Bangladesh) and Descola (South America) provide interesting testimony for the perspective of the 1980s generation of fieldworkers. An unusually intriguing account of fieldwork in Egypt by an Indian anthropologist is provided by Ghosh (1992). For a recent symposium celebrating the definitive role of fieldwork, see Sanjek (1990).
3 Cf. my anonymous review of Turnbull's *The Ik* in the Times Literary Supplement, 1974, p.131.
4 R. Firth (1975, p.10), in my opinion rightly, treats this claim with some scepticism.
5 Cf. criticism of the entirely theoretical character of Lévi-Strauss's kinship models by A.J.F. Koben, J. Verrips and L.M.J. Brunt (1974, pp.215–23).
6 Evans-Pritchard, who shared Malinowski's fascination with literally transcribed native texts (primary-source 'hard data' similar to historical documents) often also presented his subject to his students as being essentially the 'translation of culture', and (to some extent again like Malinowski in his literary phase) emphasised the discipline's links with literature and literary studies. He consequently welcomed recruits trained in English literary criticism by the legendary F.R. Leavis at Cambridge. The most famous of these was Godfrey Lienhardt (my supervisor and friend) whose *Divinity and Experience: the Religion of the Dinka* (1961)

has proved influential as perhaps the first 'post-modernist' ethnography in British social anthropology. Once this book, based on Lienhardt's D.Phil. thesis, was published, Evans-Pritchard whose close relationship with his brilliant prtegée was not untinged with ambivalence, rather characteristically remarked that it was a pity that Godfrey hadn't published his thesis in its original form rather than rewriting it so extensively. This unkind criticism has, I think some point, since Lienhardt's book does seem in places to project his own literary sensitivities onto the Dinka without producing convincing evidence that they are shared.

7 See also Elton (1967).

8 Charles Kemp first drew my attention to this striking contrast.

9 Quoted in F. Eggan, 'Social anthropology and the method of controlled comparison', *American Anthropologist*, vol. 56, 1954, pp.743–60.

10 For a vigorous critique of the work of the leading exponents of this school, see C.R. Hallpike (1973, pp.451–70).

11 For discussion of some of these issues from an American cultural perspective, see Watson (1984).

12 See e.g. J. Pitt-Rivers (1971).

13 See e.g. M. Douglas (1967 and 1970).

14 I proposed this to the British Social Science Research Council (of which I was a member) in the 1970s. But although there were already French initiatives in this direction, I could get no support from either my colleagues or the Council officials for spending 'British' funds in this way.

15 See I.M. Lewis (1996).

16 See I.M. Lewis (1997b).

17 See I.M. Lewis (1981).

18 See I.M. Lewis (1995).

19 Trained in European documentary history at Oxford, Ranger had enjoyed ample opportunity to develop this theme in central Africa where he worked in the 1960s in close association with anthropologist colleagues at what was then the University College of Rhodesia and Nyasaland, as well as others at the Rhodes-Livingstone Institute in Northern Rhodesia. These latter included W.J. Argyle, then doing fieldwork in Northern Rhodesia, who in this period published one of the most perceptive comparisons of the 'invention' of African and European nationalisms (Argyle, 1969). Argyle (published in 1971 but earlier given at seminars in Lusaka and Salisbury (now Harari)) also contributed an innovative analysis of dynastic usurpation among the Soli of central Africa, rationalised in terms of the claimed 'discovery' of original heirs who had earlier gone missing. The invention of (dynastic) tradition was indeed striking in these cases which had nothing necessarily to do with the impact of European colonisation (*pace* Ranger). Argyle did not claim any great originality for these ideas; and, indeed, their intellectual history might be traced more generally to Paul Bohannon's classic and once well-known study on genealogical invention and manipulation in lineage societies (Bohannon, 1952). Further back in the authentic anthropological tradition, Malinowski (1926) himself had, of course, presented myth in general as a 'charter' for contemporary interests and action which, as I have argued elsewhere (I.M. Lewis, 1976, p.126), is not very different from the starting point of Lévi-Strauss's great myth

analysis *oeuvre*. Malinowski had even quite explicitly analysed Trobriand myths ('traditions') invoked to legitimise rival land claims involving conflict between autocthones and powerful intruders, in a manner which is close to Argyle's work.

20 cf. Hymes (1974, p.25): 'serious ethnography is the main asset cultural and social anthropology bring today to a unified social science'.

BIBLIOGRAPHY

Note: Dates in square brackets [ ] refer to original publication.

Abbreviations
CUP   Cambridge University Press
JASO   *Journal of the Anthropological Society of Oxford*
JRAI   *Journal of the Royal Anthropological Institute*
OUP   Oxford University Press
RAIN   *Royal Anthropological Institute Newsletter*

Adam, H.M. (1983) 'Language, national self-consciousness and identity – the Somali experience', in I.M. Lewis (ed.), *Nationalism and Self-determination in the Horn of Africa* (London: Ithaca), pp. 31–42.

Ajayi, J.F.A. (1966) 'A survey of the cultural and political regions of Africa at the beginning of the nineteenth century', in J.C. Anene and G. Brown, *Africa in the Nineteenth and Twentieth Centuries* (Ibadan: Ibadan University Press).

Andrzejewski, B.W. (1982) 'Alliteration and scansion in Somali oral poetry and their cultural correlates', in V. Gorog-Karady (ed.), *Genres, Forms, Meanings: Essays in African Oral Literature* (Oxford: Journal of the Anthropological Society of Oxford), pp. 68–83.

―――― 1984. 'Somali literature', in L.S. Klein (ed.), *Encyclopaedia of World Literature in the Twentieth Century*, vol. 4 (New York: Frederick Ungar), pp. 277–9.

―――― and Lewis, I.M. (1964) *Somali Poetry* (Oxford: Clarendon).

Arens, W. (1975) 'The Waswahili: the social history of an ethnic group';, *Africa*, 45: 426–37.

Argyle, W.J. (1969) 'European nationalism and African tribalism', in P.H. Gulliver (ed.), *Tradition and Transition in East Africa* (London: Routledge & Kegan Paul).

―――― (1971) *Oedipus in Central Africa* (Natal: University of Natal Press).

―――― (1978) 'Dingiswayo Discovered: An interpretation of his legendary origins', in J. Argyle and E. Preston Whyte (eds), *Social System & Tradition in Southern Africa* (Cape Town: OUP), pp.1–18.

Asad, T. (1970) *The Kababish Arabs* (London: Hurst).
—— (1973) *Anthropology and the Colonial Encounter* (New Jersey: Humanities).
—— (1975) 'Anthropological texts and ideological problems: an analysis of Cohen on Arab villages in Israel', *Economy and Society*, 4: 251–82.
Atkinson, J.M. (1992) 'Shamanism today', *Annual Review of Anthropology*, 21: 307–30.
Augé, M. (1982) *The Anthropological Circle* (Cambridge: CUP).

Bailey, F.G. (1960) *Tribe, Caste and Nation: A Study of Political Activity and Political Change in Highland Orissa* (Manchester: Manchester University Press).
—— (1970) *Stratagems and Spoils* (Oxford: Blackwell).
Balandier, G. (1974) *Anthropo-logiques: une anthropologie de l'actuel* (Paris: Presses Universitaires de France).
Banti, G. and Giannattasio, F. (1996) 'Music and metre in Somali poetry', in R.J. Hayward and I.M. Lewis (eds), *Voice and Power* (London: SOAS).
Barclay, H.B. (1964) *Burri Al-Lamaab* (New York: Cornell University Press).
Barnes, J.A. (1951a) *History in a Changing Society* (Manchester: Manchester University Press).
—— (1951b) *Marriage in a Changing Society* (Cape Town: OUP).
—— (1954) *Politics in a Changing Society* (Manchester: Manchester University Press).
Basilov, V.N. (1984) 'The study of shamanism in Soviet ethnography', in M. Hoppal (ed.), *Shamanism in Eurasia* (Gottingen: Herodot), pp.46–63.
Bastide, R. (1968) *Applied Anthropology* (London: Harper).
Bateson, G. (1936) *Naven* (Cambridge: CUP).
Baxter, P.T.W. (1954) 'The social organisation of the Borana Galla of Kenya', unpublished D.Phil. thesis, Oxford University.
—— (1965) 'Repetition in certain Boran ceremonies', in M. Fortes and G. Dieterlen (eds), *African Systems of Thought* (London: OUP, pp.64–78.
—— (1966) 'Acceptance and rejection of Islam among the Boran of the Northern Frontier District of Kenya', in I.M. Lewis (ed.), *Islam in Tropical Africa* (London: OUP, pp.233–52.
Bernardi, B. (1952) 'The age-system of the Nilo-Hamitic peoples', *Africa*, 22: 316–32.
—— (ed.) (1973) *Etnologia e antropologia culturale* (Milan: Angeli).
—— (1993) 'Africanistica & Antropologia', *Africa* (Rome), XLVIII, 1, 1–20.
Beshir, M.O. (1974) *Revolution and Nationalism in the Sudan* (London: Rex Collings).
Biobaku, S. and Al-Hajj, M. (1966) 'The Sudanese Mahdiyya and the Niger-Chad Region', in I.M. Lewis (ed.), *Islam in Tropical Africa* (London: OUP), pp.425–41.
Black-Michaud, J. (1975) *Cohesive Force* (Oxford: Basil Blackwell).
Bloch, M. (1977) 'The past and the present in the present', *Man*, 12: 278–92.
—— (1986) *From Blessing to Violence: History and Ideology in the Circumcision Ritual of the Merina of Madagascar* (Cambridge: CUP).

Boas, F. (1989) *The Jessup North Pacific Expedition: Memoir of the American Museum of Natural History* (Leiden: E.J. Brill).

Boddy, J. (1989) *Wombs and Alien Spirits: Women, Men, and the Zar Cult in Northern Sudan* (Madison: University of Wisconsin Press).

—— (1994) 'Possession revisited', *Annual Review of Anthropology*, 23: 407–34.

Bohannon, L. (1952) 'A genealogical charter', *Africa*, 22: 301–15.

—— (1958) 'Political aspects of Tiv social organization', in J. Middleton and D. Tait (eds), *Tribes without Rulers* (London: Routledge & Kegan Paul).

Bohannon, L. and Bohannon, P. (1953) *The Tiv of Central Nigeria* (London: International African Institute).

Bovill, E.W. (1933) *Caravans of the Old Sahara* (London: OUP).

Bradbury, R.E. (1967) 'Continuities and discontinuities in pre-colonial and colonial Benin politics (1897–1951)', in I.M. Lewis (ed.), *History and Social Anthropology* (London: Tavistock), pp.193–252.

Brass, A. (1920) 'Eine neue Quelle zur Geschichte des Fulreiches Sokoto', *Der Islam*, 10.

Braukämpfer, U. (n.d.) 'Islamic principalities in south-east Ethiopia between the thirteenth and sixteenth centuries', *Ethiopianist Notes*, 1 (1 & 2), African Studies Center, East Lansing, Michigan.

Brown, R. (1973) 'Anthropology and colonial rule: the case of Godfrey Wilson and the Rhodes-Livingstone Institute', in T. Asad (ed.), *Anthropology and the Colonial Encounter* (New Jersey: Humanities), pp.173–98.

—— (1979) 'Passages in the life of a white anthropologist: Max Gluckman in Northern Rhodesia', *Journal of African History*, 20: 525–41.

Burghart, R. (1978) 'Hierarchical models of the Hindu social system', *Man*, 13: 519–36.

Burnham, P. and Ellen, R. (eds) (1979) *Social and Ecological Systems* (London: Academic).

Busia, Kofia (1951) *The Position of the Chief in the Modern Political Systems of Africa* (Oxford: OUP).

Butt, A., Wavell, S. and Epton, N. (1967) *Trances* (London).

Campbell, A. (1996) 'Tricky tropes: styles of the popular and the pompous', in J. MacClancy and C. McDonaugh (eds), *Popularising Anthropology* (London: Routledge).

Carr, E.H. (1964) *What is History?* (London: Penguin).

Cerulli, E. (1933) *Etiopia Occidentale*, 2 vols, (Rome: Sindicato Italiano Arti Grafiche).

—— (1936) *Studi Etiopici I. La Lingua e la Storia di Harar* (Rome: Istituto per l'Oriente).

—— (1959) 'Le popolozioni del bacino superiore dello Uabi-Uebi Scebeli', in *Somalia, scritti vari editi ed inediti* (Rome: Istituto Poligrafico delo Stato).

Clapham, C. (1988) *Transformation and Continuity in Revolutionary Ethiopia* (Cambridge: CUP).

Cohen, A. (1965) *Arab Border Villages in Israel* (Manchester: Manchester University Press.

—— (1969) *Custom and Politics in Urban Africa* (London: Routledge & Kegan Paul).

Cohen, G.A. (1978) *Karl Marx's Theory of History: A Defence* (Oxford: OUP).

Cohen, R. and Middleton, J. (eds) (1970) *From Tribe to Nation in Africa* (Pennsylvania: Chandler).

Colson, E. (1953) 'Social control and vengeance in plateau Tonga society', *Africa*, 23: 199–212.

Comaroff, J. (ed.) (1980) *The Meaning of Marriage Payments* (London: Academic).

—— and Comaroff, J. (1992) *Ethnography and the Historical Imagination* (Boulder: Westview).

Constantinides, P. (1985) 'Women heal women: spirit possession and sexual segregation in a Muslim society', *Social Science and Medicine*, 21(6): 685–92.

Cunnison, I. (1956) 'Perpetual kinship: a political institution of the Luapula peoples', *Rhodes-Livingstone Journal*, 20.

—— (1951) *History on the Luapula*, Rhodes-Livingstone Institute paper no. 21, Cape Town.

—— (1959) *The Luapula Peoples: Custom and History in Tribal Politics* (Manchester: Manchester University Press).

—— (1966) *Baggara Arabs* (Oxford: OUP).

Curtin, P. (1971) 'Jihad in West AFrica', *Journal Of African History*, 12 (1): 11–24.

Cutileiro, J. (1971) *A Portuguese Rural Society* (Oxford: Clarendon).

Davis, J. (1977) *People of the Mediterranean* (London: Routledge & Kegan Paul).

De Heusch, L. (1962) 'Cultes de possession et religions initiatiques de salut en Afrique', *Annales du Centre d'Etudes des Religions*, 2 (Brussels).

—— (1971) *Pourquoi l'epouser?* (Paris: Gallimard).

—— (1985) *Sacrifice in Africa* (Manchester: Manchester University Press).

De Martino, E. (1948) *Il Mondo Magico* (Torino: Boringhieri).

—— (1959) *Sud e Magia* (Milan: Il Saggiatore).

—— (1961) *La Terra del Rimorso* (Milan: Il Saggiatore).

—— (1977) *La Fine del Mondo* (Torino: Einaudi).

De Sardan, J.P. Olivier (1996) 'La violence faite aux données', *Enquête*, 3: 31–57.

Descola, P. (1994) *Les Lances du crépuscule, Relations Jivaros, Haute-Amazonie* (Paris: Plon).

—— (1996) 'A bricoleur's workshop: writing *Les Lances du crépuscule*', in J. MacClancy and C. McDonaugh (eds), *Popularising Anthropology* (London: Routledge).

D'Hertefelt, M. (1965) 'The Rwanda of Rwanda', in J.L. Gibbs (ed.), *Peoples of Africa* (New York: Holt, Rinehart & Winston).

Douglas, M. (1957) 'Animals in Lele religious symbolism', *Africa*, 27, 45–58.

—— (1967) 'Witch beliefs in Central Africa', *Africa*, 37: 72–80.

—— (ed.) (1970) *Witchcraft Confessions and Accusations* (London: Tavistock).

Dumont, L. (ed.) (1972) *Contributions to Indian Sociology*, vol. 6 (New Delhi: Vikas).

Durkheim, E. (1893) *De la division du travail sociale* (Paris: Alcan).

Eggan, F. (1954) 'Social anthropology and the method of controlled comparison', *American Anthropologist*, 56: 743–60.

Eliade, M. (1972) [1951] *Shamanism and Archaic Techniques of Ecstasy* (Princeton: Princeton University Press).

Elton, G.R. (1967) *The Practice of History* (London: OUP).

——— (1970) *Political History: Principles and Practice* (London: Allen Lane, The Penguin Press).

Elwin, V. (1955) *The Religion of an Indian Tribe* (London: OUP).

Epstein, A.L. (1978) *Ethos and Identity* (London: Tavistock).

Epstein, T.S. (1973) *South India: Yesterday, Today and Tomorrow – Mysore Village Revisited* (London: Macmillan).

Erasmus, C. and Smith, W. (1967) 'Cultural anthropology in the United States since 1900', *South Western Journal of Anthropology*, 23 (2): 111–40.

Evans-Pritchard, E.E. (1937) *Witchcraft, Oracles and Magic among the Azande* (Oxford: OUP).

——— (1940a) *The Nuer* (Oxford: Clarendon).

——— (1940b) 'The Nuer of the southern Sudan', in M. Fortes and E.E. Evans-Pritchard (eds), *African Political Systems* (London: OUP).

——— (1949) *The Sanusi of Cyrenaica* (Oxford: Clarendon).

——— (1950) 'Social anthropology: past and present', *Man*, 198: 118–24.

——— (1956) *Nuer Religion* (Oxford: Clarendon).

——— (1961) *Anthropology and History* (Manchester: Manchester University Press).

——— (1970) 'A Zande funeral custom', *Man*, 5: 126–9.

Fallers, L.A. (1954) *Bantu Bureaucracy* (Cambridge: Heffer).

——— (1957) 'Some determinants of marriage stability in Busoga', *Africa*, 27: 106–23.

——— (ed.) (1964) *The King's Men* (Oxford: OUP).

Farah, A.Y. and Lewis, I.M. (1993) *The Roots of Reconciliation* (London: Actionaid).

Fardon, R. (ed.) (1990) *Localizing Strategies: Regional Traditions of Ethnographic Writing* (Edinburgh: Edinburgh University Press).

Favret-Sbaba, J. (1980) *Deadly Words; Witchcraft in the Bocage* (Cambridge: CUP).

Field, M.J. (1960) *Search for Security* (London: Faber).

Firth, R. (1936) *We the Tikopia* (London: Allen & Unwin).

——— (1959) 'Problem and assumption in an anthropological study of religion', *Journal of the Royal Anthropological Institute*, 89: 129–48.

——— (1960) *Social Change in Tikopia* (London: Allen & Unwin).

——— (1975) 'Modern social anthropology', *Annual Review of Anthropology*, 4: 1–25.

——— (1975) 'Max Gluckman, 1911–1975', *Proceedings of the British Academy*, 61: 478–96 (London: Oxford University Press).

Fisher, H.J. (1973) 'Conversion reconsidered: some historical aspects of religious conversion in Black Africa', *Africa*, 43: 27–40.

Forde, C.D. (1950) 'Double descent among the Takö', in A.R. Radcliffe-Brown and C.D. Forde (eds), *African Systems of Kinship and Marriage* (London: OUP).

Forge, A.L. (1972) 'The Golden Fleece';, *Man*, 7 (4): 527–40.

Fortes, M. (1953) 'The structure of unilineal descent groups', *American Anthropologist*, 55: 17–51.

—— (1959) 'Descent, filiation and affinity: a rejoinder to Dr. Leach', *Man*, 59: 309 and 331.

—— (1960) 'Some reflections on Ancestor worship in Africa', Third International African Institute Seminar, paper no. 19.

—— (1970) *Time and Social Structure and Other Essays* (London: Athlone).

Fortes, M. and Evans-Pritchard, E.E. (1940) *African Political Systems* (London: OUP).

Fortes, M. and Goody, J. (eds) (1958) *The Developmental Cycle in Domestic Groups* (Cambridge: CUP).

Fortes, M. and Patterson, S. (eds) (1975) *Studies in African Social Anthropology* (Oxford: OUP).

Fortune, R. (1935) *Manus Religion* (Philadelphia: American Philosophical Society).

Frankenberg, R. (1981) 'Max Gluckman and the social anthropology of the practical world', *RAIN*, 345: 6–8.

Freedman, M. (1958) *Lineage Organisation in Southeastern China* (London: Athlone).

—— (1972) *Social and Cultural Anthropology* (Paris: Unesco).

Freeman, J.D. (1983) *Margaret Mead and Samoa* (Cambridge: Harvard University Press).

—— (1961) 'On the concept of the kindred', JRAI, 92: 192–220.

Fried, M.H. (1957) 'The classification of corporate unilineal descent groups', *JRAI*, 87: 1–30.

Friedman, J. (1975) 'Tribes, states and transformations', in M. Bloch (ed.) *Marxist Analyses in Social Anthropology* (London: Malaby), pp.162–202.

—— (1979) *System, Structure and Contradiction in the Evolution of 'Asiatic' Social Formations* (Copenhagen: National Museum of Denmark).

Fuller, C. (1979) 'Gods, priests and purity: on the relation between Hinduism and the caste system', *Man*, 14: 459–76.

—— (1992) *The Camphor Flame* (Princeton, NJ: Princeton University Press).

—— (ed.) (1996) *Caste Today* (New Delhi: OUP).

Furnivall, J.S. (1934) *Netherlands India: Study of Plural Economy* (Cambridge: CUP).

Gallini, C. (1967) *I Rituali dell'Argia* (Padua: Cedam).

—— (1988) *La Ballerina variopinta: una festa di guarigione in Sardegna* (Naples: Liguori).

—— and M. Massenzio (eds) (1997) *Ernesto De Martino nella Cultura Europea* (Naples: Liguori).

Gardner, K. (1991) *Songs at the River's Edge: Stories from a Bangladeshi Village* (London: Virago).

Gascon, A. (1995) *La Grande Ethiopie: une utopie africaine* (Paris: CNRS – 'Espaces et Milieux').

Geertz, C. (1967) 'The cerebral savage', *Encounter*, 28 (4): 25–32.

Gellner, E. (1969) *Saints of the Atlas* (London: Weidenfeld & Nicolson).

—— (1982) *Muslim Society* (Cambridge: CUP).

—— (1983) *Nations and Nationalism* (Oxford: Basil Blackwell).

—— (1985) *The Psychoanalytic Movement* (London: Paladin).

—— (1992) *Postmodernism, Reason and Religion* (new York: Routledge).

—— (1995) 'Segmentation: reality or Myth', *JRAI*, 1/4: 821–92.

Gellner, E. and Micaud, C. (1973) *Arabs and Berbers: From Tribe to Nation in North Africa* (London: Duckworth).

Ghosh, A. (1992) *In an Antique Land* (London: Granta).

Gibbon, E. (1957) *The Decline and Fall of the Roman Empire* 6 vols (london: Everyman).

Giel, R., Gezahegn, Y. and Van Luijk, J.N. (1967) 'Faith-healing and spirit-possession in Ghion, Ethiopia', paper presented to social science field research seminar, Addis Ababa, April 1967.

Gilsenan, M. (1973) *Saint and Sufi in Modern Egypt* (Oxford: OUP).

Gluckman, M. (1940) 'The Kingdom of the Zulu of South Africa', in M. Fortes and E.E. Evans-Pritchard (eds), *African Political Systems* (London: OUP).

—— (1950) 'Kinship and marriage among the Lozi of Northern Rhodesia and the Zulu of Natal', in A.R. Radcliffe-Brown and D. Forde (eds), *African Systems of Kinship and Marriage* (London: OUP).

—— (1957) *Custom and Conflict in Africa* (Oxford: Blackwell).

—— (1975) 'Anthropology and apartheid', in M. Fortes and S Patterson (eds) *Studies in African Social Anthropology* (London: Academic).

Godelier, M. (1977) *Perspectives in Marxist Anthropology* (Cambridge: CUP).

Gombrich, R. and Obeyesekere, G. (1988) *Buddhism Transformed: Religious Change in Sri Lanka* (Princeton, NJ: Princeton University Press).

Goodenough, W. (1970) *Description and Comparison in Cultural Anthropology* (Cambridge: CUP).

Goody, J. (1961) 'The classification of double descent systems', *Current Anthropology* 2: 3–26.

—— (ed.) (1968) *Literacy in Traditional Society* (Cambridge: CUP).

—— (1971) *Technology, Tradition and the State in Africa* (Oxford: OUP).

—— (1977a) *The Domestication of the Savage Mind* (Cambridge: CUP).

—— (1977b) *Production and Reproduction* (Cambridge: CUP).

—— (1995) *The Expansive Moment: The Rise of Social Anthropology in Britain and Africa, 1918–1970* (Cambridge: CUP).

Goody, J. and Braimah, J. (1967) *Salaga: The Struggle for Power* (London: Longmans).

Gordon, R. and Spiegel, A. (1993) 'South African Anthropology revisited', *Annual Review of Anthropology*, 22: 83–105.

Gough, K. (1952) 'Changing kinship usages among the Nayars', *JRAI*, 82: 71–88.

Gouilly, A. (1952) *L'Islam dans l'Afrique occidentale Francaise* (Paris: Larose).

Grimshaw, A. and Hart, K. (1995) 'The rise and fall of scientific ethnography', in A. Ahmed and C. Shore (eds) *The Future of Anthropology* (London: Athlone).

Grottanelli, V.G. (1977) 'Ethnology and/or cultural anthropology in Italy: Traditions and Developments', *Current Anthropology*, 18 (4), 593–614.

Gulliver, P.H. (ed.) (1969) *Tradition and Transition in East Africa* (London: Routledge & Kegan Paul).

Hallpike, C.R. (1973) 'Functionalist interpretations of primitive warfare', *Man*, 8: 451–70.

Hamayon, R. (1990) *La chasse a l'ame* (Nanterre: Société d'ethnologie, Paris).

—— (forthcoming) *Shamanism*, Louis H. Jordan Lectures in Comparative Religion, SOAS, 1995.

Hammel, E. (1968) *Alternative Social Structures in the Balkans* (Englewood Cliffs: Prentice Hall).

Hasan, Y.F. (1967) *The Arabs and the Sudan* (Edinburgh: Edinburgh University Press).

Hauschild, T. (1986) 'Religione e struttura sociale in Basilicata', *Basilicata* 9–16 February.

—— (1993) 'Making history in southern Italy', in K. Hasrup (ed.), *Other Histories* (London: Routledge), pp.29–44.

Heine, B. (1985) 'Notes on the Ik', *Africa*, 55 (1): 3–16.

Helander, B. (forthcoming) 'The Emperor's new clothes removed: a critique of Besteman', *American Ethnologist*.

Hinsley, F. (1973) *Nationalism and the International Political System* (London: Hodder & Stoughton).

Hjort, A. (1979) *Savanna Town: Rural Ties and Urban Opportunities in Northern Kenya* (Stockholm: Stockholm University).

Hobsbawn, E. and Ranger, T. (eds) (1983) *The Invention of Tradition* (Cambridge: CUP).

Hodgkin, T. (1963) 'Islam, history and politics', *Journal of Modern African Studies*, 1 (1).

Horton, R. (1971) 'African conversion', *Africa*, 41/2: 85–108.

—— (1975) 'On the rationality of conversion', *Africa*, 45/3: 219–35; 45/4: 373–99.

Hultcrantz, A. (1989) 'The place of shamanism in the history of religions', in M. Hoppal and D. von Sadovsky (eds), *Shamanism Past and Present*, part 1 (Budapest: Hungarian Academy of Sciences).

Humphrey, C. (1994) 'Shamanic practices and the state in northern Asia: views from the centre and periphery', in N. Thomas and C. Humphrey (eds), *Shamanism, History and the State* (Ann Arbor: University of Michingan Press), pp.191–228.

Hunwick, J.O. (1966) 'Religion and state in the Songhay Empire, 1464–1591', in I.M. Lewis (ed.), *Islam in Tropical Africa* (London: OUP), pp.296–317.

Hymes, D. (1974) *Reinventing Anthropology* (New York: Random House).

Ismagilova, R.N. (1978) *Ethnic Problems of the Tropical Africa; Can They be Solved?* (Moscow: State Printing House).

Jackson, A. (ed.) (1986) *Anthropology at Home* (London: Tavistock).

Jacobson, A. (1967) *Marriage and Money*, Studia Ethnographica Uppsaliensia no. 28 (Uppsala: University of Uppsala).

Johnson, J.W. (1974) *Heellooy, Heellellooy: The Development of the Genre Heelloo in Modern Somali Poetry* (Bloomington: Indiana University Press).

────── (1996) 'Musico-moro-syllabic relationships in the scansion of Somali oral poetry', in R.J. Hayward and I.M. Lewis (eds), *Voice and Power: The Culture of Language in North-East Africa* (London: SOAS), ALC supplement 3.

Jones, A.H.M. and Monroe, E. (1935) *A History of Ethiopia* (Oxford: Clarendon).

Jones, G.I. (1963) *The Trading States of the Oil Rivers* (London: OUP).

Kahn, J.S. (1980) *Minangkabau Social Formations: Indonesian Peasants and the World Economy* (Cambridge: CUP).

────── (1981) Review in *Man*, 16 (4): 713–14.

Kapferer, B. (1983) *A Celebration of Demons* (Bloomington: Indiana University Press).

Karp, I. and Maynard, K. (1983) 'Reading the Nuer', *Current Anthropology*, 24 (4): 481–92.

Kenyatta, Jomo (1938) *Facing Mount Kenya* (London: Heineman).

Kessler, C.S. (1977) 'Conflict and sovereignty in Kelantanese Malay spirit seances', in V. Crapanzano and V. Garrison (eds), *Case Studies in Possession* (New York: Wiley).

Knutsson, K.E. (1967) *Authority and Change* (Goteborg: Etnografiska Museet).

Koben, A.J.F., Verrips, J., Brunt, L.N.J. *et al.* (1974) 'Lévi-Strauss and empirical inquiry', *Ethnology*, 13: 215–23.

Kroeber, A. (1948) *Anthropology* (London: Harrap).

Kroeber, T. (1961) *Ishi in Two Worlds: A Biography of the Last Wild Indian in North America* (Berkeley: University of California Press).

Kuklick, H. (1978) 'The sins of the fathers: British anthropology and African colonial administration', *Research in the Sociology of Knowledge, Sciences and Art*, 1: 93–119.

────── (1991) *The Savage Within: The Social History of British Anthropology, 1885–1945* (Cambridge: CUP).

Kuper, A. (1973) *Anthropology and Anthropologists: The British School 1922–1972* (London: Routledge).

────── (1986) 'Lineage theory: a critical retrospect', *Annual Review of Anthropology*, 11: 71–95.

────── (1994) 'Culture, identity and the projection of a cosmopolitan anthropology', *Man*, 29/3: 537–54.

────── (1999) 'South African Anthropology: An Inside Job' in *Among the Anthropologists: History and Context in Anthropology* (London: Athlone), chapter 9.

Kuper, L. and Smith, M.G. (eds) (1969) *Pluralism in Africa* (Berkeley: University of California Press).

La Barre, W. (1970) *The Ghost Dance: The origins of Religion* (New York: Doubleday).

Laderman, C. (1991) *Taming the Wind of Desire: Psychology,Medicine, and Aesthetics in Malay Shamanistic Performances* (Berkeley: University of California Press).

Laitin, D. (1977) *Politics, Language and Thought: The Somali Experience* (Chicago: Chicago University Press).

Lanternari, V. (1983) 'L'apocalisse come problema antropologico: Ernesto de Martino' in *Festa, Carisma, Apocalisse* (Palermo: Sellerio Editore).

—— (1997) *La mia allienza con Ernesto De Martino* (Naples; Liguori Editore).

Larose, S. (1977) 'The meaning of Africa in Haitian vodu', in I.M. Lewis (ed.), *Symbols and Sentiments* (London: Academic).

Last, M. (1979) 'Some economic aspects of conversion in Hausaland', in N. Levtzion (ed.), *Conversion to Islam* (New York: Holmes & Meier).

—— (1991) 'Spirit-possession as therapy', in I.M. Lewis, A.A. Safi and S. Hurreiz (eds), *Women's Medicine: The Zar-Bori Cult in Africa and Beyond* (Edinburgh: Edinburgh University Press), pp.49–63.

Launay, R. (1983) *Traders Without Trade: Responses to Change in Two Dyula Communities* (Cambridge: CUP).

Leach, E. (1954) *Political Systems of Highland Burma* (London: Bell).

—— (1957) 'Aspects of bridewealth and marriage stability among the Kachin and Lakher', *Man*, 57: 50–5.

—— (1961) *Rethinking Anthropology* (London: Athlone).

—— (1962) 'On certain unconsidered aspects of double descent systems', *Man*, 62: 130–4.

—— (1976) *Culture and Communication* (Cambridge: CUP).

—— (1984) 'Glimpses of the unmentionable in the history of British social anthropology', *Annual Review of Anthropology*, 13: 1–23.

Leclerc, G. (1972) *Anthropologie et Colonialisme* (Paris: Fayard).

Leighton, A.M., Lambo, A.T. and Hughes, C.C. *et al.* (1963) *Psychiatric Disorder among the Yoruba* (New York: Cornell University Press).

Leiris, M. (1958) *La possession et ses aspects theatraux chez les ethiopiens de Gondar* (Paris; Plon).

Levine, D.N. (1965) *Wax and Gold: Tradition and Innovation in Ethiopian Culture* (Chicago: University of Chicago Press).

—— (1974) *Greater Ethiopia* (Chicago: Chicago University Press).

Lévi-Strauss, C. (1963) *Structural Anthropology* (New York: Basic Books).

—— (1970) *The Raw and the Cooked* (London: Jonathan Cape).

—— (1966) *The Savage Mind* (London: Weidenfeld & Nicolson).

Levtzion, N. (1968) *Muslims and Chiefs in West Africa* (Oxford: OUP).

Lewis, B. (1971) *Race and Color in Islam* (New York: Harper & Row).

Lewis, H.S. (1965) *A Galla Monarchy: Jimma Abbba Jifar, Ethipia, 1830–1932* (Madison: University of Wisconsin Press).

Lewis, I.M. (1961) *A Pastoral Democracy* (London: OUP) [Revised edition due 1999 (Münster; Lit)].

—— (1962a) 'Historical aspects of genealogies in Northern Somali social structure', *Journal of African History*, 3: 35–48.

—— (1962b) 'Marriage and the family in northern Somaliland', *East African Studies*, 15, Kampala.

—— (1963) 'Dualism in Somali notions of power', *JRAI*, 93: 109–16.

—— (1965a) 'Problems in the comparative study of unilineal descent', in M. Banton (ed.), *The Relevance of Models for Social Anthropology* (London: Tavistock).

——— (1965b) *The Modern History of Somaliland: From Nation to State* (London: Weidenfeld & Nicolson).

——— (1965c) 'Review of P.L. van den Berghe', *Annals of the American Academy of Political and Social Science*, 357: 187.

——— (1966a) 'Spirit possession and deprivation cults', *Man*, 1/3: 307–29.

——— (ed.) (1966b) *Islam in Tropical Africa* (London: OUP) [New edition 1980 (London: Hutchinson)].

——— (ed.) (1968a) *History and Social Anthropology* (London: Tavistock).

——— (1968b) 'Nationalism and tribalism in contemporary Africa' in R.C. Olembo (ed.), *Human Adaptation in Tropical Africa* (Nairobi: East Africa Publishing).

——— (1969a) 'Spirit possession in northern Somaliland', in J. Beattie and J. Middleton (eds), *Spirit Mediumship and society in Africa* (London: Routledge & Kegan Paul).

——— (1969b) 'Sharif Yusuf Barkhadle: the blessed saint of Somaliland', *Proceedings of the Third International Congress of Ethiopian Studies* (Addis Ababa), pp.75–82.

——— (1969c) 'From nomadism to cultivation: the expansion of political solidarity in southern Somalia', in M. Douglas and P. Kaberry (eds), *Man in Africa* (London: Tavistock), pp.59–78.

——— (1971) *Ecstatic Religion* (London: Penguin) [Revised edition 1989 (London: Routledge)].

——— (1976) *Social Anthropology in Perspective* (Harmondsworth: Penguin) [rev. ed. 1985 (Cambridge: CUP)].

——— (1981) 'Why me?' (review of J. Favret-Saada, *Deadly Words: Witchcraft in the Bocage*), *London Review of Books*, 1 July, pp.11–12.

——— (ed.) (1983) *Nationalism and Self-Determination in the Horn of Africa* (London: Ithaca).

——— (1986) *Religion in Context* (Cambridge: CUP) [Revised edition 1996].

——— (1987) *Prospettive di Antropologia* (Rome: Bulzoni).

——— (1988) *A Modern History of Somalia: Nation and State in th Horn of Africa* (Boulder: Westview) [Published previously as (1965b)].

——— (1989) [1971] *Ecstatic Religion*, rev. edn (London: Routledge).

——— (1990) 'Spirits at the house of childbirth' (review of Janice Boddy, *Wombs and Alien Spirits*, *Times Literary Supplement*, 1–7 June, p.590.

——— (1993) *Possessione, Stregoneria, Sciamanismo* (Naples; Liguori).

——— (1994) *Blood and Bone: The Call of Kinship in Somali Society* (New Jersey: Red Sea).

——— (1995) 'Review of D. Parkin, *Sacred Void*', *Africa*, 65 (3): 482.

——— (1996) [1986] *Religion in Context*, 2nd edn (Cambridge: CUP).

——— (1997a) 'Review of P. Stoller, *Embodying Colonial Memories*' *JRAI*, 3 (2), p.397.

——— (1997b) 'Review of S.J. Rasmussen, *Spirit Possession and Personhood among the Kel Ewey Tuareg*', *Zeitschrift fur Ethnologie*, 122, pp.299–300.

——— (1997c) 'Clan, conflict and ethnicity in Somalia: humanitarian intervention in a stateless society', in D. Turton (ed.), *War and Ethnicity: Global Connections and Local Violence* (Rochester: Rochester University Press), pp.179–202.

——— (1998a) 'Doing violence to ethnography: some comments on Catherine

Besteman's distorted reporting on Somalia', *Cultural Anthropology*, 13/1: 1000–8.

—— (1998b) *Saints and Somalis* (London: Haan; and New Jersey: Red Sea Press).

Lewis, I.M., Hurreiz, S. and As-Safi, A. (eds) (1991) *Womens' Medicine: The Zar-Bori Cult in Africa and Beyond* (Edinburgh: Edinburgh University Press).

Lewis, O. (1951) *Life in a Mexican Village: Tepotzlan Revisited* (Urbana: Illinois University Press).

Lienhardt, G. (1961) *Divinity and Experience: The Religion of the Dinka* (Oxford: OUP).

Littlewood, R. (1996) *Reason and Necessity in the Specification of the Multiple Self*, Royal Anthropological Institute Occasional Paper no.43.

Lloyd, P.C. (1955) 'The Yoruba lineage', *Africa*, 25: 235–52.

Loizos, P.L. (1975) 'Change in property transfer among Greek Cypriot villagers', *Man*, 10 (4): 503–23.

Lot-Falck, E. (1973) 'Le chamanisme en Siberie: essai de mise au point', *Bulletin de l'Asie du sud-est et monde insulindien*, 4 (3): 1–10.

—— (1977) 'A propos du terme chamane', *Etudes mongoles et siberiennes*, 8 (Nanterre).

Loudon, J.B. (1959) 'Psychogenic disorders and social conflict among the Zulu', in *Culture and Mental health* M.K. Opler (ed.) (new York: Macmillan).

Luling, V. (1965) 'Government and social control among some peoples of the Horn of Africa', M.A. thesis, University College London.

—— (1967) 'Some spirit possession cults in Mogadiscio and its vicinity', paper presented to social science field research seminar, Addis Ababa, April 1967.

—— (in preparation) 'A southern Somali sultanate'.

Macfarlane, A. (1970) *Witchcraft in Tudor and Stuart England* (London: Routledge & Kegan Paul).

—— (1978) *Origins of English Individualism* (London: Routledge & Kegan Paul).

Mackenzie, W.J.M. (1967) *Politics and Social Science* (London: Penguin).

Makris, G.P. (1996) 'The Tumbura cult in Khartoum', *Africa*, 66/2: 159–82.

—— (forthcoming) *Changing Masters: Spirit Possession and Identity Construction among Descendants of Slaves in the Sudan*.

Malinowski, B. (1922) *Argonauts of the Western Pacific* (London: Routledge & Kegan Paul).

—— (1926) *Myth in Primitive Psychology* (London: Routledge & Kegan Paul).

—— (1938) *Methods of Study of Culture Contact in Africa, Memorandum XV* (London: International African Institute).

Maquet, J.J. (1960) *The Premise of Inequality in Ruanda* (London: OUP).

Marcus, G.E. and Cushman, D. (1982) 'Ethnographies as texts', *Annual Review of Anthropology*, 11, 25–69.

Markakis, J. and Ayele, N. (1978) *Class and Revolution in Ethiopia* (Nottingham: Spokesman).

Martin, B.G. (1976) *Muslim brotherhoods in Nineteenth-Century Africa* (Cambridge: CUP).

Massenzio, M. (1995) *Storia e Metastoria* (Lecce: Argo).

Mastromattei, R. (1988) *La terra reale: Dei, spiriti, uomini in Nepal* (Rome; Valerio Levi).

—— (1997) 'Psicopatie e fondamento', in C. Gallini and M. Massenzio (eds), *Ernesto De Martino nella Cultura Europea* (Naples; Liguori), pp.247–58.

Mathey, P. (1996) 'A glimpse of Evans-Pritchard through his correspondence with Lowie and Kroeber', *JASO*, 27/1: 21–45.

Mead, M. (1928) *Coming of Age in Samoa* (New York: William Morrow).

Middleton, K. and Tait, D. (eds) (1958) *Tribes Without Rulers* (London: Routledge & Kegan Paul).

Minogue, K. (1967) *Nationalism* (London: Batsford).

Mintz, S.W. (1996) 'Enduring substances, trying theories: the Caribbean region as *Oikoumenê*', *JRAI*, 2/2: 289–312.

Mohamad, A.M. (1980) *White Nile Arabs* (London: Athlone).

Moore, S.F. (1994) *Anthropology and Africa* (Charlottesville: Virginia University Press).

Muller, E.W. (1981) *Der Begriff 'Verwandschaft' in der Modernen Ethnosoziologie* (Berlin: Reimer).

Munson, H. (1995) 'Segmentation: reality or myth', *JRAI*, 1/4: 829–32.

Murdock, G.P. (1949) *Social Structure* (New York: Macmillan).

—— (1951) 'British social anthropology', *American Anthropologist*, 53: 465–73.

—— (1972) 'Anthropology's mythology', *Proceedings of the Royal Anthropological Institute, 1971*: 17–24.

Murphy, R. (1972) *The Dialectics of Social Life* (London: Allen & Unwin).

Murphy, R. and Steward, J. (1956) 'Tappers and trappers: parallel process in acculturation', *Economic Development and Culture Change*, 4: 335–55.

Nabokov, I. (1997) 'Expel the lover, recover the wife: symbolic analysis of a South Indian exorcism', *JRAI*, 3 (2): 297–316.

Nadel, S.F. (1946) 'A study of shamanism in the Nuba Hills', *JRAI*, 76: 25–37.

—— (1947) *The Nuba* (London: OUP).

Nakane, C. (1970) *Japanese Society* (Berkeley: University of California Press).

Newbury, C. (1988) *The Cohesion of Oppression: Clientship and Ethnicity in Rwanda (1860–1960)* (New York: Columbia University Press).

O'Brien, D.B. (1971) *The Mourides of Senegal* (Oxford: OUP).

Ohnuki-Tierney, E. (1987) *The Monkey as Mirror: Symbolic Transformations in Japanese History and Ritual* (Princeton, NJ: Princeton University Press).

Okeley, J and Callaway, H. (eds) (1992) *Anthropology and Autobiography* (London: Routledge).

Olderogge, D.A. (1957) 'Osman dan Fodios Aufstand und seine Bedeutung', *Akten des XXIV Orientalistenkongresses*, Munich.

Orent, A. (1967) 'The Dochay cult of Kafa', paper presented to social science field research seminar, Addis Ababa, April 1967.

Ortner, S. (1984) 'Theory in anthropology since the sixties', *Comparative Study of History and Society*, 26/1: 126–66.

Panoff, M. (1977) *Ethnologie: le deuxieme souffle* (Paris: Payot).

Paques, V. (1964) *L'arbre cosmique dans la pensee populaire et dans la vie quotidienne du nord-ouest africain* (Paris; Institut d'Ethnologie).

Parkin, D. (1970) 'The politics of ritual syncretism: Islam among the non-Muslim Giriama of Kenya', *Africa*, 40: 217–33.

—— (1972) *Palms, Wine and Witnesses* (London: Intertext).

—— (1991) *Sacred Void: Spatial Images of Work and Ritual among the Giriama of Kenya* (Cambridge; Cambridge University Press).

Parry, J. (1980) 'Ghosts, greed and sin: the occupational identity of the Benares funeral priests', *Man*, 15: 88–111.

—— (1994) *Death in Benares* (Cambridge: CUP).

—— (1995) 'On hierarchical complementarity', Henry Myers Lecture.

Perrin, M. (1995) *Le Chamanisme* (Paris: Presses Universitaires de France).

Person, Y. (1968) *Samori: Une Revolution Dyula* vol. 1 (Dakar: Ifan).

Peters, E. (1960) 'The proliferation of segments in the lineage of the Bedouin in Cyrenaica', *JRAI*, 90: 29–53.

—— (1972) 'Shifts in power in a Lebanese village', in R. Antoun and I. Harik (eds) *Rural Politics and Social Change in the Middle East* (Bloomington: Indiana University Press).

Pitt-Rivers, J. (1971) 'On the word "caste"' in T. Beidelman (ed.), *The Translation of Culture* (London: Tavistock).

—— (1977) *The Fate of Shechem or the Politics of Sex* (Cambridge: CUP).

Polier, N and Roseberry, W. (1989) 'Tristes Tropes: post modern anthropologists encounter the Other and discover themselves', *Economy and Society*, 18: 245–64.

Prince, R. (ed.) (1982) 'Shamans and endorphins', *Ethos*, 10/4.

Prunier, G. (1996) *The Rwanda Crisis* (London: Hurst).

Radcliffe-Brown, A.R. (1935a) 'On the concept of function in the social sciences', *American Anthropologist*, 37: 392–402.

—— (1935b) 'Patrilineal and matrilineal succession', *Iowa Law Review*, 20: 283–303 [Reprinted in Radcliffe-Brown, A.R. (1952).]

—— (1952) *Structure and Function in Primitive Society* (London: Cohen & West).

Radcliffe-Brown, A.R. and Forde, C.D. (eds) (1950) *African Systems of Kinship and Marriage* (London: OUP).

Ranger, T. (1993) 'The Invention of Tradition Revisited: the case of Colonial Africa', in T. Ranger and O. Vaughan (eds) *Legitimacy and the State in 20th century Africa* (London, Macmillan).

Rasmussen, S.J. (1995) *Spirit Possession and Personhood among the Kel Ewey Tuareg* (Cambridge, CUP).

Read, R.E. (1968) *The High Valley* (London: Allen & Unwin).

Reisman, P. (1977) *Freedom in Fulani Social Life: An Introspective Ethnography* (Chicago: Chicago University Press).

Redfield, R. (1930) *Tepoztlan, A Mexican Village* (Chicago: University of Chicago Press).

Reyna, S.P. (1994) 'Literary anthropology and the case against science', *Man*,

29/.3: 555–82.

Riches, D. (1975) 'Cash, credit and gambling in a modern Eskimo economy', *Man*, 10: 21–33.

Ricoeur, P. (1963) 'Structure et hermeneutique', *Esprit*, 322 (November): 596–627.

Sahlins, M (1961) 'The segmentary lineage: an organization of predatory expansion', *American Anthropologist*, 63: 322–45.

—— (1989) *Islands of History* (London and New York: University of Chicago Press).

Said, E. (1978) *Orientalism: Western Conceptions of the Orient* (London: Routledge).

Salamone, F.A. (1975) 'Becoming Hausa: ethnic identity change and its implications for the study of ethnic pluralism and stratification', *Africa*, 45: 410–24.

Samatar, S. (1982) *Oral Poetry and Somali nationalism* (Cambridge; Cambridge University Press).

Sangren, P.S. (1988) 'Rhetoric and the authority of Ethnography; "postmodernism" and the social reproduction of texts', *Current Anthropology*, 29: 405–35.

Sanjek, R. (ed.) (1990) *Fieldnotes: The Makings of Anthropology* (Ithaca; Cornell University Press).

Saunders, G.R. (1984) 'Contemporary Italian cultural anthropology', *Annual Review of Anthropology*, 13: 447–66.

—— (1997) 'Un appuntamento mancato: Ernesto De Martino e l'antropologia Statunitense', in C. Gallini and M. Massenzio (eds), *Ernesto De Martino nella Cultura Europea* (Naples: Liguori), pp.35–58.

Schapera, I. (1942) *A short history of the Bakgatla-bagakgafela*, Cape Town University, School of African Studies, Communications no. 3.

—— (1947) *The Political Annals of a Tswana Tribe*, Cape Town University School of African Studies, Communications no. 18.

—— (1950) 'Kinship and marriage among the Tswana', in A.R. Radcliffe-Brown and D. Forde (eds) *African Systems of Kinship and Marriage* (London: OUP).

—— (1962) 'Should anthropologists be historians?' *JRAI*, 92: 143–56.

—— (1952) *The Ethnic Composition of Tswana Tribes* (London: Athlone).

—— (1956) *Government and Politics in Tribal Societies* (London: Watts).

—— (1970) *Tribal Innovators: Tswana Chiefs and Social Change, 1795–1940* (London: Athlone).

Schlee, G. (1985) 'Interethnic clan identities among Cushitic-speaking pastoralists', *Africa*, 55: 17–38.

Schmidt, B. (1996) *Creating Order: Culture as Politics in Nineteenth and Twentieth Century South Africa* (The Hague: CIP).

Schneider, D.M. (1961) 'The distinctive features of matrilineal descent groups', in D.M. Schneider and K. Gough (eds), *Matrilineal Kinship* (Berkeley: University of California Press), 1–32.

Sered, S.S. (1994) *Priestess, Mother, Sacred Sister: Religions Dominated by Women* (new York: OUP).

Shack, W. (1966) *The Gurage* (London: OUP).

Sharp, J. (1980) 'Two separate developments: anthropology in South Africa', *RAIN*, 36: 4–5.

Shepherd, M. (1962) 'Comparative psychiatric Treatment in different Countries', in D. Richter, J.M. Taylor, Lord Taylor and O.L. Zangwill (eds), *Aspects of Psychiatric Research* (London: OUP), pp.110–24.

Shihab, Ad-Din. (ed. and trs. R. Basset) (1897–1909) *Futuh al-Habasha* (Paris: Ernest Lereux).

Shirokogoroff, S.M. (1935) *The Psychomental Complex of the Tungus* (London: Kegan Paul).

Siikala, A.L. (1978) *The Rite Technique of the Siberian Shaman* Finnish Folklore Communications, no. 220 (Helsinki).

Simmons, W.S. (1979) 'Islamic conversion and social change in a Sengalese village', *Ethnology*, 18 (4): 303–23.

Skinner, E.P. (1966) 'Islam in Mossi society;', in I.M. Lewis (ed.) *Islam in Tropical Africa* (London: OUP), pp.350–73.

Smith, A. (1971) *Theories of Nationalism* (London: Duckworth).

Smith, H.F.C. (1966) 'A neglected theme of West African history: the Islamic revolutions of the nineteenth century', *Journal of the Historical Society of Nigeria*, 2 (1).

Smith, M.G. (1960) *Government in Zazzau* (London: OUP).

—— (1962) 'History and social anthropology', *JRAI*, 92: 75–85.

Smith Bowen, E. (Laura Bohannon) (1954) *Return to Laughter: An Anthropological Novel* (New York: Harper).

Snow, D.A. and Machalek, R. (1984) 'The sociology of conversion', *Annual Review of Sociology*, 10: 167–90.

Solivetti, L.M. (1994) 'Family, marriage and divorce in a Hausa community: a sociological model', *Africa*, 64 (2): 252–71.

—— (1996) *Equilibrio e controllo in una societa tradizionale: la valle del Niger nella Nigeria del Nord* (Rome: Istituto Italo-Africano).

Southall, A. (1954) *Alur Society: A Study in Processes and Types of Domination* (Cambridge: Heffer).

—— (1976) 'Nuer and Dinka are people: ecology, ethnicity and logical possibility', *Man*, 11: 463–91.

—— (1973) 'Amin's military coup in Uganda: great man or historical inevitability?' Third International Congress of Africanists, Addis Ababa.

Srinivas, M.N. (1952) *Religion and Society among the Coorgs* (Oxford: OUP).

—— (1997) 'Practicing social anthropology in India', *Annual Review of Anthropology*, 26: 1–24.

Stenning, D.J. (1954) *Savannah Nomads* (London: OUP).

Sternberg, L. (1925) 'Divine election in primitive religion', *Proceedings XXI International Congress of Americanists*, Goteburg, pp.472–512.

Stewart, J.H. (1955) *Theory of Culture Change* (Champaign, IL: University of Illinois Press).

Stirrat, R.L. (1977) 'Demonic possession in Roman Catholic Sri Lanka', *Journal of Anthropological Research*, 33: 133–57.

Stocking, G. (ed.) (1978) *Selected Papers form the American Anthropologist, 1921–1945*. (Washington: American Anthropological Association).

—— (ed.) (1984) 'Functionalism historicized', in *History of Anthropology*, vol. 2. (Wisconsin: University of Wisconsin Press).

————(1995) *After Tylor: British Social Anthropology, 1881–1951* (Wisconsin: University of Wisconsin Press).

Stoller, P. (1995) *Embodying Colonial Memories: Spirit Possession, Power and the Hauka in West Africa* (London: Routledge).

Strathern, A. (1971) *The Rope of Moka* (Cambridge: Cambridge University Press).

Swantz, M.L. (1970) *Ritual and Symbol in Transitional Zaramo Society* (Uppasala: Gleerup).

Thomas, K. (1963) 'History and anthropology', *Past and Present*, 24 (April): 3–24.

Torrey, E.F. (1966) 'The Zar cult in Ethiopia', paper presented to Third Congress of Ethiopianists.

Tremearne, A.J.N. (1914) *The Ban of the Bori* (London: OUP).

Trimingham, J.S. (1949) *Islam in the Sudan* (London: OUP).

————(1959) *Islam in West Africa* (London: OUP).

————(1964) *Islam in East Africa* (London: OUP).

————(1968) *The Influence of Islam upon Africa* (London: Longmans).

Tubiana, M.J. (1964) *Survivances Preislamiques en Pays Zaghawa* (Paris: Institut d'Ethnologie).

Tubiana, J. (ed.) (1980) *Modern Ethiopia, from the Accession of Menilek to the Present* (Rotterdam: A.A. Balkema).

Turnbull, C. (1974) *The Mountain People* (London: Cape).

Ullendorff, E. (1960) *The Ethiopians* (London: OUP).

————(1968) *Ethiopia and the Bible* (London: OUP).

Vail, L. (ed.) (1989) *The Creation of Tribalism in Southern Africa* (London: Currey).

Van den Berghe,P.L. (1964) *Caneville: The Social Structure of a South African Town* (Connecticut: Weslayan).

————(1971) 'Pluralism and the polity', in L. Kuper and M.G. Smith (eds), *Pluralism in Africa* (Berkeley: University of California Press).

Vansina, J. *et al.* (1964) *The Historian in Tropical Africa* (London: OUP).

————(1965) *Oral Tradition* (London: Routledge & Kegan Paul).

Verger, P. (1969) 'Trance and convention in Nago-Yoruba spirit mediumship', in J. Beattie and J. Middleton (eds) *Spirit Mediumship and Society in Africa* (London: Kegan Paul).

Vidyarthi, L.P. (1977) 'The rise of social anthropology in India (1774–1972): a historical appraisal', in K. David (ed.), *The New Wind: Changing Identities in South Asia* (Paris: Mouton).

Watson, G. (1984) 'The social construction of boundaries between social and cultural anthropology in Britain and North America', *Journal of Anthropological Research*, 40 (3): 351–66.

White, L. (1949) *The Science of Culture* (New York: Grove).

Wilson, G. (1939) *The Constitution of Ngonde* (London: OUP).

Wilson, G. and Wilson, M. (1945) *The Analysis of Social Change* (London: OUP).

Wilson, M. (1936) *Reaction to Conquest* (London: OUP).

Woldetsadik, T. (1967) 'The cult of Damwamwit and the Mwayat Organisation, paper presented to social science field research seminar, Addis Ababa, April 1967.

Worsley, P. (1957) *The Trumpet Shall Sound* (London: MacGibbon & Kee).

Wyllie, R.W. (1973) 'Introspective witchcraft among the Effutu', *Man*, 8 (1): 74–9.

Yap, P.M. (1960) 'The possession syndrome: a comparison of Hong Kong and French findings', *Journal Mental Science*, 106: 137–44.

Zolla, E. (1986) *L'Amanta invisible, l'erotica sciamanica nelle religioni, nella letteratura e nella legittimazione politica* (Venice: Marsilio).

INDEX

Addis Ababa, 66, 67, 77, 84
Adorcism, 106
Afar people, 67
Africa, xiii; and nationalism, 10, 58; and 'Plural society', 63, 64, 68; sub-Saharan, 13, 17, 97, 100, 102; and 'tribalism', 59, 60, 74-5;
Agnates, 44,
Ahmad Gran, medieval Muslim leader, 70
American Indians, 125, 126, 129, 130
Amharas, 22, 66, 67, 70, 73, 78, 79, 89-90
Ancestor cults, 42,
Andrzejewski, B.W.,72-4,77
Apartheid, 6, 24, 25, 80, 131
Arab League 77
Arabia, 39
Arabic 70-73,
Arabs, 62, 70-2, 77, 98
Ashanti, 47, 63

Bantu, 47, 64, 137
Baxter, Paul, 87, 88, 98
Bedouin (of Cyrenaica), 38, 39-55
Bemba (tribe),61
Bernardi, Bernardo, 27, 36, 46, 142
Black Studies, 129, 138

Boas, F., 122, 126, 127
Boddy, J., 140
Bohannon,L., 38-55
Bomoh, Malay shaman and ritual specialist, 111-112
Borana, 88, 92
Botswana, 65
Buddhism, 107
Buryat, 109

Camels, 73
Cargo cults, 18, 134
Carr, E.H., 123, 124
Caste (India), 1, 134
Castaneda, Carlos, 125
China, 48, 50
Christianity, 31, 69, 70, 84, 89, 90, 91, 93, 94, 98, 100, 102, 120, 134
Colonisation, xiii,xiv, 5; and decolonisation, xiii, 58; and precolonial frontiers in Africa, 60, 61; and spirit possession, 22, 91, 93; and 'tribalism', 59, 74, 75
Cosmology, 59, 87, 88, 93, 99, 102, 107
Cross-cousins, 52
Cultural anthropology (American), 23, 115, 117, 123, 124-129